PRAISE FOR *GHOSTS OF EVEREST*

"Makes for fascinating reading, and, with its well-chosen illustrations and handsome design, *Ghosts of Everest* is the standout."
—*The Washington Post Book World*

"A beautifully illustrated book . . . offers refreshing insights. . . . Debunks widely held theories."
—*The Wall Street Journal*

"Riveting. . . . The firsthand account of the five men who examined Mallory's remains is powerful reading, and you know they will be forever changed by the discovery. . . . The book contains astonishing photographs."
—*Boston Globe*

"A taut narrative. . . . A work of historical importance that reads like a detective thriller."
—*Publishers Weekly*

"Intriguing . . . riveting detail."
—*Christian Science Monitor*

"Enthralling. . . . The story is so compelling we're rooting for Mallory and Irvine. . . . A splendid read."
—*Los Angeles Daily News*

"A truly amazing account. . . . A good read for adventure lovers and a historical standout among the escalating numbers of Everest climbing books."
—*Library Journal*

"For those wanting the definitive record of the Mallory story to date, *Ghosts of Everest* is the book to have."
—*The Seattle Times*

"A glossy, gripping and stunningly photographed account."
—*Minneapolis Star-Tribune*

"A gripping story. . . . A historic thriller. . . . Riveting."
—*Denver Post*

"An engrossing account."
—*Seattle Post-Intelligencer*

"*Ghosts of Everest* adds a great deal of knowledge that helps add some facts to a romantic historical legend."
—Steve Eyman, Cox News Service

"As this story shifts back and forth between the expeditions, it blends the real and imagined into one dramatic narrative, a well-researched and well-written book that reports the largely successful findings of a dangerous expedition."
—*Tampa Tribune-Times*

"These accounts, taken straight from members of the 1999 Mallory and Irvine Rescue Expedition, will certainly slake the reader's thirst for the gritty details."
—*Rock & Ice*

"A compelling detective story. . . . A gorgeous book. . . . Exquisitely photographed."
—*The Globe and Mail* (Toronto)

"Eloquent . . . cuts through one of the century's last enigmas with forensic skill."
—*The Sunday Times* (London)

DETECTIVES ON EVEREST

THE 2001 MALLORY & IRVINE RESEARCH EXPEDITION

JOCHEN HEMMLEB WITH ERIC SIMONSON

CONTRIBUTIONS FROM DAVE HAHN, LARRY JOHNSON, RILEY MORTON,
JAKE NORTON, BRENT OKITA, ANDY POLITZ, JOHN RACE,
TAP RICHARDS, AND JASON TANGUAY

THE MOUNTAINEERS BOOKS

Published by
The Mountaineers Books
1001 SW Klickitat Way, Suite 201
Seattle, WA 98134

First edition, 2002

Published simultaneously in Great Britain by Cordee, 3a DeMontfort Street, Leicester, England, LE1 7HD

Manufactured in the United States of America

Project Editor: Kathleen Cubley
Editor: Don Graydon
Copyeditor: Kris Fulsaas
Cover design: Ani Rucki
Interior design and layout: Jennifer LaRock Shontz
Cartographer: Jennifer LaRock Shontz
Photographer for chapter opener photos: Jim Fagiolo

CHAPTER OPENER PHOTO CAPTIONS

page 20: *Three oxygen tanks recovered from vicinity of 1922 British ABC Camp*

page 26: *From various expeditions (clockwise from top left): tent pole from 1924 British Camp; felt or "walk" mitten found near exit from gullies leading through the Yellow Band (probably from '24 Mallory and Irvine attempt); olive green wool glove; white wool sock with black stitching found in vicinity of Camp VI Everest North Ridge/Upper North Face; Chinese piton; Norton's sock with name on outer cuff*

page 36: *1933 British cooking implements*

page 44: *1933 British backpack frame with 1975 Chinese wand*

page 64: *1922 British expedition (clockwise from top): leather webbing (purpose unknown); deteriorating zinc-carbon battery; 1922 crampon; machined solid metal cap, surface cut with thirteen slots (purpose unknown)*

page 84: *Recovered from 1975 Chinese Camp VI: tent; aluminum badge removed from leg of tripod; survey basket belonging to tripod identical with one placed on the summit in 1975*

page 100: *1924 British tent poles, cotton guylines with wooden tighteners, scraps of tent with metal eyelets*

page 126: *1933 British tinned foods*

page 150: *1960 Chinese oxygen tank and face mask*

page 164: *Chinese equipment: ice ax found at 1975 Camp VI site but in all probability from 1960 Chinese expedition, whose Camp VI was only a few yards away; crampon used both in 1960 and 1975; gloves used both in 1960 and 1975*

Cover photographs: *International rescue: Phurba Sherpa (left) and Dave Hahn (right) at the Mushroom Rock, 28,120 feet, on Everest's Northeast Ridge, May 24, 2001* (Photo © Andy Politz)
   Inset: *Last blessing: George Mallory (left) and Geoffrey Bruce (right) at the Puja ceremony, Rongbuk Monastery, April 1924* (Photo © Noel Odell, courtesy of Peter Odell)
Frontispiece: *Mount Everest: Chomolungma, Goddess Mother of the world* (Photo by Chris Curry © Hedgehog House, New Zealand)

Photographers and Picture Sources: We gratefully acknowledge all those who provided photographs for use in this book. We have made every attempt to trace copyright holders and gain permission for such use. We apologize for any errors or omissions.

Library of Congress Cataloging-in-Publication Data

Hemmleb, Jochen, 1971–
   Detectives on Everest: the story of the 2001 Mallory & Irvine research expedition / Jochen Hemmleb with Eric Simonson; contributions from Dave Hahn . . . [et al.].
      p.   cm.
Includes bibliographical references (p.   ) and index.
   ISBN 0-89886-871-8 (pbk.)
   1. Mountaineering expeditions—Everest, Mount (China and Nepal) 2. Leigh-Mallory, George Herbert, 1886-1924. 3. Irvine, Andrew, 1902-1924. 4. Mount Everest Expedition (1924) I. Simonson, Eric R. II. Hahn, Dave. III. Title.
GV199.44.E85 H45 2002

915.49'6—dc21   2002005274

The world's highest archeological site: Mount Everest's North Face, as seen from the 23,120-foot North Col *(Photo © Jake Norton)*

CONTENTS

Keeper of the past: Mount Everest's Northeast Ridge, view up toward the First Step and summit *(Photo © Andy Politz)*

ACKNOWLEDGMENTS

THE 2001 MALLORY & IRVINE RESEARCH EXPEDITION would not have been successful without the hard work and support of many individuals and organizations.

We acknowledge and thank the Mallory family for their kind spirit and cooperation in working with us to find a permanent home for the collection of Mallory's personal items recovered in 1999. The collection has been transferred to the Royal Geographical Society in London.

The American Foundation for International Mountaineering, Exploration, and Research (AFFIMER) supported both the 1999 and 2001 expeditions and also lent assistance with the handling of the Mallory collection during the interim period. We thank board members Larry Huntington, Scott Franz, Dan Mann, Charlie Peck, and Steve Potter for their generosity and hard work.

Three very successful public exhibitions of the Mallory collection were arranged in the United States, and the team thanks Susan Norton and Nancy Beers Parsons of the National Geographic Society in Washington, D.C.; Erica Stone and Norbu Tenzing of the American Himalayan Foundation in San Francisco, California; and Redmond Barnett and Patty Blankenship of the Washington State History Museum in Tacoma, Washington.

Our sponsors were crucial to making the 2001 trip happen. Although we dealt with companies, the personal efforts of individual employees made all the difference. In particular, we thank Keith Black, Darren Bradley, Jean Cobb, Jon Cox, Mark Delaplane, Ashley Devery, Dick Dickerson, Terri DiLibero, Kim Emery, Jennifer Gombas, Linda Grebe, Jean Hample, Craig Hartman, Kurt Heisler, Steve Hudson, Marcus Hutnak, Tina Ingle, Debbie Lazenby, Rick Leduc, Frank Meyer, Ric Nelson, Kim Oberto, Don Pickard, Gareth Richards, Janice Rosado, Anna Schreiber, Greg Schwarz, Robert Sever, Christian Stolz, Bill Sweasy, Jackie Thompson, Blake Waltrip, Eric Weiss, Donna Snyder White, Rand Whitney, Kim Wiemer, and Brooke Wilson. A complete list of the companies that sponsored our expedition is found in Appendix II.

Our Internet cybercast would not have been possible without the assistance of Anya Zolotusky, Laurel Harkness, and Ken "Tup" Wright at Zaaz in Seattle, and Activate video web hosting. Riley Morton, our field technician, did a great job both during and after the expedition.

At The Mountaineers Books, thanks to Helen Cherullo for her continued support and to Don Graydon, David Emblidge, and Kathleen Cubley for their editing assistance. We appreciate the opportunity to work with them.

Thanks to International Mountain Guides and its customers for the several treks and climbing programs that subsidized our expedition. We appreciate the assistance of Schelleen Scott in promoting these, and guides Heidi Eichner, Heather Macdonald, Craig John, and Jason Tanguay, who led them.

Our hosts in China, Tibet, and Nepal helped us conduct a smooth expedition. Thanks to Ying Daoshui, Wang Yongfeng, and Li Guowei at the Chinese Mountaineering Association in

Beijing, and in Lhasa, Dou Chang Shen and Yang Zhen at the China-Tibet Mountaineering Association. Our liaison officers, Liu Feng and Li Ruihia, were of great assistance. In Kathmandu, we owe thanks to Ang Jangbu and Sonam Gyalpo at Great Escapes and to their great Sherpa team.

Finally, the 2001 Mallory & Irvine Research Expedition would not have been possible without the tireless efforts of Erin Copland Simonson. She thought we were nuts to go back again, but that did not stop her from working very hard to give us the best shot.

In addition, Jochen Hemmleb thanks those individuals who supported his ongoing research after 1999: Daniel Anker, Peter Arens and Claudia Friese at ZDF (Mainz, Germany), Peter Gillman, Don Goodman, David Hambly, Tom Holzel, Sandy Hunter, Erich Keller at Swissphoto (Zurich, Switzerland), Clemens Kratzer at Alpin (Munich, Germany), Muneo Nukita, Simone Rieker and her team at Reisefieber (Bad Homburg, Germany), Jan Richter at H5B5 (Munich, Germany), Audrey Salkeld, Iain Scollay at Granada Media (London, United Kingdom), Rebecca Stephens, Julie Summers, Huw Thomas and Joanna Wright at the Royal Geographical Society (London, United Kingdom), Ed Webster, and, in particular, the members from the 1960 and 1975 Chinese Everest expeditions: Xu Jing, Qu Yinhua, Wang Fuzhou, Zheng Shusheng, Wang Zhenhua, Liu Dayi, Jin Junxi, Xia Boyu, Wu Peilan, and Zhang Junyan.

PREFACE

THERE ARE PLACES IN THIS WORLD that are like time capsules. Places where the past is preserved, so we can look back and relive a bygone age or event. Who has not marveled at the artifacts recovered from the *Titanic?* Sometimes they are plain and simple items—plates, cutlery, a bottle. So why do we feel such a strange, almost magical fascination when looking at them? Is it because we can so easily associate these ordinary items with our everyday life? Is it because it required extraordinary efforts to recover such ordinary objects? Is it because their well-preserved state seems for a moment to break the irreversible time continuum, bringing a sense of timelessness and immortality?

In the world of mountains and mountaineering, the North Face of Mount Everest is such a place. For eighty years it has witnessed every stage in the development of high-altitude climbing, from the early pioneers who braved the mountain clad in tweeds and nailed boots to the high-tech adventurer of today. And the traces of the past are still up there: a tent where climbers spent a stormbound night, some clothing bearing the name tag of a famous pioneer, the ice ax that cut steps on a first ascent . . .

But Mount Everest and the people who attempt to scale its slopes change. Just as the traces of the past are slowly erased by the winds, the spirit of the pioneers is vanishing and the story of their adventures slowly forgotten.

We were determined to keep the legacy of the early Everest expeditions alive. In this shared goal, the two of us came from different perspectives, myself as an Everest historian,

Eric Simonson as a long-standing organizer of Himalayan expeditions. In 1999 Eric led a group of experienced climbers, which also included me as researcher, to the North Face of Mount Everest in pursuit of mountaineering's most enduring mystery: Were George Mallory and Andrew "Sandy" Irvine, two British climbers who disappeared near the summit of Everest in 1924, the first to reach the top of the world's highest mountain?

On May 1, 1999, our team's journey into the past led to the ultimate encounter with history when we found the frozen body of George Mallory at 26,760 feet (8,155 m).

The discovery created worldwide interest. Thousands of visitors came to see exhibitions of the artifacts we had brought down from the mountain: Mallory's snow goggles, letters and notes, an old oxygen bottle. The book about our expedition, *Ghosts of Everest,* enjoyed widespread success and was translated into seven languages.

Although our expedition fulfilled its mission of rekindling interest in the early Everest attempts, it also left us with a lot of unanswered questions. After all, we had not solved the riddle of Mallory and Irvine's final climb. There was more to be learned about the early attempts, more clues to be found on the mountain, more stories to be told. We needed to go back.

This book is the sequel to our team's journey into the past. Our 2001 Mallory & Irvine Research Expedition returned to the North Face of Mount Everest not only to search for more answers to the mystery, but also to look for traces of other pioneering expeditions, each of them an inspiring adventure in its own right. George Finch and Geoffrey Bruce's historic first climb using oxygen in 1922. Frank Smythe's daring solo attempt in 1933. The dramatic nighttime ascent by three Chinese in 1960. Some aspects of these stories, brought to light by new discoveries on the mountain, in archives, and from interviews, are told here for the first time.

This book is a story of pioneers past and present. It seeks to recapture the spirit and adventure of the early Everest North Face expeditions by following their routes on the mountain, studying the artifacts we found along the way, and listening to the pioneers' own words.

And it tells of the people who followed the footsteps of the pioneers. Our expedition team, a varied group of people coming from very different backgrounds, joined in an unusual quest to become time travelers in search of history high on the slopes of the world's highest mountain—detectives on Everest.

Note: Unless quoted from dispatches published on the team's website (*www.mountainguides.com*) or stated otherwise, communications between and from the individual members were transcribed from taped interviews and e-mail correspondence during and after the 2001 expedition. These quotes appear without source citation throughout the book. —J.H.

HIGH MYSTERY

The image will stay with me forever: It was May 1, 1999. Looking through my telescope at Rongbuk Base Camp on the Tibetan side of Mount Everest, the whole upper North Face of the mountain filled my view. In the midst of the vast expanse of scree and snow at 27,000 feet (8,230 m), I could make out five tiny figures strung out in a straight line, slowly inching their way forward. They epitomized the unusual goal of an unusual expedition—to search for traces of two missing British climbers, George Mallory and Andrew "Sandy" Irvine, who had vanished near the summit of Mount Everest in 1924. With their disappearance they had left the mountaineering world its most famous riddle, were the two actually the first to reach the top, twenty-nine years ahead of Edmund Hillary and Tenzing Norgay?

It was a debate that began practically the day the 1924 British Everest expedition returned from the mountain. At first, opinions among mountaineers and historians were optimistic. Noel Odell, the team's geologist, who had last seen the climbers high on the mountain's Northeast Ridge, thought there was "a strong probability that Mallory and Irvine succeeded." He believed the pair had been just 800 feet (240 m) below the summit when he saw them, above any major difficulties.

Others cited Mallory's skill and determination. It was his third attempt to reach the top and, because he was already thirty-seven, probably his last. For his mentor, Geoffrey Winthrop Young, there was no doubt, "Difficult as it would have been for any mountaineer to turn back with the only difficulty past—to Mallory it would have been an impossibility . . . the mountain was first climbed, because Mallory was Mallory."[1]

Within the first year after the 1924 expedition, however, opinion veered the opposite direction. A majority no longer believed in a success. They doubted Odell's sighting, or at least argued that its time—12:50 P.M.—put Mallory and Irvine impossibly behind schedule. They cited Irvine's relative inexperience and pointed to the overall length and seriousness of the route. After the next expedition in 1933, which turned back from its summit attempt at about 28,100 feet (8,565 m), one member summed up the general chorus, "All mountaineers hope that Mallory and Irvine reached the summit of Everest, yet it cannot be denied that the facts are against their having done so."[2]

Yet with no *conclusive* proof either way, the issue remained one of conjecture. The unresolved question continued to occupy mountaineers and historians. Although Hillary and Tenzing's ascent in 1953 made the history books, the debate about Mallory and Irvine was never put to rest completely, and diverging opinions still abounded. During the first solo ascent of Everest in 1980, South Tyrolean Reinhold Messner passed below Mallory's route and, judging from afar, saw "real proof that Mallory and Irvine, with their comparatively primitive equipment, failed there in 1924."[3] Five years later, in 1985, Catalan Toni Sors and five companions climbed the Northeast Ridge under the extra burden of deep monsoon snow, but afterward, Sors surprisingly concluded that he thought Mallory and Irvine could have done it.[4] The mystery would not go away . . .

Finding conclusive evidence that Mallory and Irvine had indeed reached the top of Mount Everest in 1924 would mean rewriting history. As far as we know, none of the world's fourteen highest peaks—the summits higher than 26,250 feet (8,000 m)—had been climbed before 1950. A success by these early pioneers would have to be regarded as a triumph of human spirit over nature, given their comparatively primitive equipment and the obstacles they had to overcome. Everest itself was *terra incognita,* with unknown climbing difficulties and weather, and little was known about the problems of living in the rarefied air of high altitudes. Attempting the highest summit in the world in such circumstances was a huge step into the unknown, comparable with sailing the uncharted oceans centuries earlier or challenging the North and South Poles.

But until 1999 there were few pieces of hard evidence to work with. The expedition of 1933 found Irvine's ice ax at 27,730 feet (8,450 m) on the Northeast Ridge. In 1975 a Chinese climber, taking a short walk from his camp at 26,900 feet (8,200 m), stumbled upon a corpse he later described as an "English dead." The body was dressed in old clothing that was torn to ribbons by years of exposure to the elements, and from its age and location, the body could only have been Mallory or Irvine. Finally, in 1991 American mountain guide Eric Simonson discovered an old discarded oxygen cylinder from the 1924 expedition, not far from the ice-ax site.

Each discovery rekindled and nurtured the debate about Mallory and Irvine's possible fate, but none was able to solve the question of whether the pair had reached the summit before they died. Hope for an answer rested on the possible recovery of one of the cameras the climbers were known to have carried. Any film in these cameras stood a good chance of being preserved in the cold and dry environment at 27,000 feet (8,230 m). It could therefore still yield printable images of the pair's highest point, perhaps even the ultimate grail—the summit.

Before 1999, only once in the seventy-five years since Mallory and Irvine's disappearance had a systematic search for the climbers and their cameras been attempted. The other expeditions before the Second World War had the summit as their sole objective, and after the Chinese occupation of Tibet began in 1950, the north side of Everest (where Mallory's route lay) was sealed off to foreigners for almost three decades. In the fall of 1986 a search team led by Americans Andrew Harvard and David Breashears, instigated by the pioneers of the quest, American businessman Tom Holzel and British mountaineering historian Audrey Salkeld, went to Everest. Bad weather and the death of Sherpa Dawa Nuru eventually prevented them from reaching the suspected search area high on the mountain.

In the years after, ideas for a renewed search effort were put forward by several parties. I had studied the mystery and history of Everest's north side for more than a decade, in the process compiling what Salkeld called "one of the most comprehensive Everest archives in private hands." Rather late in the research, I learned that Briton Graham Hoyland, a BBC employee and grandnephew of 1924 expedition member Howard Somervell, had equally promoted the idea of another search for a number of years.

Foundations for the 1999 Mallory & Irvine Research Expedition were eventually laid in August 1998. American Larry Johnson, then marketing director of a small publishing company in Pennsylvania and an avid student of the Mallory mystery, came upon my research on the Internet and presented it to mountain guide Eric Simonson, one of the most experienced Himalayan expedition organizers. Simonson also had a strong interest in the history of Everest. At the same time, the BBC consented to a film project based on Hoyland's ideas, and after overcoming a number of organizational and logistical hurdles, both parties joined forces.

The expedition team consisted of leader Eric Simonson; high-altitude climbers Conrad Anker, Dave Hahn, Jake Norton, Andy Politz, and Tap Richards; expedition doctor Lee Meyers; and me and Larry Johnson as researchers. The accompanying six-member film crew included Hoyland, producers Peter Firstbrook (BBC) and Liesl Clark (PBS/*NOVA),* cameramen Ned Johnston and Thom Pollard, and sound recordist Jyoti Rana.

We met with unusually benign conditions on Mount Everest. There had been little precipitation the previous winter, which left the upper mountain abnormally clear of snow. If there had ever been a chance of finding anything, it was during the 1999 expedition.

The 1999 Mallory & Irvine Research Expedition: (standing, from left) Lee Meyers, Conrad Anker, Andy Politz, Dave Hahn, Thom Pollard, Jake Norton, Tap Richards, Eric Simonson; (kneeling, front) Jochen Hemmleb (key persons not shown: Larry Johnson, Graham Hoyland.) *(Photo © Schelleen Scott)*

As I watched the mountain from Base Camp on May 1, 1999, the five climbers high on the North Face had just started traversing into the search area, a steeply sloping basin beneath the point where Irvine's ice ax had been found in 1933. A few minutes earlier, Jake Norton had found an old blue oxygen cylinder from the 1975 Chinese expedition, which indicated the vicinity of the camp from where one of their climbers had stumbled across the ominous "English dead."

Every climber now followed his own hunches. Hahn cruised solitarily along the crest of an ill-defined rock rib in search of further evidence of the Chinese camp. Politz's curiosity drove him to climb up well into the gullies of the Yellow Band, a cliff band looming above the basin. Richards and Norton headed downhill, crisscrossing the slope for any traces. Anker was lowest, quickly descending to the bottom edge of the basin, where it broke off in a series of steep crags, the natural boundary of the search zone.

Anker had just turned around to climb back uphill and stopped to remove his crampons when a piece of blue-and-yellow fabric caught his attention. Drawing nearer, Anker happened to look over his right shoulder and suddenly spotted "a patch of white that was whiter than the rock around [it] and also whiter than the snow."[5]

When he reached it, he saw it was a body. But it did not take him long to realize that it was not a body from recent times: a bleached heel bone, an old hobnailed leather boot, and tattered natural-fiber clothing all indicated that it must have been there for a long time.

The body was lying facedown on a sloping ledge, pointing uphill. The head and upper torso were frozen solidly into the gravel that had accumulated around it over the decades. Most of the clothing on the back was missing, shorn away by the wind. The exposed skin was bleached white by the sun. There were signs of a fall: arms were stretched out in a self-arrest position and the right leg was broken just above the boot top, the lower part bent at a sharp angle. The body was tangled up in a length of climbing rope, the broken strands fluttering in the breeze.

But who was it?

From the existing information and theories, the team had believed that if any body were ever to be found, it would be Sandy Irvine's, mainly because it was his ice ax that had been found many years earlier on the ridge above. Soon the men started searching the body's clothing for any cameras, personal effects, and means of identification. Jake Norton finally turned over a name tag on the neck. He looked at it, then paused in surprise.

"Wait, this says 'George Mallory' . . ."[6]

The climbers had encountered mountaineering history, and in doing so had themselves become part of it. Like no other name in the mountain's history, Mallory's was associated with Everest. The whole essence of climbing the world's highest mountain was projected on his life and character. Mallory's famous quip, "Because it's there," in answer to the question of why he wanted to climb Everest, seemed to express in a single phrase the whole simplicity and absurdity of mountaineering. With his inability to find a lasting satisfaction in everyday life and his conflicting passions, torn between the love for his family and his obsession with the mountain, Mallory embodied the deep inner struggle of many dedicated mountaineers—and the tragedy in 1924 brought fully home the consequences of Mallory's choice. He left behind a wife and three young children. In his twenties, Mallory's romantic good looks and athletic physique had earned him the nickname of "Sir Galahad"—a fitting analogy, even more so in retrospect, because this was King Arthur's knight who had disappeared when he touched the holy grail. It was the stuff of legend. And with the graceful and charismatic image preserved in black-and-white pictures from a bygone age, Mallory would never grow old.

With the discovery of his remains, all this changed. A marblelike figure, partly disintegrated into bone, yet so definitely human—this was the new image the world would have of George Mallory. Suddenly he was tangible. His personal belongings and his clothing, the latter damp after taken from its snowy enclosure and with an

Mallory's wristwatch and pocketknife
(Photos by Jim Fagiolo © Mallory & Irvine Research Expedition)

Mallory's goggles *(Photo by Jim Fagiolo © Mallory & Irvine Research Expedition)*

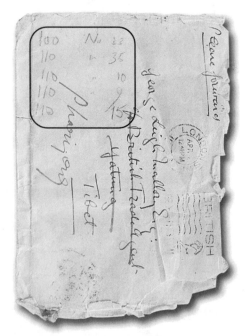

Envelope of "Stella" letter. Note pencil notations. *(Photo by Jim Fagiolo © Mallory & Irvine Research Expedition)*

organic smell that none of the team will ever forget, transformed the man from legend to mortal being. In the words of his discoverer, Conrad Anker, "George Mallory is now someone I've met."

Amazingly, the historic discovery did little to solve the mystery surrounding the man, had Mallory and Irvine reached the summit? No camera was found, and there were no further clues with the body or in the near vicinity. There still existed the possibility that Irvine carried one of their cameras, but his final resting place was yet to be discovered somewhere on the vast, windswept slopes of the North Face.

Notes on an envelope Mallory had carried with him indicated the pair probably had more oxygen available for their summit day than previously believed. No oxygen set was found with the body, but the clamp attaching the mask to Mallory's leather helmet had been tucked away in a pocket. This suggested that Mallory had taken off the set and had been climbing beyond the time when his supply had run out. Also found in a pocket were Mallory's goggles, which hinted at a descent late in the day, perhaps after climbing very high on the ridge.

But such optimistic notions were counterbalanced by profound disagreement about whether Mallory and Irvine could have surmounted the most difficult part of their route, the Second Step, a 100-foot (30-m) cliff on the Northeast Ridge with a vertical slab in its upper part. In 1999 Conrad Anker had assessed the obstacle and nearly succeeded in free-climbing it, using only the hand- and footholds the rock offered. Mallory and Irvine would have had to do the same. After initial hints at the opposite, Anker eventually considered it improbable that the pair could have climbed the Second Step with the techniques and equipment they had in 1924.

On the other hand, Andy Politz had revisited the area from where geologist Noel Odell had seen Mallory and Irvine for the last time on June 8, 1924, climbing a rock step high on the Northeast Ridge. From the perspective Politz obtained, he found he could reconcile Odell's account with only a place *above* the Second Step—suggesting that the pair had climbed it nevertheless.

Faced with inconclusive evidence, the question whether Mallory and Irvine reached the summit was for the time being at a dead end. The search on the mountain was over and the case remained "not proven."

Yet for the team members, deeply affected by their discovery of mountaineering's most legendary figure, a large part of the adventure had only just begun.

Matchbox and tin of meat lozenges
(*Photos by Jim Fagiolo © Mallory & Irvine Research Expedition*)

Letters and handkerchief, in which they were wrapped (*Photo by Jim Fagiolo © Mallory & Irvine Research Expedition*)

CHAPTER 1

UNDER THE MAGNIFYING GLASS

If the 1999 Mallory & Irvine Research Expedition team had scrutinized Everest's North Face with the eyes of detectives, we were now put under the magnifying glass ourselves. Eric Simonson confessed that he had not been ready for the worldwide excitement generated by our 1999 expedition. "Despite my thirty years of expedition climbing and high-altitude mountain guiding, I now realize I was quite naïve going into this trip," he said. "I remember walking up the East Rongbuk Glacier the day before our search, hearing my inner voice screaming at me, telling how terribly unprepared we were for what was perhaps to come. That was certainly an understatement. Little did we realize the amount of interest in the story, and the onslaught of publicity." Our discovery of George Mallory's body had created an excitement far beyond the climbing world and put *us* in the center of widespread attention, admiration, and controversy.

Much of this was focused on the four persons who featured most prominently in the media's portrayal of the expedition and its success: expedition leader Eric Simonson, myself as historian, Internet correspondent Dave Hahn, and Mallory's discoverer, Conrad Anker. In the end, however, no one among the team would remain unaffected.

I had gone into the expedition as a student, about to finish my master's degree in geology—and I am still amazed when I remember what awaited me after our return. The pace of my life accelerated, as if someone had put me atop a rocket and lit the fuse. It was a rush; there was hardly time to think. The nine days I was home in Frankfurt before flying to Seattle to work on the expedition book, I had the national press on my doorstep every day. Suddenly I found myself being treated as one of the central figures in this historic event.

Simonson's public role had irrevocably changed—"from a highly respected expedition organizer to a part of mountaineering history," as one writer put it. Soon Simonson found himself the spokesperson for the team, presenting our story as well as that of Mallory and Irvine to a broad audience.

Lectures by Simonson and the other team members filled halls in the United States, and in Mallory and Irvine's home country, the interest was predictably huge. When I gave a lecture at the Royal Geographical Society in London, more than 800 came. Touring Great Britain sometimes also meant an unexpectedly close encounter with history: After my very first presentation, in Bristol, an old woman approached the podium and introduced herself as the daughter of Geoffrey Bruce, one of Mallory and Irvine's colleagues from the 1924 expedition. The public admired the boldness of the old explorers, was thrilled by the 1999 team's detective work, and was moved by how the discovery seemed to bring back to life George Mallory and his time. A great majority was supportive of our efforts to solve the mystery of Mallory and Irvine's last climb, and they appreciated the care and respect the search team had afforded Mallory's remains. The artifacts we brought back were put on display by the National Geographic Explorers Hall in Washington, D.C., and at the Washington State History Museum in Tacoma, Washington, where they attracted thousands of visitors. Six books were published and two films produced in the aftermath of the expedition. Each presented a different angle of the story and differing conclusions about what might have happened in 1924, and all enjoyed widespread attention.

The overwhelming media exposure was an eye-opening experience. Dealing with it provided a huge challenge, especially for Simonson: "My naïveté was soon replaced by wariness as I saw our photos reprinted without permission, conversations misquoted, or the team's goals and intentions misrepresented." Simonson's position as leader of the expedition singled him out for criticism regarding some of the team's actions, in particular the publication of pictures of Mallory's remains. Admittedly the team made a mistake in the hasty way the pictures were first published: by way of a photographic agency that in turn sold it to the highest bidder, in this case a British tabloid newspaper. It was a mistake the team regretted, and apologies were made in public and in private.

As for their publication in general, we knew there was a fine line between due respect for the dead and our obligation to document and present a historic discovery. In the immediate aftermath of our find, we had been confronted with a flood of responses and requests for images—and the very mixed reactions after our decision to publish them clearly showed that the pictures meant different things to different people. Some considered them tasteless and sensationalistic; others saw their poignancy and historical significance.

The pictures not only documented the find, they also defined a reality, the conclusion of Mallory's final climb and its "how" and "where." Moreover, the pictures did so in an uncompromising way, which was bound to hurt feelings. In a sense, they destroyed the myth. Mallory, the legend, was after all mortal. But one picture in particular, Jake Norton's image of Mallory's outstretched corpse with the summit of Everest behind, symbolized as did nothing else the personal struggle between the man and his mountain. The team had wanted to tell Mallory's story anew by adding a chapter to it, and the image told this new chapter with a clarity and intensity no verbal description could.

Jake Norton pondered over the controversy raised by his pictures, "In the wake of the criticism, I have asked myself time and again, 'Did we do the right thing?' And from my heart has always come the same resounding answer, 'Yes.' But, alas, we are human, and prone to mistakes. Certainly, not everything we did in 1999 was the epitome of perfection. Had we the ability, we would go back and change such decisions. In reality, we cannot. I am reminded of a thought prevalent in Buddhism: correct intent over correct action. The idea is that no one can ever hope to live life without their actions causing some pain or problem for someone, somewhere along the line. But one can live with correct intent, always intending to do the right thing, although inadvertent mishaps may occur. I know we went into every action in 1999 with correct intent—to honor and cherish the memory of George Mallory and Sandy Irvine. And we have held this in our hearts and minds throughout."

Those closest to Mallory, his one surviving daughter, Clare (who died in 2001), and his son, John, were among the calmest and kindest of our critics. Clare wrote the foreword to our 1999 expedition account, telling of how the discovery brought back old feelings of love and loss. John was initially upset by the publication of the pictures of his father's body, but in a touching letter to Simonson three months later, he concluded:

> *I think I now understand better than I did some of the difficulties you must have had in trying to deal with the media as well as running a major mountaineering venture. If my family were over critical and misrepresented your motives, please forgive us. I certainly do appreciate the way the corpse was buried, which must have been exceedingly hard work at that altitude. Those involved deserve special praise.[1]*

The media's reactions to the discovery, especially by its representatives within the climbing community, were also revealing, as Dave Hahn observed, "In the wake of our trip, I sometimes found myself angry that so many who had so little to do with the actual discovery were so eager to write about it, lecture about it, profit from it, and pontificate about it. They were going to use it to put forward whatever theories they had about this or that. They were going to use it to make points about modern climbers and guides and commercial interests and religion, philosophy and society, and, most importantly, . . . themselves."

Although a lot of this did not come as a real surprise, the vehemence of some of the criticisms was astonishing. Just allowing for the possibility that Mallory *could have* reached the summit qualified for being burned at the stake in Reinhold Messner's castle. Other authors included my research in their works—but without credit. Reprinted expedition dispatches were in some cases edited so that my name did not show up in them.

The media singled out Anker as the "hero" of the Mallory discovery, frequently so by overlooking the others' contributions to what had essentially been a team effort— a fact sometimes overlooked by Anker himself. Soon he stood separate from the rest of the team, and we knew little about how he was personally affected by what must have been a turning point in his life. Even more so, in his case this was soon outweighed by a far more incisive, tragic event. Only five months after Mallory's discovery, while attempting to climb and ski down 26,337-foot (8,027-m) Shisha Pangma in Tibet, Anker's team was engulfed by an avalanche. It injured him badly and took two lives— his closest friend, world-class alpinist Alex Lowe, and cameraman Dave Bridges.

What was it in the discovery of a climber high on the slopes of Mount Everest that created so much emotion even seventy-five years after his disappearance?

Of course, there is the mystery of whether Mallory and Irvine had reached the summit of Mount Everest before they died. The discovery had rekindled a historic debate, and the various theories were debated fiercely. But we soon sensed that the quest for an answer to this historical riddle, as well as the fascination and contro-versy it created, were an expression of something deeper and more profound. Just the image of two lone Englishmen clad in tweeds and nailed boots pitting themselves against the highest mountain created a feeling of awe and admiration, independent of whether or not one believed they had reached the top.

Perhaps the story of Mallory and Irvine is so poignant and provoking because it embodies a spirit that has widely been lost over the past seventy-five years. And the discovery of Mallory at the end of the twentieth century could be seen as a timely reminder of this vanishing spirit.

Today's world of technology allows us to live with an unprecedented level of comfort, but at the same time has separated us from many natural challenges needed to build trust in human qualities. The story of Mallory and Irvine's last climb is in many ways an antithesis to today's life. They had braved the biggest natural chal-lenge with a minimum of technology and comfort, and they needed to trust human qualities such as determination, judgment, and instinct more than their equipment. There was also a purity and simplicity in their story—two men with a clearly defined goal and purpose.

When I and the other members of the 1999 expedition recounted the story of Mallory and Irvine in the many slide shows and lectures we gave during the year 2000, we could feel among the audience a positive longing for adventure, challenge, and the sense of purpose and direction it can bring to life. Mallory's story came as a much-sought, perhaps even much-needed inspiration, engendering a positive spirit.

By discovering Mallory on Everest, the members of the 1999 Mallory & Irvine Research Expedition had become forever connected with the man, his story, and his spirit. Simonson could see the lasting effect this would have on our lives, "The previous eighty-odd expeditions that I had done in the last thirty years all had a beginning and an end. This 'bookend' quality was always one of the things that had positively distinguished each expedition experience for me. In contrast, the 1999 Mallory & Irvine Research Expedition put us in the middle of a story that predates my birth by decades, and that will continue long after we are dead and gone."

As Simonson once put it, it had become "the expedition that never ends."

CHAPTER 2

TRACKING DOWN MALLORY'S SPIRIT

In the excitement and fascination immediately after the discovery of Mallory's body, many believed that the mystery of Mallory and Irvine's final climb was still unsolved, and plans were quickly formulated for another search within the next two years.

But as the months passed, a majority began to agree with what many mountaineers had believed for a long time: No, they said, Mallory and Irvine could never have climbed the Second Step in 1924, let alone reached the summit. Theirs had been a gallant effort, inspiring—but, in the end, just another failed attempt with another two dead climbers in the long list of Everest victims. The case was closed.

Was it really?

There was one man in particular among the 1999 team who did not accept the prevailing opinion: Andy Politz.

The first reason was Politz's own experiences on Mount Everest. He had visited the mountain seven times, climbing on each of its three great ridges and faces. In 1991 he reached the summit by the North and Northeast Ridges, the route Mallory and Irvine had attempted. On the crux of the Second Step, Politz used the ladder installed by the Chinese in 1975, but nonetheless gained more insights into the difficulties of a free ascent than expected. During his first try, the badly anchored device came loose, wildly swinging around and threatening to throw him off down the North Face.

"For the second attempt, I chose to use the crack in the corner to the left rather lavishly," Politz remembered. "My weight was bearing on the ladder, for sure, but the pendulum effect was countered by arm bars and hand jams in the crack."

Politz estimated the crack would be in the 5.7 to 5.8 range of difficulty if free-climbed, and at the exit he found "the mother of all fabulous hand jams." Conrad Anker also had initially rated the pitch 5.8 after his near-free ascent in 1999, but later he revised it to 5.10 after comparison with other climbs he had done in Yosemite and Utah. This put the pitch at the upper limits of a skilled weekend climber of today, and obviously beyond the standards of 1924.

The length of the ladder showed Politz that the difficult part was less than 16 feet (5 m) high. He could not see why Mallory and Irvine would not have helped each other on the Second Step crux with a shoulder stand, in which the lead climber uses his partner to gain 5 or 6 feet (about 2 m). It would have been a common technique of the times, and the Chinese resorted to such tactics on that very pitch almost four decades later.

Then in 1999, on the day Mallory's body was found, Politz solitarily climbed up the North Ridge to reach the area from where Noel Odell had caught his famous last sighting of Mallory and Irvine on June 8, 1924. In the years after, Odell had started to waiver in his belief on which of the prominent rock steps of the Northeast Ridge he had seen the pair. Did he see them surmounting the Second Step, as he initially believed? Or had they only been at the lower First Step? Or had they even been above the two steps, on an outcrop later named the Third Step, as historian Audrey Salkeld once suggested? Could Odell have confused one step with another?

Politz remembered the perspective from Odell's viewpoint, "From where I stood I could see the three steps. . . . And the question was whether from that perspective the steps all lined up or separated significantly enough? . . . Well, I tell you, you're so magnetically drawn to the view and those steps are definitely separated. There is only one place that could be described as being 'at a very short distance from the base of the final pyramid,' as Odell wrote—and this is the Third Step."[1]

In the light of Conrad Anker's near-free ascent of the Second Step, after which he declared it improbable that Mallory and Irvine could have done the same, Politz's observations received little attention. This showed the one-sided way the case is often observed. The Second Step was obviously impossible in 1924—so Odell could not have seen Mallory climbing it or a feature even higher up the ridge.

But with no *real evidence* to discount Odell's sighting, the opposite opinion is equally possible. Odell saw Mallory and Irvine climbing the Second or Third Step—so it must have been possible for them to pass the crux somehow, somewhere (for a detailed discussion of the Second Step and Odell's sighting, see "Interlude: Mallory & Irvine—The Puzzles," between chapters 7 and 8).

It is this one-sided way of thinking that Politz recognized as the second reason for his diverging opinion, "Today we are so dependent on technology and equipment, and we take our knowledge so much for granted that we think ours is the only way to get things done. When we look at the incredible abilities of traditional cultures, which often had little gear, we marvel at how a human could do this. Rather than being incredulous to these cultures' capabilities, maybe we should inquire about what our amazement tells of our culture.

"The common argument I have heard is, Mallory and Irvine could not have reached the summit because they did not have the gear, experience, knowledge, or strength to pull it off. There is a quiet comment made here—the implication that *we* do have it. Which is right. But the element not accounted for in this argument is the heart and soul of the participants. There is a spiritual element to experience that will make up for a good bit of gear, knowledge, and strength."

To fully understand what might have happened on Mallory and Irvine's final climb, Politz felt it necessary to throw overboard the present-day views, instead trying to see the events with 1920s eyes. What kind of climber had Mallory been? What background had formed Mallory's skills and attitudes?

One of Politz's friends from his hometown of Columbus, Ohio, a Scot named Gavin Anderson, connected him with the Karabiner Mountaineering Club in Manchester, England. Anderson, a longstanding member of the club, had repeated many of Mallory's climbing routes. There was no uncertainty about Mallory having ascended these routes, compared to his having climbed Mount Everest, because they were recorded in guidebooks and other accounts. By climbing these routes himself, Politz hoped to ascertain Mallory's boldness and gymnastic and technical ability to make a guess whether he could have surmounted the Second Step. Politz even invited Anker to join him, but unfortunately he was not available at the time.

Upon landing in Manchester, Politz's first stop was the little village of Mobberley, Cheshire. This was where Mallory spent his childhood years. His father continued a family tradition as vicar of the centuries-old Saint Wilfrid's church. The church's square stone tower, with its castle ambience, would surely have held great appeal for a young kid enamored with steep ground and high places. Inside was a stained-glass window made in George Mallory's memory, depicting him beside the heroes of England: King Arthur and Sir Galahad. What a place to start gaining insights into the man!

It took nearly a week for Politz's baggage to catch up with him. But the Karabiner Mountaineering Club and especially its president, Duncan Lee, were gracious, helping out with outdoor clothes and gear. Lee had already mapped out an itinerary of climbs, based out of the club's hut in Wales.

In the early years of rock climbing in Great Britain, Pen-y-Pass in the region of Snowdonia, north Wales, was a center of activity. The hotel situated at the pass had housed many climbing parties, brought together by one of Britain's premier mountaineers at the time, Geoffrey Winthrop Young. He and Mallory soon became close friends after they first met in 1909, and one can easily see how Young's ideas and skills as a climber must have inspired and guided young Mallory.

Young's broad, in-depth knowledge is perhaps best reflected in his manual, *Mountain Craft,* a classic insight into the mountaineering experience, judgment, and

Mallory rock climbing on the Moine Arête, Aiguille Verte, French Alps *(Photo by Geoffrey Winthrop Young © The Alpine Club, London)*

gear of the 1920s. It shows that the climbers of Mallory's and Young's times did things differently from how we do them today—and it is remarkable that physiological, psychological, and social aspects of climbing appear first in the book, before any aspects of technical equipment.

On their first day of climbing, Lee and Politz visited a crag called Lliwedd, which features three routes by Mallory: *Bowling Green Buttress, Garter Traverse,* and *Mallory's Pipe,* all rated Very Severe (about 5.7 by today's standards). During the first ascent of *Bowling Green Buttress* in 1919, Mallory was with his wife, Ruth, David Pye, and Claude Elliot. The crux proved to be a steep, shallow corner, and the last few feet were done with the aid of a jammed ice ax—long before "dry tooling," the usage of ice tools on rock pitches, had become part of climbing vocabulary.

Politz and Lee did the climb in modern rock boots, with modern ropes and protection. As they edged up the slabby, thinly fractured and dense rock, they could not help but be impressed with Mallory and his partners. The route required far more balance and nerve than they thought it would, and they tried to imagine doing it in ancient footwear such as nailed boots or tennis shoes.

A fine, grassy ledge system at the top of the first pitch allowed a traverse left to the top of *Mallory's Pipe*. Legend has it that Mallory climbed it alone to retrieve a favorite pipe he had forgotten on the Bowling Green ledges. Certainly it looked like a reasonable solo in tight-fitting, sticky-soled rock shoes. To have done so in contemporary gear, Mallory must have been very comfortable with ascending and descending difficult rock.

George Mallory (right) and Siegfrid Herford at Pen-y-Pass in 1913. Herford was considered the best British rock climber of his time. *(Photo by Geoffrey Winthrop Young © The Alpine Club, London)*

Andy Politz climbs just above the crux of Mallory's Ridge *(Photo © Duncan Lee)*

As a third route, Politz and Lee chose *Mallory's Ridge,* a 400-foot (120-m) route rated Very Severe, leading to the summit of Y Garn. The year before Mallory's first ascent together with Harold Porter in 1911, another climber had fallen and died on the route. Prior to the climb, Mallory had inspected the crux on a rope from above, so in order to maintain standards of "fair play," he let Porter lead this pitch during the eventual ascent.

The ridge begins innocently enough with a vegetated, loose scramble up blocky ground from its base. The crux is where the ridge rears up in a broad buttress, a vertical step of some 60 feet (20 m), barring progress across the whole width of the line. To proceed, the climber slides delicately off to the right into an obvious fault.

As Politz belayed Lee on the crux, he could imagine the first-ascent party quietly struggling to gain some safeguards. Today's approach of dispatching a route in a few long pitches is rooted in speed, because each additional stance requires time to set up and take down. The fewer belays, the faster the climb. In the early days, without pitons and carabiners to attach the climber to the rock, belays were made whenever there was a suitable stance to brace oneself against a fall. For this, both leader and second had to be able to move safely together over any unprotectable sections and quickly assess the possibilities of the terrain for a natural anchor.

The climbing above the crux yet again stopped Politz short. He found himself needing to lieback off the ridge crest, having to step very high and forcing himself out of balance. He struggled with the images in his head—the dead fallen climber, the poor shoes Mallory and Porter would have been wearing, no gear to place for anchors, and the intricate nature of the climbing.

If the demanding nature of Mallory's routes needed any more confirmation, Politz and Lee's fourth and last climb provided it. *Eastern Gutter* on Llechog was another Very Severe first ascent by Mallory and Porter, in 1911—but the groove required far more focus, judgment, skill, and calm than is generally needed for this grade. The remoteness of the location, with its two-hour approach, would have made it very difficult to obtain help in case of an accident. There were few places for protection, and the climbing was continuously steep. Once there came a point where the only way to keep from falling off was to keep moving.

Later, Politz summed up his general impressions, "When done in modern style, these early climbs are an interesting journey into the history of our sport. When climbed with the gear and style of the first-ascent party, the climber is assured an adventure. By no means should these climbs be seen as casual undertakings—and anyone attempting them without ever having climbed at today's higher standard, without today's knowledge, training, and confidence, could be in for an utterly harrowing experience."[2]

Of course, none of this actually proved that Mallory *did* climb the Second Step on Everest's Northeast Ridge. Yet in Politz's opinion, there was now a greater possibility that he *could* have. By experiencing the climbs of Mallory and his peers, to Politz they came across as technically skilled, focused, and intuitive. In dealing with the stresses of unprotected climbing, exposure, and routefinding, they had been exceptional. All in all, the routes were more demanding than their technical grade implied. Those who made the first ascent must have possessed the maturity of climbers capable of climbing routes several grades more difficult.

But there was more to be gained from Politz's visit to Great Britain. Like so many climbers, Politz had grown up with tales of British mountaineers and their exploits. And as a boatbuilder he had an interest in the British Navy, with its evolving ship design and management. But he was completely unprepared for the general public he met in Great Britain, the people he encountered during climbing, in pubs, or after his lectures. Politz found a toughness in this society that had produced the attitudes of the early explorers, a stoicism developed in the face of hardship. Whether history had formed the nation, or people had molded history, mattered little.

With their long tradition of land and sea exploration, the British regarded it almost as a given right that they would lead the quest for the last unchallenged corners of the world. Searches for Sir John Franklin's lost expedition to the Northwest Passage had indirectly opened the race for the North Pole, eventually won by Americans. When Robert Falcon Scott met his tragic end after being beaten to the South Pole by Norwegians, it must have been almost too much for the British Empire to bear. The highest mountain in the world, Mount Everest, thus became the Third Pole—and one senses that the British were determined not to fail there. In fact, Politz could still sense a widespread belief among the general public that Mallory and Irvine did indeed succeed.

Certainly, it was somewhat wishful thinking. Yet people knew just how difficult the years before the early Everest expeditions, the years of World War I, had been. Such level of hardship sculpts a great strength, cohesiveness, and resourcefulness in people. In overcoming the unbelievable trials of the time, the British had shown great capabilities and virtues—and men of this society, such as Mallory and Irvine, were seen as embodying them.

"England will always hold some who are not content with humdrum routine and soft living," wrote the London *Morning Post* after the climbers' deaths. "The spirit which animated the attacks on Everest is the same as that which has prompted arctic and other expeditions, and in earlier times led to the formation of the Empire itself."[3]

Mallory's colleague, Howard Somervell, saw his friend's personal role in this context. "I verily believe his death, as that of his well-loved and splendid companion, is a clarion call to our materialistic age, which so terribly needs the true unselfish spirit typified by George Mallory alike in his life and in its ending."[4]

Perhaps it is overstating it only a little to say that Mallory carried and was carried by the hopes and dreams of a whole nation.

The lessons Politz learned in Great Britain were manifold. Although the circumstances of Mallory's death might still be put down to an ordinary mountaineering accident, the other circumstances of his last climb could not be measured against conventional standards.

Politz experienced the seriousness of what a climber's initiation in the 1920s had been. Among the British, he felt the spirit that had made the British Empire and shaped generations of bold explorers. What had played out between Mallory and Mount Everest on June 8, 1924, was not only the result of one man's private obsession with a mountain—it was influenced by a whole age and society. There was a wealth of factors that in one way or another would have had a bearing on Mallory's mindset before he set out on his last climb, and that make it all the more difficult to guess at his actions and decisions that day.

Then Politz remembered again one item that he and the others from the search team had found with Mallory in 1999: Mallory's sunglasses. Mallory had stowed them away in one of his pockets. But why? Had he taken them off during a snow squall, even if they would have protected his eyes and enhanced visibility? Or had it been dark already, sometime after seven o'clock? If Mallory had been last seen high on the mountain shortly before 1:00 P.M. and had died in the evening, what had he been doing in the intervening hours?

Being so close to the Third Pole, with his country wanting this success so badly, and with the personal future this success would ensure, would Mallory have turned around? *Could* he have turned around?

"What I am striving for is to grasp the lesson within the story of Mallory and Irvine, and to illustrate this lesson with an image from the camera they carried on the summit day," Andy Politz once said in summarizing his quest. As for the first part, his visit to Great Britain told him part of the lesson. For the second part, he and his partners from 1999 needed to go elsewhere—back to Mount Everest.

CHAPTER 3

CLOUDS BEFORE THE MOUNTAIN

"I was deeply torn about whether to go back to Everest and continue the search," Eric Simonson remembered. "It would have been so easy after 1999 to walk away from it all and not to take the same risks again. I knew the chances of two big successes in a row were small, that there was no guarantee of another significant find—but a significant chance of failure or worse!"

In his thirty years as mountain guide, Simonson often worked toward distant goals with the hope his efforts would pay off one day. To him and the team, the discovery of Mallory's body had been such a day. Was he about to squander all the opportunity, support, and good will the event had created? Such questions entered Simonson's head in summer 2000, as he faced the prospect of again putting together an expedition to solve the mystery of Mallory and Irvine.

Despite lamenting about an "ungodly race," in spring 2000 the BBC's Graham Hoyland organized another search expedition for Irvine and the famous camera. With logistical support from New Zealander Russell Brice, one of the most experienced expedition leaders on Everest, Hoyland's team set out with high hopes. But a series of storms covered the upper slopes in too much snow to find anything. That left our team's option of going back in 2001 still viable.

Putting a big expedition together may start with a dream, but it is soon rooted in the day-to-day reality of organizing people, gear, money, transportation, and dozens of other tasks and items. It was clear from the beginning that there was no point in returning to Everest for a poorly funded and half-baked search. We needed a lot of money, pure and simple, to mount the kind of professional research expedition we hoped to do. And so the adventure began far away from Everest, in the office of Simonson's company, International Mountain Guides, in Ashford, Washington.

Eric Simonson *(Photo © Jake Norton)*

When she had worked on Wall Street, Erin Copland probably never thought she would someday be up to her elbows in expedition spreadsheets, making deals involving sleeping pads, camp furniture, and food that came in little bags. She staunchly supported the 1999 expedition, and she and Simonson got married later the same year. Now, despite the birth of their daughter in March 2000, Erin entered the fray again. On one hand, she could see the business possibilities, while on the other hand she quietly resigned herself to the fact that her husband had gone nuts . . . again.

Right from the start, the Simonsons encountered fund-raising challenges. To attract sponsors and return to them some value for their investment, the team needed visibility. This in turn required support from the media, secured by weaving a complicated series of deals between the media's representatives, the team, and the sponsors.

One major funding source for the team in 1999 had come from selling the broadcast rights to BBC in Great Britain and PBS/*NOVA* in the United States. For 2001, Simonson worked hard on a similar deal with Granada Media in England. He made two trips to London for negotiations and, based on a handshake deal, thought that a consortium of Channel 4 (GB), PBS/*NOVA* (USA), and National Geographic TV (international rights) was going to pull through and provide a large part of the financing.

We had happily forgotten about our previous experiences with TV companies.

For Internet coverage, important to all sponsors for visibility, we thought we had a deal with MountainZone.com and its parent company, Quokka Sports.

That was before the demise of many Internet companies in late 2000.

There were hurdles outside the United States, too. Permits and a commitment of cooperation needed to be secured from the Chinese Mountaineering Association (CMA) in Beijing as well as from the China-Tibet Mountaineering Association (CTMA) in Lhasa. Although permission to climb Mount Everest costs less from China than from Nepal, logistics in China are more expensive—and most of it has to be paid in advance. Still, the good relationship with the Chinese that Simonson had established over the years kept the amount of red tape at bay, and negotiations went smoothly.

Although we would approach Mount Everest through Chinese Tibet, the start of our journey would be in the Nepalese capital of Kathmandu. There, advance payments had to be made to some of the key Sherpas we wanted for the expedition, because otherwise they might be lured off by other teams. Simonson planned for the biggest Sherpa group he had ever taken to the Himalayas: eighteen climbers and five cooks. Again, Simonson's established working relationships with local organizations ensured vital support. His longtime agents, Ang Jangbu and Sonam Gyalpo at Great Escapes Trekking in Kathmandu, worked on the details of the Sherpa team,

equipment organization, and permits for legal shipment of the team's oxygen and communication equipment into Nepal and China.

Simonson's attitude remained surprisingly idealistic. "While I still didn't quite know how we were going to pay for it all, I just went ahead, hoping that all the twelve-hour days Erin and I spent on expedition business would eventually pay off."

At the time, if anything was relatively trouble-free, it was the selection of the climbing team. Everybody from 1999 had decided to return, with one exception; Conrad Anker had stated immediately after the 1999 expedition that he had no interest in further pursuing the historical quest.

Of the 1999 five-person search team, Dave Hahn, thirty-nine, had continued his nomadic life as ski patroller and mountain guide. Home was Taos Ski Valley, New Mexico; Ashford, near Mount Rainier, Washington; and the ice fields of Antarctica's Mount Vinson. Although Hahn's guiding career was not particularly affected by the finding of Mallory, the 1999 expedition had otherwise been a watershed in his life.

The 2001 Mallory & Irvine Research Expedition: (standing, from left) Brent Okita, Lee Meyers, Jake Norton, Dave Hahn, Tap Richards, Eric Simonson; (kneeling, from left) John Race, Andy Politz, Jochen Hemmleb (not shown: Jason Tanguay, Heidi Eichner, Riley Morton, Larry Johnson)
(Photo © Jake Norton)

Brent Okita holding the front portion of a 1922 hand-forged iron crampon that he discovered en route to modern Advanced Base Camp *(Photo © Brent Okita)*

John Race *(Photo © John Race)*

An illness that had plagued him throughout the 1999 trip and turned his summit day into a near nightmare was recognized as an intolerance to gluten. His body had not been able to properly absorb nutrients, including iron to build the oxygen-carrying red blood cells. After a fundamental change in his diet, Hahn began to regain his strength. As an ultimate test, he went back to Everest and climbed it from the South Side in spring 2000—his third time to the summit.

Jake Norton and Tap Richards, still our youngsters at twenty-seven, had embarked on quite different paths: Norton, whose pictures of Mallory were published worldwide, had turned his passion for photography into a small business, which he now ran between guiding trips. Richards, on the other hand, kept working as a full-time guide on Mount Rainier and abroad. He and his girlfriend, Heidi Eichner, had recently settled into a house in Seattle. In autumn 2000, the two climbed Cho Oyu, the world's sixth-highest peak.

Andy Politz, forty-one, still lived in Columbus, Ohio, with his wife and their two sons. In "real life," he kept working for a utility company maintaining gas pipelines and regularly taught outdoor activities at an alternative school. Politz also found time for his hobbies, sailing and boat-building.

The 2001 expedition got two newcomers, both with considerable Everest experience. Forty-year old Brent Okita came from Enumclaw, Washington, where he lived with his wife. He worked as a mountain guide on Mount Rainier, in Alaska, and the European Alps, and during the winter as ski patroller at Washington's Crystal Mountain ski area. In 1991, he climbed Everest by the North Ridge and on the descent survived a night without tent or sleeping bag at 27,750 feet (8,460 m).

John Race, thirty-two, lived in Leavenworth, Washington. From there he ran youth outdoor programs for his company, Northwest Mountain School. Beside this, "JR" guided on Mount Rainier and in Alaska. He went to Everest in 1994, where he reached the First Step on the Northeast Ridge in an attempt to rescue two stricken climbers.

Two nonclimbing members completed the main crew: Lee Meyers, fifty-four, from Columbia, Missouri, was again our expedition doctor. He had his job as an emergency room physician, but now saw his occupation as a means to regularly return to the mountains of the world: After 1999 he accompanied several other expeditions, including one to Cho Oyu in Tibet.

And I joined the team again as historian and researcher, contributing my knowledge of the early Everest expeditions and being responsible for the documentation and analysis of any artifacts found on the mountain.

If our team possessed any special strength or advantage, it was the bond of friendship between everyone. We all shared a common background, either from work as mountain guides or through the experience of 1999, and the mutual respect resulting from it kept us together.

If it took a bond of friendship to get the team together, it still took money and gear to get us to the mountain. Although gear was abundant, money was still short. Eventually, four of Simonson's trusted partners—Lowe Alpine Systems, Eureka, Slumberjack, and Vasque—jumped in with both cash and equipment. Eureka also designed a new high-altitude tent specifically for the expedition, and another company, Metrotech, added a couple of metal detectors as its contribution.

But just as everything seemed to be off to a good start, an unexpected blow struck from a completely different direction.

After the controversy over the publication of pictures of Mallory's body in 1999, there was no doubt among the search team members about the need for direct dialogue with the members of the Irvine family. For example, I had been in personal communication with Sandy Irvine's grandniece and biographer, Julie Summers. Up until this time, there had not been any hints that the family was opposed to a search. In fact, they had remained silent when the BBC went back to Everest earlier in 2000.

In late November, however, the first statements were heard that the family "would prefer that Irvine's body be left in peace." Soon after, the British Alpine Club published an official memorandum "for help in identifying appropriate conduct to be observed should Sandy Irvine's body be found." It reinforced the family's claims to all personal artifacts found on the body, as well as full control over release of information and photographs. Also, it backed the family's concerns about the handling of the remains, and to strengthen this point brought up a new accusation—that the 1999 search team had "damaged" Mallory's body.

The accusation was unfounded. Although from some descriptions of the team's actions, it might be assumed there was an actual breaking of the body, no such damage occurred and the complaint is unsupported by the film and photographic evidence.

Another point of criticism centered around the fact that the search team had returned to the site and disinterred Mallory, apparently to salvage more artifacts. The British Alpine Club was quick to point out that disinterring is illegal in the United Kingdom and other countries. Yet Andy Politz and Thom Pollard, the PBS cameraman, had not returned to recover more items. Rather, they had returned to close the case of Mallory's camera forever.

The team had not carried metal detectors on the day Mallory was found. Their climb from Camp V was originally intended to be only a reconnaissance for a full-scale search from Camp VI later on. If they had not gone back with a metal detector, the expedition could never have said with absolute certainty that there was no camera at or near the body. In this context, disturbing the burial site again during the same research expedition seemed a lesser evil than leaving it to endless speculation about any undiscovered contents, very possibly inviting a return party to search the site once more. During the investigation, Politz and Pollard treated the remains with the same care and respect the first team did. Afterward, they restored the site—a protective layer of rocks over the body—to its original state. They read again Psalm 103, which the Bishop of Bristol in England had given the expedition for a committal service.

Again, we had tried to find a compromise between due respect for the dead and our obligation as researchers. A thorough investigation to solve the questions that had arisen from the initial discovery should ensure that Mallory could rest in peace once and for all. But the memorandum misrepresented this intention in a way that cast doubt on the expedition's work and tarnished the reputation of its members.

On top of it all, the documentary deal with Granada Media in Great Britain fell apart, leaving the expedition without any financing from the media sector. At the same time, in the United States, prospects on the Internet sector were equally grim: Quokka Sports and MountainZone were heading for bankruptcy.

The expedition found itself against the wall, and there were many moments in these "dark days of November" when throwing in the towel was thought to be imminent.

But such adversity seemed to create a renewed surge of energy within the team. There was a grim determination to make the expedition happen against all odds, paired with an almost mock refusal to give in to those who continued to misrepresent our intentions. Said Simonson, "The more I thought about it, the more our expedition's return to Everest represented an obligation to seek truth for history. We all had huge respect for George Mallory and Sandy Irvine. We felt they would have wanted us to try to find out what had happened to them on Everest—and we knew there were a great many people who wanted to know the end of the story. We just had to go back."

No support from the media? Well, then we would do the Internet cybercast and expedition film ourselves. From the former MountainZone staff we recruited webmaster Anya Zolutusky and video technicians Riley Morton and Ken "Tup" Wright. Morton, twenty-five, had graduated from Western Washington University with a degree in outdoor media and was starting his one-man business, Soulstice-films. He would act as on-site producer on the mountain, while Dave Hahn and John Race invested in video and sound gear for the filming.

The other team members also bundled their resources, providing what they could in terms of personal and group gear as well as money. Some managed to strike smaller sponsorship deals, and there were even a few dedicated fans among the public who made some donations.

In the end, it was the commercial climbers and trekkers organized by International Mountain Guides that pulled the 2001 Mallory & Irvine Research Expedition out of its fund-raising crisis. They included two trekking groups to Advance Base Camp, led by guides Heidi Eichner and Heather Macdonald. Another group of climbers under the leadership of Craig John and Jason Tanguay was to attempt the North Col and the North Ridge to 26,250 feet (8,000 m). Additionally, a Singaporean-Brazilian team operated under the expedition's permit, as did nonguided clients Terry LaFrance from Albany, New York, and Mike Otis from

Phoenix, Arizona. These two were to climb separately from the search team, but would use the camps and other facilities put in place by the expedition. Together, these paying clients covered a good third of the expedition's overall budget.

Far away in Germany, I was somewhat removed from the frenzy, so I could not know the finer details of what was going on. To the very last day, I was half convinced that everything would fall apart and we would not go. How and where had the others managed to scrape together the money and resources? Even when I boarded the plane to Kathmandu, I did not know—but by then I did not ask anymore.

In fact, back in Washington State, Erin Simonson was still closing the last deals when the team was already out the door—and for her husband, the wheeling and dealing was not finished either. Eric Simonson recalled the last hectic hours the team spent on American soil. "At the Los Angeles airport, I put a ten-thousand-dollar charge on my credit card to cover all our excess baggage—and with that we were off."

CHAPTER 4

ON THE TRAILS OF HISTORY

There was no ship or seasickness. There was no five-week walk through dense jungles, over high Himalayan passes, and across arid deserts. No, the 2001 Mallory & Irvine Research Expedition had it pretty easy compared with the early British Everest expeditions. We simply hopped on planes near our homes and, some forty-eight hours later, with sore rear-ends and swollen ankles, we touched down with a resonant *thud* upon the tarmac of Tribhuvan International Airport in Kathmandu, Nepal.

Bodnath Stupa, Kathmandu, the religious center for Tibetans living in Nepal
(Photo © Jochen Hemmleb)

The first crux of the 2001 expedition lay only minutes from the tarmac, in the baggage claim area where some 117 duffel bags, boxes, and containers, filled to the brim with tents, stoves, oxygen, and other equipment, awaited the team. With excitement brewing, the main team of Eric Simonson, Dave Hahn, Andy Politz, Tap Richards, Brent Okita, Lee Meyers, and John Race were met by Jake Norton and me, who had arrived in the Himalayan capital earlier. After collecting amounts of gear bordering on the absurd, the team cleared customs and boarded a bus to the smoggy, hectic streets of downtown Kathmandu.

After a twenty-minute ride, navigating through the narrow alleys and busily avoiding oncoming vehicles, people, and sacred cows, the expedition arrived at Great Escapes Trekking, the Nepalese agency that arranges the details of any Himalayan excursions by Simonson's company, International Mountain Guides. Here our group met the Nepali team that would become the backbone of the expedition in the months to come.

With twenty-three Nepalis total, the expedition's Himalayan experience was greatly augmented. All the Nepali climbers had been on previous expeditions, and many of them had climbed Everest before. Additionally, most of the Nepali team members were old friends and climbing partners of the western members. Head cook Pemba Sherpa was on his thirteenth expedition with Simonson. For Pa Nuru Sherpa, who was the Sherpa team's leader *(Sirdar),* the 2001 trip was his fifth for International Mountain Guides.

The 2001 Mallory & Irvine Research Expedition included other Himalayan ethnic groups as well: Man Bahadur Tamang joined his third International Mountain Guides trip and hoped to make his third summit of Everest. "MB," as we called him, had been with Simonson and Norton on Cho Oyu in 1997, and again with Simonson on Everest's Southeast Ridge in 1998; he has also climbed Makalu. Tara Bir Yakha, a Limbu from Dhankuta, joined the trip as assistant cook to Pemba. Although his home is less than 3,000 feet (900 m) above sea level, Tara had been an expedition cook on many trips and repeatedly reached 21,200-foot (6,460-m) Advance Base Camp without any trouble.

Arrival in Kathmandu marked the true beginning of the 2001 Mallory & Irvine Research Expedition. The two-year hiatus since the discovery of Mallory's body had not taken the edge off the team's passion for the mystery, as I found out right away. When Jake met me at the airport, I thought, "Take it easy. Don't shift immediately into research mode. Take time to enjoy each other's company first." We went to our hotel rooms—and five minutes later had air photos and maps scattered all over the place. The ghosts of Everest had not let us off the hook one iota.

Occupied by last-minute tasks and excited by the adventure ahead, it was easy to forget the huge undertaking on which we would soon embark. The search team

SHERPAS—THE TRUE HEROES OF THE HIMALAYAS

The idea of climbing the great Himalayan peaks is not traditional for the Nepali people. For them, the Himalayas were (and, to many, still are) literally the "Abode of Snow." They were a kingdom of the mountain gods, and to tread upon their snowy summits was to trespass on the divine.

With the rush of western explorers in the Indian subcontinent in the mid-1800s, however, came the subsequent desire to climb and "conquer" the Himalayan giants. The early *sahibs,* as the locals of the Indian subcontinent called foreigners (mainly the British), understood immediately that assistance from the tough local people would prove invaluable in their attempts to climb these high mountains. The first Nepali people hired for expedition work in the early 1900s were the Sherpas living in Darjeeling, India. Over the years, the Sherpas were hired again and again as climbing partners and assistants in the Himalayas. When Sherpa Tenzing Norgay summited Everest with Edmund Hillary in 1953, the existence of this small population of Nepali hill people hit the world news.

Over the past fifty years, the term "Sherpa" has taken on a new meaning in the western world. Rather than designating a Himalayan ethnic group, "Sherpa" is often used to refer to anyone anywhere who carries loads in the mountains. This is a misinterpretation.

The Sherpas came to Nepal from Tibet some five hundred years ago over the Nangpa La (*la* means "pass") near Cho Oyu. The word *Sherpa* itself was originally less a proper name and more a locator: *shar* in Tibetan means "east" and *pa* means "people." Thus, when asked who they were, the Sherpas would reply *"shar pa"*: "We are people from the east." After crossing the 19,000-foot (5,800-m) Nangpa La, the Sherpas settled primarily in the Solu Khumbu region of Nepal, at the foot of Mount Everest. Other Sherpas now live in the Nepali districts of Rolwaling, Helambu, the Arun Valley, and Kathmandu, and in Darjeeling, India. The Sherpas, who lived at high altitudes day in and day out, were perfectly fit for high-altitude work. Over time, their bodies had become adjusted to this environment, developing broader chests and increased lung capacity.

Geography and politics also assisted in the Sherpas' rapid rise to Himalayan fame. When Nepal opened its doors to the world in 1950, the Southeast Ridge was discovered as the most hospitable route to the world's highest summit. Everest was the understandable focal point of Himalayan mountaineering efforts, and the Sherpas were poised right at its base.

Until recently the Sherpas have reaped little reward and received disproportionately minute praise for their Himalayan efforts, despite the fact that most of today's expeditions would not be successful without them. Edmund Hillary, Reinhold Messner, Chris Bonington, Jim Whittaker, George Mallory, and Sandy Irvine—these are all somewhat household names in the West. Unfortunately rare, however, is knowledge of Nawang Gombu, who was the first to summit Everest twice. Or Ang Rita, who has climbed Everest ten times without supplemental oxygen, by three different routes. Or Babu Chiri, who first spent twenty-one hours on the summit of Everest in 1999, and the following year made an unprecedented sixteen-hour, fifty-six-minute speed climb from Base Camp to the summit along the Southeast Ridge.

Sadly, while we were on the mountain in late April 2001, we received the news that this great alpinist was killed in a crevasse fall while guiding on another expedition to the south side of Everest. Babu's death was the latest in a long list showing the heavy sacrifice that native climbers have made for the world's obsession with the highest mountain: Starting with seven porters lost in an avalanche in 1922, almost a third of Everest's 171 fatalities (as of spring 2001) have been Nepali.

When speaking of recognition of the Sherpas, it is important to note that not all Nepalis who climb in the Himalayas *are* Sherpas. Some of Nepal's thirty-six ethnic groups, such as the Rana Tharu, live in the southern lowlands and are not known for their Himalayan prowess. However, many groups inhabit the valleys of the Himalayas, growing up in villages similar to those of the Solu Khumbu region. Although the Sherpas are still the unrivaled leaders in Himalayan climbing, others—Tamang, Rai, Limbu, Magar, Gurung, et cetera—are rapidly making their presence felt in the Himalayan climbing scene.

would not simply be climbing Everest, but hoped to live at Camp VI (26,900 feet/ 8,200 m) for days at a time and scour the slopes of Everest's North Face in search of traces of Mallory and Irvine. Simonson, always the rational one and not one to pad reality, brought the team to focus immediately. As Jake Norton recalled, "We had just cracked beers and were theorizing about what we might find, and where, when Eric said, 'Guys, we gotta acknowledge that this is big time, and it is not unlikely that when we get back here in ten weeks, one of us may not be along. Anyone of you guys could die up there on this trip. I don't want to be morbid or anything, but let's keep that in mind, OK?' It was definitely a reality check. Not that any of us took Everest lightly or anything, but it is always an eye-opener to have the possibility of death thrust into the forefront of a conversation."

With that weighty thought in our minds, we began discussing the details of the months to come. The first team dinner of the 2001 Mallory & Irvine Research Expedition rapidly became a brainstorming session, wiping away the distractions of hunger and jet lag. All who had been there in 1999 had spent the past two years pondering the final days of Mallory and Irvine, and surmising about future searches. Okita and Race, on the other hand, were new to the research and had a full share of questions. What was the terrain like in the search zones? Where exactly was Mallory found?

It was obvious that, from many standpoints, the team was far better prepared this year than in 1999. First and foremost, the climbers knew what they would encounter on the mountain. Everyone had been to Everest at least once and had either reached the top or climbed high on the Northeast Ridge. They were familiar with the terrain of the search area.

As "walking Everest fact-file," it was my job once more to compile anything that would help us in the search for camps and other traces from the ancient expeditions. The other team members freely shared their photos and information from the 1999 search. At the Royal Geographical Society in London, I made an evaluation of all high-altitude photos taken during the early British expeditions. The most valuable addition to the research material was a set of high-resolution air photos of Everest's upper North Face, made specifically for the expedition by Swissphoto of Zurich. They showed the potential search areas at the scale of 1:1,000—1 millimeter ($\frac{1}{25}$ inch) on the images approximated 1 meter (10 feet) in nature, and objects as small as 25 centimeters (10 inches) could be discerned on them. We had learned from our experiences and mistakes two years ago and had armed ourselves accordingly.

The next days were spent with final preparations. The city of Kathmandu has gone through enormous changes over the past few years. Modernity has made inroads into the medieval capital with increased intensity, bringing with it elements of the convenience and availability we have come to expect in the West. The impact these conveniences have made on major Himalayan expeditions—such as the 2001

A *Vaishnava,* follower of the god Vishnu
(Photo © Jake Norton)

Mallory & Irvine Research Expedition—is huge. No longer is it necessary for all food and equipment to be carted some 9,000 miles from the United States to Nepal. To the already huge quantity of equipment and supplies the team brought from the United States, much more was to be added from the markets of Kathmandu. From potato chips to aluminum snow pickets to toilet paper, a lot was bought locally.

Walking the streets and markets of Kathmandu alters one's sense of time, centuries intertwined like a crazy quilt. On an excursion to buy solar panels, car batteries, and other materials needed for the team's electronic setup, Jake Norton headed into the market of Bagh Bazaar in downtown Kathmandu. He later wrote in his journal:

One would think—after [making] ten trips to Nepal and [spending] two school programs here—that [for me] the novelty and wonder of Kathmandu would have worn off; that the smog, poverty, and inherently chaotic nature of the city would have transitioned from exciting to annoying. But, fortunately, it is just the opposite, and I continue to marvel at the sounds, sights, smells, and sensations throughout this place. . . . The scene was familiar and yet still exciting. Silk saris flowed like water in the breeze while half-dead dogs scurried out of the way of honking taxis. A thousand-pound sacred cow lounged in the busy intersection of the bazaar, completely disregarding the frustrated people trying to get by. A porter carrying computers down the street accidentally kicked over the wicker basket in which a club-footed man sporting a goiter the size of a football was collecting handouts. I passed a leper, his limbs wrapped in gauze, lying in the dust on the corner near the Nepal Solar Electric Company—where I was to spend more than 100,000 rupees, or about the annual income of two average Nepali people. It was madness, a clashing of centuries and mixture of worlds, the collision of the twenty-first century and the seventeenth. . . . It was Kathmandu in all its complexity and harshness, and, as always, it was challenging, refreshing, and wonderful.

Then the packing began. The yard of Great Escapes Trekking became something of a disaster area, its green grass covered with what seemed to be the entire contents of a supermarket and outdoor equipment store. A pile of seventy tents overflowed onto plastic trash bags spilling staple foods, snacks, and freeze-dried meals. Pemba and Pa Nuru shouted orders to the other Sherpas, directing the organizational melee. Blue packing barrels, already bursting with their payload of sleeping bags, stoves, and tents, were compacted again and again to fit "just one more" item inside. Thirty bright red propane bottles were delivered by a fleet of three-wheeled auto-rickshaws and stacked neatly near the mountain of Pemba's kitchen gear. *Dokos,* triangular wicker baskets, piled high with goodies from Asan Tole Bazaar—tomatoes, ginger, spices of all kinds, chives, lettuce, cucumber—found a safe haven in the back

Packing up for Everest
(Photo © Jochen Hemmleb)

of a huge container truck, right next to the delicate cargo of 3,200 eggs. It was a monstrous undertaking, but—somehow—packing all the food and equipment needed to sustain some forty people in Tibet for twelve weeks took less than one day.

Afterward it was time for relaxation and final errands in the tourist heart of Kathmandu: Thamel. Once a residential area full of classic Newari architecture, pagoda-style temples from the seventeenth century, and bustling markets, Thamel has become the Himalayan equivalent of Times Square. It is the absolute definition of a free-market economy, with hawkers shouting their wares at every tourist. "Change money? Carpet buy? I give you my best price, Madame. Smoke? Hashish? You like incense? Hello, taxi?" If it is bought or sold, it will be found in Thamel. And so everybody swarmed out in search of some last bits and pieces: toothpaste, prayer flags, playing cards, postcards, snacks, a few more books for the expedition library. Soon it was time for the farewell dinner at one of our favorite hangouts, the Northfield Café. It was the last meal in a western setting we would have for the next two and a half months.

The morning of March 15 was a clear one, and the bus with the team members on board set off for the Friendship Highway and the border of Tibet. After forty-five minutes in the dusty boulevards and alleyways of Kathmandu, we began to climb out of the smog of the valley east toward the hill town of Dhulikhel, a small mountain hamlet that has found renewed economic vigor in the tourist resorts dotting its hillsides. This renewal, however, has come with a price, both for Dhulikhel and for Nepal as a whole. The region is one of the poorer in the nation. In recent years, the Maoist party of Nepal has gained sweeping popularity in such areas, its promises of social and

The 2001 Mallory & Irvine Research Expedition Sherpa team at Rongbuk Basecamp *(Photo © Jake Norton)*

economic equality striking a poignant chord with Nepal's most destitute citizens. Dhulikhel itself was the site of a major firefight between police and Maoist guerillas in April 2000, and the district as a whole is a continued hotbed of political unrest.

Fortunately for us, all was quiet as we passed. The ribbon of pavement that is the "Friendship Highway" between Nepal and Tibet cuts a modern swath through ancient terrain. Countless terraces edge the steep hillsides that are pockmarked with the scars of landslides, an unfortunate reminder of the population pressures facing Nepal's delicate geography. In the fields flanking the highway, bright yellow flowers of mustard plants stand in stark contrast to the vivid green of rice paddies and wheat fields. All around, life goes on as it has for centuries. Farmers till their fields with oxen and water buffalo, and carry their harvest to market in baskets traditionally carried on a tump line, a strap across the forehead. The Kavre Palanchok district, where Dhulikhel is located, exemplifies the geographic diversity of Nepal. Weaving through farms in sweltering heat at 2,000 feet (600 m) above sea level, it is hard to imagine that a mere 50 miles (80 km) to the north lies the snowy crest of the Great Himalaya.

After three hours of bouncy busing heading northeast, we arrived in a favorite spot, the town of Lamusangu. Perched on the banks of the Bhote Kosi (*kosi* means "river"), Lamusangu has the best *daal bhat* in the region. This hearty meal of rice (*bhat*), lentils (*daal*), vegetables (*tarkaari*), and meat (*maasu*) is the meal of choice for most of Nepal's 25 million people, twice a day, for all of their lives. For the thrifty visitor, *daal bhat* is the way to eat. In the local restaurants, an all-you-can-eat meal costs as little as 50 rupees (75 cents U.S.). We settled onto benches overlooking the rushing waters and dined happily with the flies.

After Lamusangu, the highway begins to climb steadily, following the Bhote Kosi toward its source on the Tibetan Plateau. A major hydro project has recently been completed on the Bhote Kosi. In recent years, with the help of many nongovernmental organizations (NGOs)[1] and huge foreign aid, including assistance from the Chinese government, Nepal has begun to tap its vast hydroelectric potential. Every year, another river finds its waters dammed to provide for the electrical needs of the growing economy—much to the chagrin of foreign-owned rafting companies—bringing the advantages and pitfalls of electricity to this impoverished region.

Here, the road itself is evidence of how difficult, and dubious, hydro projects can be in the Himalayas. Rushing tributaries cascade down the hillsides from all directions, carrying their mud into the lake behind the dam. Access to the power plant is difficult. Every few kilometers, with the bus rocking, tilting, and jolting at all angles, the team crosses a landslide, the pavement ripped down the hillside by monsoon torrents unleashing their fury.

After five hours of butt-busting driving, we finally arrived in Kodari at the Tibetan border. The village, in fact just a row of ramshackle buildings beside the road,

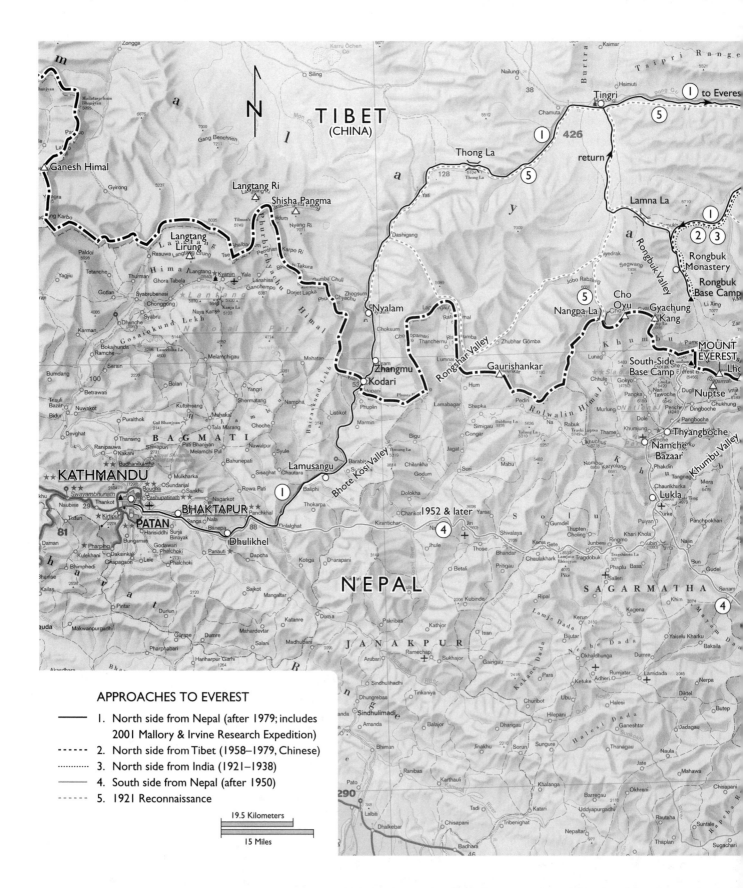

APPROACHES TO EVEREST

—————   1. North side from Nepal (after 1979; includes 2001 Mallory & Irvine Research Expedition)

- - - - -   2. North side from Tibet (1958–1979, Chinese)

············   3. North side from India (1921–1938)

—————   4. South side from Nepal (after 1950)

- - - - -   5. 1921 Reconnaissance

19.5 Kilometers

15 Miles

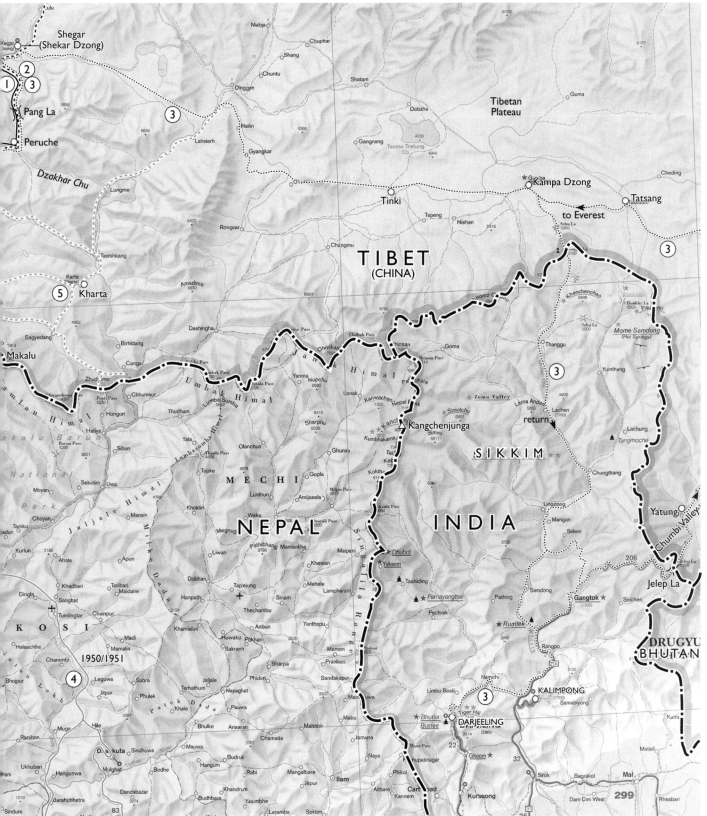

Lulu

Kegar Dzong

Shegar
(Shekar Dzong)

② ③
①
Pang La

Peruche

Dzakhar Chu

Lungme

Tashihkang

Karta
Kharta

⑤ Kharta

Sagyedang

Makalu

Zhudrmo

Chhumsur

Pong Pass
4230

Hongon

Thudham

Chhimsur

Hatiya

Yala

Sibun

Barun Pass

National

Park

Moyan

Sekidim   Uwa

Tamku

Choyan

Kurlun   Ahale

Apun

Khadbari   Toribari
Maidane

Dingla   Satighat
Tumlingtar   Chainpur

Helauchha

KOSI

Charambi

1950/1951

④   Leguwa   Sabra

Bhojpur   Jitpur   Phulek

Ranibas   Muga   Hile

Dhankuta   Sindhuwa

Ukhubari   Hangunwa   Mulghat

Sindure   Dandabazar
Bodhe

Barahchhetra

Mabja   Chuphar

Shang

Chuntu

Dinggye   ③   Hsilin

Lahsierh   Gyangkar

Rongxar

Chngmu

Dashingha

Amadme

Birhldang

Canga

Umbak Himal

Lumba Sumba

Olanchun

Topke

Lunthun

Khoklin

Waku

Megnug

Liwan

Dobhan   Tap'ejung

Hanpath

Khamlalun   Anbun

Huwaku   Pokhari

Sakrani

Jaljale   Phidim

Terhathum   Nayaghat

Bhulke   Ansaran

Chamaita

Mauwa   Budruk

Hangum   Rabi   Mangalbare   Jitpur

Budhbara   Khandrum   Yasimbhe   Laramba   Soktim

Shatam

Tibetan
Plateau

Dobzha   Guma

Gangnang   Tsomo Tretung
Co

Tepeng   Niehan

Tinki

③

Kampa Dzong

Tatsang

to Everest

Sebu La
5000

Thanggu

③

Khanchenchao

Donkhy La

Mome Samdong
(Hot Springs)

Yumthang

TIBET
(CHINA)

Chabuk Pass

Ohmikang   Hsinsan

Hsinsan Pass   Goma

Yanma   Nupchu

Lonak

Sharphu

Kanwachen   Nepal Peak

Kumbhakarna   Tak

Ghunsa

Gopla   Kab

Amijasela   Koktha

Milan Pass

Jaljale Himal

Kangchenjunga

Simvu

Siniolchu

Zema Valley

Lama Anden

Lachen

return

SIKKIM

Lachung   Tangmoche

Chungthang

Lingdong

Mangan

Selem

INDIA

Yatung

Chumbi Valley

MECHI

NEPAL

Pathibhang   Mamankhe

Maipeni

Khewan

Mehele   Lampharam

Sinam   Yanthapu

Thechambu

Memen   Pranbun

Bharpa

Pauwa

Mabir

Sandakapur

Maimuwa

Mabu

Jamuna

Naya

Phikal

Pokhari   Dhubdi

Yuksom

Tashiding

Pamayangtse

Pechrek

Rumtek

Pathing

Samdong

Gangtok   Sirichen

Rangpo

Namchi

Limbu Basti

Bhutia
Bustee

Tiger Hill

DARJEELING

Ghoom

Car Road

Kannem   Kurseong

Bhupatinagar

Aitbare

Samabiyong

KALIMPONG

Jelep La

DRUGYU
BHUTAN

Kumi

Matiali

Bagrakot   Mal

Dam Dim West   Rheabari

299

(Base map © Mairs Geographischer verlag, Ostfildern)

Zhangmu, Tibet, street scene *(Photo © John Race)*

is a quintessential border town: poverty stricken, dirty, and rife with dashed hopes and meager livings. It was time to stretch legs and backs. Some of us walked a half hour to the door of Liping Monastery high above the village, where we were greeted happily by the abbot and a young monk. After a brief tour of the monastery, we made a few offerings for good fortune and then climbed a small tower to gaze across the border toward Zhangmu, Kodari's neighbor on the other side.

The following morning we passed through Nepali customs, crossed the Friendship Bridge, and, signing in with a Chinese military officer, crossed the border into Chinese Tibet. Crammed in the back of a Chinese truck, we bounced along the wildly pot-holed dirt road across the no-man's-land between the border post and Zhangmu. The town is located at 7,550 feet (2,300 m), set at an impossibly steep angle along a hillside, its houses seemingly stacked on top of each other and clustering around a single winding main road. The sky-high flanks of the surrounding mountains are scarred by landslides, and one almost expects the whole village to slide down into the canyon at any moment.

The street life of Zhangmu is perhaps what its Nepalese counterpart, Kodari, had hoped for; a place where all kinds of business go on everywhere, all kinds of goods pile high in the shops, and one can buy everything—from groceries to garments, from liquor to love.

Beyond Zhangmu, the Friendship Highway is but a narrow track scratched into the steep sides of the Bhote Kosi gorge. Huge junipers, evergreens, and rhododendrons cling precariously to the slopes, nourished by cascading waterfalls. Some 1,000 feet (300 m) below rush the torrents of the river, ever carving a deeper and more volatile canyon. The road itself is a patchwork of landslides connected by occasional strips of stable soil. Beyond the lush forests and steaming waters, we could already see far off and far above the characteristic brown of the arid Tibetan Plateau.

After four hours of driving north, our first destination in Tibet was the village of Nyalam, at 12,300 feet (3,750 m) on the edge of the plateau. Nyalam is an old trading town on the commerce route between Tibet, Nepal, and the Indian subcontinent to the south. Most locals in Nyalam speak both Tibetan and Nepali, and many are married to former Nepali citizens. We

The road up the Bhote Kosi gorge *(Photo © Jochen Hemmleb)*

John Race filming Tibetan Buddhist prayer flags and mani stones near Nyalam, Tibet
(Photo © Jake Norton)

pulled up in front of the Snow Land Guest House and were welcomed by the glowing smile of the owner, Tashi, an old friend of the entire expedition. Charming and successful, Tashi and his wife, Pema, are living evidence of Nyalam's past. He is a native of Nyalam, Pema is a Sherpani who grew up in the Khumbu region of Nepal.

The town's architecture reflects the influence of cultures from more recent times. Concrete blocks inhabited by Chinese military intermingle with traditional Tibetan houses with their brightly painted and decorated fronts. Nyalam sits in a glorious location, encircled by craggy peaks often termed "the Tibetan Alps." At 20,000 to 22,000 feet (6,100 to 6,700 m), these peaks are the "little guys" of the Himalayas, and are often forgotten by modern climbers. Many summits are both unnamed and unclimbed. For the 2001 team, Nyalam's altitude and proximity to high-altitude hiking was a perfect opportunity to acclimate. We spent two nights in the town, fending off headaches with beer (not recommended!) and daily excursions into the high country (recommended, unless one tried to keep up with the two-legged steam engine named Andy Politz!).

After Nyalam, the next destination—Tingri, some 125 miles (200 km) to the east-northeast—was a six- to eight-hour drive on rough Tibetan gravel roads. Halfway to Tingri, the team got its first full view of the Great Himalaya from atop the 17,000-foot (5,180-m) Thong La. It was a clear though windy and cold day, and we were rewarded with an eye-popping panorama. The horns of Gaurisankar, Ganesh, Langtang, and other peaks created a saw blade of granite and glaciers ripping the horizon. Dominating all was the gleaming white massif of Shisha Pangma, at 26,337 feet (8,027 m) the world's fourteenth-highest peak and the lowest of the 8,000-meter giants. From a research perspective, the view was encouraging. Much rock poked through the snow and ice, indicating once again a dry winter in the Himalayas.

More bouncing and dust-showering along the road down the far side of the pass brought us at last to Tingri, located beside a hillock in the midst of a dry salt plain at 14,400 feet (4,390 m). According to an ancient tale, an Indian named Tamba Sangay, dissatisfied with his native place, had once asked the Lord Buddha what he should do. The Lord Buddha told him to take a stone and throw it far, and where the stone fell, Sangay should spend his life. Sangay did as he was told, throwing the stone so far that no one saw where it fell. Many months he looked in vain until he passed over the mountains into Tibet. There he came to a place where, although it was winter, there was a large black space bare of snow—and in the middle of it was the stone. The local people had heard it as it came flying across the sky from India and hit the ground with a ringing sound, *ting!* So the surrounding country came to be called Tingri, "the Hill of the Ting."[2]

Once a monastery town, Tingri is now but a dusty stop of a few houses along the main Tibetan highway. Due to its proximity to Nangpa La, the pass that served

Trucks being loaded with gear in Tingri, Tibet
(Photo © John Race)

as the major escape route for Tibetan refugees fleeing the Chinese occupation, Tingri is also the home of a major Chinese military base—an unmistakable sign of the region's troublesome recent past. And Tingri is also host to more dramatic views. Due south from town rises the monstrous dome of Cho Oyu, the "Goddess of Turquoise," at 26,907 feet (8,201 m) the world's sixth-highest peak. Slightly east is the dark bulk of Gyachung Kang, which misses the magic 8,000-m mark by only 48 meters (160 feet). And still farther east rises the pyramid of Chomolungma, Sagarmatha, Mount Everest . . . "the Goddess Mother of the World."

The day at Tingri was spent with more walks in the surrounding fields and hills, much to the delight of the locals. Photos from Norton's Polaroid camera became most-wanted gifts for everyone, and for the rest of our hike, he, Race, and I were surrounded by a laughing, noisy—and smelly!—crowd of children. To them, encountering these nylon-clad whites must have been just as exotic, a bridge across cultures and time.

That night we gathered for dinner at the Everest View Hotel. If anything aside from the mountain view stands out as refreshing in the windblown town of Tingri, it is the smells of food cooking at the hotel's restaurant. Run by a Chinese couple from Sichuan Province, it is a favorite stop for the expedition, providing a delicious respite from the harsh Tibetan Plateau. As we sat together, discussions revolved like the lazy Susans on the tables, spilling theories about the Mallory and Irvine mystery like peanuts from the members' chopsticks. We started getting tuned to our mission.

The following day, March 20, marked the final stage of our journey to Base Camp. The Sherpas had started ahead the previous day, together with three trucks of gear and additional equipment from International Mountain Guides' storage room in Tingri. Now, on a misty morning, the team followed, driving east along the Tibetan Highway to shortly before Shegar (formerly Shekar Dzong), where a steep switchback road leads south and up to 16,800-foot (5,120-m) Pang La.

Crossing the pass was not as pleasant as in 1999. The harsh wind blew with intensity, whipping up dust to sting the eyes and burn the throat. The sudden altitude gain left us breathless, and it was colder, too, much colder than the balmy day we had enjoyed two years earlier. But the view was the same, ripe with drama, and excitement filled the air. From the top of the pass, we gazed longingly at the spectacular sight ahead. Like shark's teeth, rising in defiance of gravity, rise Makalu, Lhotse, Cho Oyu, Gyachung Kang, and Everest. The summit was shrouded in clouds, but they couldn't hide the mountain's towering dominance. It was a view of which one never tires. And here we finally found ourselves firmly in the footsteps of Mallory and Irvine. They, too, had gazed upon this sight seventy-seven years before, undoubtedly with similar excitement, apprehension, and wonder.

As is common on Himalayan passes, Pang La's summit is crowned with prayer flags and other remnants of Tibetan devotion to the dominant Himalayan faith, Tibetan Buddhism. When embarking upon an expedition such as this, rife with danger, one feels that propitiating any and all deities, regardless of the religious affiliation, is probably a good idea. Noting this, the team gladly threw "windhorses," small paper flags imprinted with Tibetan Buddhist prayers, as an offering to the gods.

On the other side of the pass, the road winds its way downward over scree slopes and through a narrow gap in a rock ridge to the village of Peruche in the broad valley of the river Dzakhar Chu (*chu* means "river"). The green of the irrigated fields on the riverbanks contrasted sharply with the reddish and ocher slopes above, and as the road continues west-southwest to Chosang at

Tingri Tibetans delighted with their Polaroid photos
(Photo © Jake Norton)

Coming down the Pang La in Tibet with views of (left to right) Makalu, Lhotse, Everest, Gyachung Kang, and Cho Oyu on the horizon *(Photo © Jake Norton)*

the entry of the Rongbuk Valley, this brief lushness was soon replaced by barren gravel plains, overlooked by the dark-gray trapezoid of Everest's final pyramid lurking over the intervening ridges.

At 16,350 feet (4,980 m), Rongbuk is the last place most people would think of to spend a life of religious devotion. Monastic settlements existed in the area for centuries, but the religious center, the Rongbuk Monastery, was founded only in 1902 by a lama from the Nyingmapa sect of Tibetan Buddhism. Hardly surprising, it was renowned for its solitude. With the onslaught of tourists since Tibet was reopened to foreigners in 1979, that all changed. A hotel was built in 1999 to house tourists and earn money for the monastery, and jeeps bursting with view-seekers from faraway nations whisk by daily. Destroyed during China's Cultural Revolution, the monastery has now been restored to much of its former beauty—although one is left with the uneasy feeling that this was not done out of pure reverence for Tibetan culture and religion.

What has not changed, however, is the dramatic feel of Rongbuk. Walking by the monastery's domed *chortens* (reliquaries for the high lamas) and flapping prayer flags, we gazed once again with wonder at Mount Everest looming in the distance. At this close range, the mountain is unreal in its size, filling the head of the valley. As Tap Richards recounted, "There you are at 16,500 feet, gasping for breath as you get out of a jeep. And then you look up and see that there is almost 13,000 feet more of mountain to climb up. . . . It is daunting."

Daunting, yes. But also intriguing, inviting, and altogether mesmerizing. Hearts thumping with excitement, we boarded our jeeps for the final time and drove the remaining miles through mounds of glacial moraine to Rongbuk Base Camp.

THE MOUNTAIN—
A SHORT EVEREST PROFILE

Name: Mount Everest, also known as Chomolungma (Tibetan for "Goddess Mother of the World"), Qomolangma (Chinese), and Sagarmatha (Nepalese for "Heavenly Mountain"); other local names and spellings are also known

General appearance: Prodigious mountain mass of black-gray, brown, and ocher rocks (mudstone, shale, limestone, greenschist, and granite); lopsided pyramid with three main ridges (Northeast, Southeast, and West) and three faces (North-northwest, East-southeast, and Southwest), surrounded by four glaciated valleys (Main and East Rongbuk, Kangshung, and Khumbu)

Height: 29,037 feet (8,850 m), but growing a few millimeters each year

Age: Composed of rocks between about 550 and 440 million years old (Cambrian to Ordovician period on the geologic timescale); growing period started about 50 million years ago (lower Tertiary period), with a peak at around 5 million years ago, and continues

Origin: Formed as part of the Himalayan mountain chain during the collision of India and Asia, caused by continental drift

Location: Latitude 27° 59' 17" N, longitude 86° 58' 06" E; straddling the border between Chinese Tibet in the north and the Kingdom of Nepal to the south

Climbing the world's highest mountain has always held a huge appeal for both mountaineers and the general public: It was seen as the epitome of human challenge and adventure.

That Mount Everest was the highest of them all was confirmed in 1852 during the Great Trigonometrical Survey of India (GTS), a huge campaign to map and measure the farthest regions of the British Empire. Measuring with theodolites over great distances, they determined for "Peak 15" an average altitude of 29,002 feet

Sunset accents the massive North Face of Mount Everest. *(Photo © Jake Norton)*

(8,839 m)—remarkably close to the latest established figure of 29,037 feet (8,850 m), measured with satellites and receivers of the global positioning system (GPS).

In 1856, the Royal Geographical Society of London received the results from the superintendent of the GTS, Andrew Waugh. In ignorance of any local name, he suggested the peak be named after his predecessor—Sir George Everest.

On the other side of the Himalayan chain, however, the Tibetans had long known the Rongbuk Valley near the mountain as a place for spiritual attainment. They named the peak and the surrounding country Chomolungma, and Jesuits had already put it on a map after a general survey of the Chinese empire between 1708 and 1716.

The first ideas of an expedition to Mount Everest had been nurtured at the turn of the twentieth century, but none of these became reality. In 1913 a young British Army officer named John Noel undertook an illicit journey to southern Tibet from Sikkim, India, coming to within 40 miles (65 km) of Everest—nearer than any westerner had been at the time. Six years later, he gave a lecture of his adventure before the Royal Geographical Society and brought the issue of scaling the world's highest peak back into public discussion. It set in motion the wheels of bureaucracy that led to permission from the Indian and Tibetan governments of a first reconnaissance expedition to Mount Everest in 1921.

Half of the massif was located in Nepal, which was closed to foreigners at the time. Thus the only way lay through Tibet, and it was from this side that the British made their first attempts to climb the mountain—including the 1924 expedition with Mallory and Irvine.

After the Second World War and the occupation of Tibet by the Chinese in 1950, the situation reversed. Nepal opened its borders, and a new way was found to the mountain from the south. It was by this way that Edmund Hillary and Tenzing Norgay finally made the first confirmed ascent of Mount Everest on May 29, 1953.

Since then, the route from Nepal via the Khumbu Glacier, Western Cwm, South Col, and Southeast Ridge has become the most common on Everest. Since the reopening of the Tibetan side in 1979, however, the classic route of the first expeditions by the East Rongbuk Glacier, North Col, North Ridge, and Northeast Ridge has rapidly gained popularity.

Although both have now achieved the status of "normal routes," the two are very different. The ascent from the south has the famous Khumbu Icefall as a major hurdle at the beginning, and the summit day along the Southeast Ridge is only a moderately difficult climb, mostly over snow. Only for the last quarter mile is it the quintessential knife-edge with its famous sting in the tail, the short but steep Hillary Step.

By contrast, the north side reserves most of its trials for the last day, all at altitudes higher than 27,000 feet (8,230 m). The summit climb via the Northeast Ridge offers brittle rock for a starter, followed by two 100-foot (30-m) rock steps with an awkward, exposed traverse between them thrown in for good measure. It even has the icing on the cake—literally, because the route finishes with steep snow and mixed ground on the final pyramid. The ridge, with its maze of towers, steps, ramps, and ledges, makes for difficult orienting, and it is often a long way down. In addition, the last camp on the north side is 1,000 feet (300 m) higher than its southern counterpart, Camp IV on the South Col at 25,940 feet (7,906 m). This forces climbers to spend more time in the so-called "Death Zone" above 8,000 meters, where the human body does not regenerate, not even during sleep.

What both "normal routes" on Mount Everest share is the climbing season. April and May are considered the best months for an ascent from either side. It is the time before the rainy monsoon, when temperatures are getting warmer but precipitation is still low. The months after the monsoon, September and October, also offer suitable climbing conditions. There is usually more snow on the mountain after the monsoon, but a firm snow cover can make some of the routes on the North Face actually easier, providing better going underfoot than the downsloping, gravel-strewn slabs.

Although the monsoon has the warmest temperatures, and a common weather

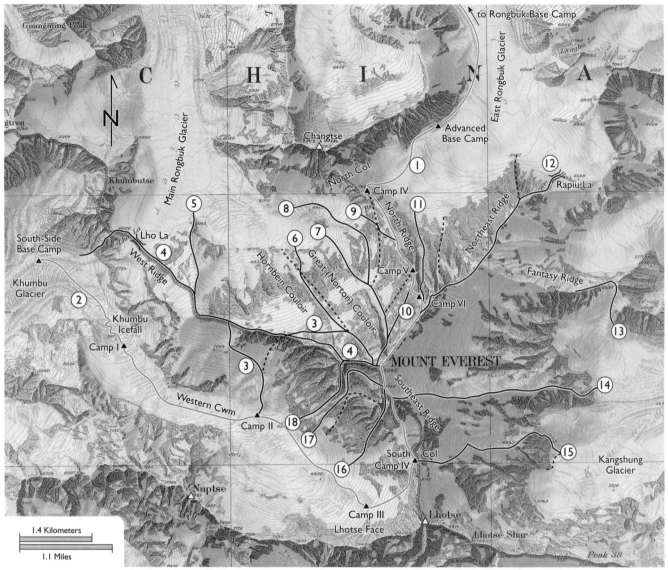

(Base map made by Swissphoto Surveys under direction of Bradford Washburn. Reproduction with permission of the Boston Museum of Science.)

—— STANDARD ROUTES (year of first ascent)
1. North/Northeast Ridge (1960)
    Pre-WWII British attempts, Chinese expeditions
2. Southeast Ridge (1953) Hillary & Tenzing

—— MAJOR CLIMBING ROUTES (year of first ascent)
3. West Ridge/North Face (1963)
4. West Ridge direct (1979)
5. West Ridge from Tibet (1986)
6. Hornbein Couloir direct (1980)
7. Great (Norton) Couloir direct (1984)
8. Great (Norton) Couloir left side (1991)

9. North Face to North Ridge (1985)
10. North Face Traverse (1980)
11. North Couloir (1996)
12. Complete Northeast Ridge (1995)
13. Fantasy Ridge (unclimbed)
14. East Face, American Buttress (1983)
15. East Face "Neverest Buttress" (1988)
16. South Pillar (1980)
17. Southwest Face (1975)
18. Southwest Pillar (1982)

------ VARIATIONS, ATTEMPTS

window in August sometimes allows an ascent, the massive snowfalls create difficult and hazardous conditions most of the time. In winter, on the other hand, storms often strip the mountain bare of snow, but temperatures become extremely low. The party that made the first winter ascent, in 1980, recorded minus 40 degrees Celsius (minus 40 degrees Fahrenheit) on the South Col . . . inside their tents!

Most ascents of Mount Everest take place during the pre-monsoon, followed by the post-monsoon season. Until 2001, there have also been five winter ascents and two during the monsoon.

For the two decades after the first ascent in 1953, the sole objective of most expeditions to Mount Everest was the summit. "To have conquered the top of the world" was a matter of national pride for mountaineering's leading nations and their climbers. Hillary's route was repeated, and the Chinese claimed "their" North Ridge in 1960, very probably becoming the first to succeed via the route of the early British attempts. Junko Tabei from Japan was the first woman to summit Everest, in 1975 by the Southeast Ridge.

Then climbers began gradually to turn their eyes to the unclimbed faces and ridges of the mountain. Americans made a start in 1963 when they reached the summit by the West Ridge and upper North Face. By descending Hillary's route, they also became the first to traverse Everest. In the late 1960s, the Japanese began to attempt the mighty Southwest Face, dominating the Western Cwm, which was eventually climbed by the British in 1975. Four years later the complete West Ridge route was climbed, in 1980 the North Face, and in 1983 the East Face. The complete Northeast Ridge was the last major route to be climbed, in 1995.

The decade between 1978 and 1988 saw a new spirit of mountaineering on Everest. To the new pioneers, reaching the summit was no longer the primary goal— they wanted to climb the mountain "by fair means," without supplementary oxygen and the vast technology of large expeditions. This change in attitude led to the first ascent of Mount Everest without bottled oxygen, by Reinhold Messner and Peter Habeler in 1978, the first entire solo ascent of the mountain by Messner in 1980, and some audacious new routes on the North and East Faces by small teams.

But somehow, inexplicably, this new spirit vanished by the 1990s, and large expeditions returned. Their concept and clientele had changed, though. Rather than elite mountaineers, it was now rich adventurers who, for big money, sought the thrill of a lifetime by being guided to the summit of the world's highest peak. And there were the smaller nations, which now saw the chance to put one of their countrymen on the summit with the help of experienced expedition organizers. Nowadays almost every ascent is made by either of the two standard routes; new lines or the repetition of one of the other great faces and ridges are a rare exception. It seems as if the motivation for climbing Mount Everest has come full circle.

It is the highest mountain of all—and that makes it extraordinary.

CHAPTER 5

TRASH AND TREASURES

Jake Norton had been on his way down from Advance Base Camp when he felt the need to answer a call of nature. Leaving the well-trodden trail along the moraine of the East Rongbuk Glacier, he disappeared among the mounds of rubble and meltwater lakes in search of a sheltered spot. Looking across one of the frozen ponds, something strange caught his eye—an oblong, cylindrical object protruded vertically from the ice, far too symmetrical for a rock. The object was made of metal, its brown hue pockmarked by years of freezing, thawing, and rusting. But it was not another can, another piece of trash—it was a treasure, one of the oldest relics that can be found on Everest: an oxygen bottle from the British expedition of 1922.

We had returned. For everybody on our team, coming into Rongbuk Base Camp on March 20, 2001, brought a sense of déjà vu. There was the familiar bay in the moraine at the edge of the outwash plain. There was the cluster of yellow tents, dwarfed by the gray snout of the Main Rongbuk Glacier. And there was Mount Everest, majestically looming over the head of the valley. It is a desolate wasteland of stone, dust, snow, and water—yet with the savage beauty of raw, unbound nature.

Rongbuk Base Camp and the North Face of Mount Everest (*Photo © John Race*)

The first days after our arrival were spent making Base Camp our home. The Sherpas had already pitched the members' tents, everybody's own haven of privacy and solitude, as well as two large canvas pyramids that served as kitchen and storage room. We then erected two oblong army tents, one as mess tent and the other for housing the communication and research equipment. Power for radios, laptop computers, and satellite phones came from three truck batteries, charged by solar panels and a windmill. Later we attached to the communication tent a smaller, third tent, which became the studio for Riley Morton, our video technician, and occasionally the hospital for our doctor Lee Meyers's worst cases.

Relaxing at Rongbuk Base Camp
(*Photo © Jake Norton*)

In the early days of the expedition, many suffered from the usual altitude headaches and sore throats, which made living at 17,000 feet (5,180 m) an unpleasant experience. Once we had been to the higher camps, however, Base Camp transformed into the place where the air was thick, nights were restful, and food tasted great—in short, a place for rest and recuperation.

It was a remarkably cohesive and harmonious group assembled to spend the next two months together on the slopes of the world's highest mountain. Personality clashes and acrimony, which seemingly have become such a large part of today's expedition life (and resulting mountaineering literature), were notably absent.

Even those who had not been on the first research expedition had no trouble fitting in, despite their differences in character. For his young age, John Race had remarkable strength and experience. His youthful enthusiasm found its expression outwardly in a constant stream of comments, jokes, and one-liners. If others showed their commitment to the project simply by "walking their talk," Race went a step further and walked his talk talking. Brent Okita was almost the exact opposite. From his Japanese father he had inherited calmness and modesty, underlined by gentle eyes and a soft voice. Behind the quiet exterior, however, hid a bundle of suppressed energy, determination, and competitiveness. Together with Jake Norton, Race and Okita formed our second group of climbers, who headed up the mountain on March 27.

Two days earlier, the first train of yaks, the scruffy Tibetan pack animals, and herders had arrived from the villages in the lower Rongbuk Valley. They turned Base Camp into a bazaar. Everywhere people gesticulated over the countless bags and boxes, the voices mixing with the ringing of yak bells. Prices were negotiated, weights checked and rechecked with makeshift scales, followed by more negotiating. More

Yaks on the East Rongbuk Glacier near Camp II (*Photo © Jochen Hemmleb*)

shouting and gesticulating usually meant, "I think this load is too heavy!" So the load was packed anew, lifted again onto the animal's back, only to be thrown off by the yak—which was a yak's way of saying, "I think it's too heavy, too." When all was said and done, fifty-six loaded yaks and nineteen herders were ready to leave for Camps I to III, followed by our first climbing team of Dave Hahn, Tap Richards, Andy Politz, and fifteen Sherpas. Another train of forty-two yaks was to follow on March 29, and a third train of thirty-two yaks four days later.

We watched as the crowd of people and animals slowly moved on over the gravel flats and disappeared in the trench on the left side of the Main Rongbuk Glacier. They would follow this for 3 miles (5 km) before turning left into the side valley of the East Rongbuk Glacier, the way to Advance Base Camp and the upper mountain.

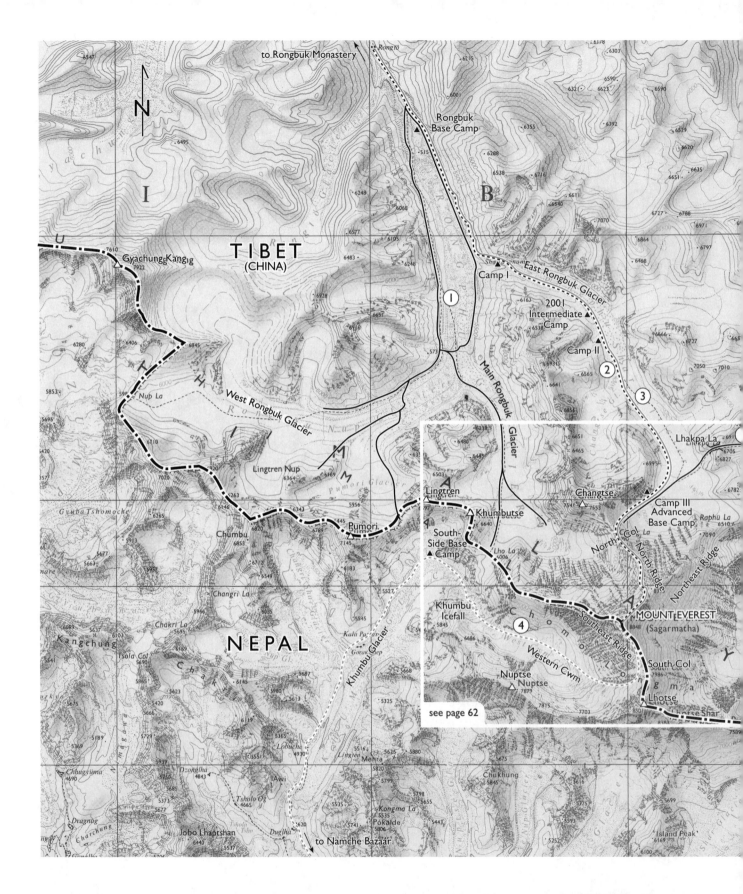

to Rongbuk Monastery

Rongbuk
Base Camp

TIBET
(CHINA)

B

East Rongbuk Glacier

Camp I

2001
Intermediate
Camp

Camp II

②

③

Gyachung Kang

West Rongbuk Glacier

Nup La

Lingtren Nup

Pumori

①

Main Rongbuk Glacier

Lhakpa La

Changtse

Camp III
Advanced
Base Camp

Raphu La

North Col

North Ridge

Northeast Ridge

Lingtren

Khumbutse

South-
Side Base
Camp

Lho La

Khumbu
Icefall

Western Cwm

④

MOUNT EVEREST
(Sagarmatha)

Southeast Ridge

South Col

Lhotse

Nuptse

Nuptse

Lhotse Shar

see page 62

Chumbu

Gyubu Tshomoche

Changri La

Chakri La

Kangchung

Kala Pattar

Gorak Shep

NEPAL

Khumbu Glacier

Lobuche

Dzonglha

Awi

Tsholo Og

Dragnag

Jobo Lhaptshan

Duglha

Mehra

Kongma La
Pokalde

Chukhung

Island Peak

to Namche Bazaar

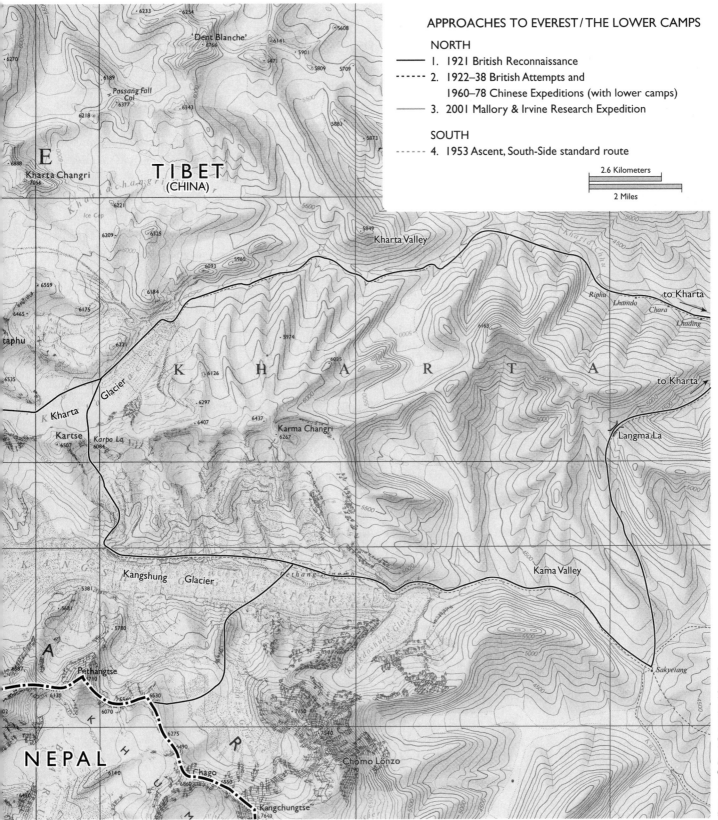

APPROACHES TO EVEREST / THE LOWER CAMPS

NORTH
1. 1921 British Reconnaissance
2. 1922–38 British Attempts and
   1960–78 Chinese Expeditions (with lower camps)
3. 2001 Mallory & Irvine Research Expedition

SOUTH
4. 1953 Ascent, South-Side standard route

2.6 Kilometers

2 Miles

TIBET
(CHINA)

'Dent Blanche'

Passang Fall
Col

Kharta Changri

Kharta Valley

to Kharta

to Kharta

K H A R T A

Langma La

Glacier

K Kharta

Kartse

Karpo La

Karma Changri

K A N G S

Kangshung   Glacier

Kama Valley

Sakyetang

A

Pethangtse

NEPAL

Chago

Chomo Lonzo

Kangchungtse

(Base map © Royal Geographical Society)

1921: THE BRITISH FIND THE WAY

The route via the Main and East Rongbuk Glaciers is now the standard approach to Mount Everest from the north—and it is one of the enduring riddles in the history of the mountain's exploration why the British reconnaissance expedition of 1921 missed it.

The aim of this very first Everest expedition had come down to basics. Explore and survey the mountain's surroundings, find a way *to* the mountain, and find—if possible, even attempt—a way *up* the mountain. The newly formed Mount Everest Committee appointed as leader Lieutenant-Colonel Charles K. Howard-Bury, who had paved the expedition's way with his persistence in negotiations with Indian and Tibetan government officials about permission to travel their countries.

Because it was a reconnaissance, its members were a mixed group of scientists and climbers. The former included Henry T. Morshead and Edward O. Wheeler as surveyors, Dr. A. M. Heron as geologist, and Dr. Alexander F. Wollaston as doctor and naturalist. The climbing team at first seemed a sound balance of experience and strength; Harold Raeburn and Dr. Alexander M. Kellas, both Scots in their mid-fifties, formed the core because of their distinguished mountaineering and exploration record in the Himalayas and elsewhere. Their younger counterparts were Guy H. Bullock, thirty-two, and George Mallory, then thirty-five.

But it was the age of the more experienced members that nearly became the expedition's undoing. They had left Darjeeling, India, in mid-May 1921, and trekked northeast through Sikkim to cross the Jelep La into Tibet. The changing climate, from humid rain forests to the arid desert of the Tibetan plateau, and the hardships of the trek, compounded by awful food, hit the eldest members hardest. Both Raeburn and Kellas suffered from dysentery, and the latter grew so weak that he needed to be carried on a stretcher. Eventually, as they approached the town of Kampa Dzong (*dzong* means "fort"), his heart gave out. He was buried on the hillside above the town, within sight of Mount Everest. As Raeburn's condition did not improve, he was forced to return to Sikkim, accompanied by Wollaston. Now seriously depleted in their force, the others moved on.

West of Kampa Dzong, the expedition entered unknown territory—in the words of Mallory, they were "about to walk off the map."

Past the fort of Shekar Dzong, spectacularly situated on a rock pinnacle, the party reached Tingri Dzong, where they decided to split. One group explored the surroundings of Cho Oyu, following the ancient trade route to the Khombo La (now Nangpa La), a pass on the border to Nepal, while another went southwest as far as Nyalam and the Rongshar Valley. Mallory and Bullock, on the other hand, turned southeast from Tingri to the Lamna La, which brought them to the Rongbuk Valley leading to Everest. (See map on pages 52 and 53.) Soon they were greeted by a spellbinding sight of their elusive goal. Mallory later wrote:

At the end of the valley and above the glacier Everest rises not so much a peak as a prodigious mountain-mass. There is no complication for the eye. The highest of the world's great mountains, it seems, has to make but a single gesture of magnificence to be lord of all, vast in unchallenged and isolated supremacy.[1]

Over the following three weeks they explored the Main Rongbuk Glacier and its western tributary. From a nearby peak they could see that a broad buttress at the left side of Everest's North Face formed a feasible way to the upper Northeast Ridge of the mountain, which in turn led to the summit. The base of the buttress was a high saddle between Everest and its northern neighbor, Changtse, which they called Chang La or North Col. Because its western face appeared too steep, hopes rested on an easier approach from the other side. And here Mallory and Bullock made a grave mistake: They assumed the valley on the other side could only drain to the east.

Consequently, the party then traveled for more than 100 miles (160 km) to the Kharta and Kama Valleys on the eastern side of the massif. The latter leads to the fearsome Kangshung or East Face of Everest, which Mallory immediately dismissed as a way of ascent and left it to "other men, less wise." By mid-August they had climbed up the Kharta Glacier, where Bullock realized their mistake; this route did not lead to the saddle between Everest and Changtse. There was another glacier between them and the Rongbuk Valley, draining to the north. And they remembered a stream they had encountered on the eastern side of the Main Rongbuk Glacier three weeks earlier . . .

Having thus discovered the true nature of the approaches to Everest from the north and east, Mallory and Bullock retreated down to the village of Kharta for a rest, where they were joined by the returning Howard-Bury, Wheeler, Morshead, and Raeburn. Partly to fulfill the goal of finding a way up the mountain, partly to compensate for his failure in recognizing the significance of the East Rongbuk Valley, Mallory decided on a last attempt to reach the North Col via a pass at the head of the Kharta Glacier. They once again set up camp at 20,000 feet (6,100 m) in the upper valley, but got stuck there for three weeks by the rains and snows of the monsoon. Perhaps nothing illustrates better the miserable living conditions and the toughness of the men than Bullock's diary entry of September 12, 1921, "There was at least 6 inches of snow. . . . Having only brought one coat, which was wet, spent the evening in a sweater. Luckily I had two."[2]

On September 23, all except Raeburn reached the pass and camped there in 34 degrees Fahrenheit of frost (minus 37 degrees Celsius). The next morning, only Mallory, Bullock, and Wheeler felt fit to continue. Accompanied by ten porters, they made it a short day by descending to the East Rongbuk Glacier before camping again at 22,000 feet (6,700 m).

The 1921 expedition's camp on the Kharta Glacier, with Lhotse in the center and Mount Everest on the right *(Photo by A. F. R. Wollaston © Royal Geographical Society, London)*

It was three tired climbers and three tired porters who embarked on the final stage of the way on September 25. Fortunately the going was straightforward; only the last slopes were steep and covered in deep snow. By 11:30 A.M., after four and a half hours of climbing, they had made it and stood in the howling wind on the shelf of the North Col at 23,180 feet (7,066 m).

The men were too weary to be triumphant—but they should have been. The expedition of 1921 had seen Mount Everest from every side, had identified a practicable approach from the north, and finally had seen a feasible route to the summit. They had paved the way.

The stream coming out of the East Rongbuk Valley does not look particularly impressive from the opposite side of the Main Rongbuk Glacier, where Mallory and Bullock had camped. But from this vantage point, one cannot fail to notice the glistening white shark fins of ice in the back of the valley—and it remains a riddle why the 1921 party did not realize that they marked a huge glacier giving access to the mountain.

The entry into the East Rongbuk Valley is a steep climb of some 500 feet (150 m) over loose moraine rubble to the terraces overlooking the left shore of the East Rongbuk River. Our 2001 expedition called this the "fun hill," which was best tackled by pointing one's nose to the ground and monotonously plodding up until the worst was over. Others took a more aggressive approach, and we could regularly

The sangas at Camp I, East Rongbuk Valley
(Photo © Jochen Hemmleb)

hear Tap Richards turning up his portable cassette player before stomping up the slope, bawling to the tunes of the aptly named rock band Rage Against the Machine.

The trail then leads along the terrace to several flat spots between boulders and a couple of *sangas,* low stone enclosures that serve as windbreaks. This was the British Camp I of 1922 and after, at around 18,100 feet (5,500 m). When Edmund Hillary and George Lowe visited the East Rongbuk Valley during a spirited round trip from Nepal in 1952, they had found an old battery still among the camp's relics, and in 1960 the Chinese discovered some food tins and a rotten pair of shoes. However, the continuous use of the site by later expeditions and trekking groups have long since erased any further traces.

Beyond, the East Rongbuk Valley becomes a classically U-shaped glacial trough, overlooked by vertical faces of turreted and shattered black-brown shale. It is a bleak, daunting scenery, especially in bad weather. After my first hike up the valley, I spoke laconically of "suicide day." Normally when trekking in bad weather, I can at least find joy in the exercise itself. But walking across the endless undulating boulder fields in driving sleet, I ceased to feel even this. The whole world was a muddy black and white, devoid of any color, lifeless and depressing. I once thought, "This would have been a good day to die."

Our expedition placed the first camp, Intermediate Camp, at 19,330 feet (5,890 m) beside a pond in the right lateral moraine. Kelsong, our Tibetan helper from Nyalam, kept a lonely vigil there for several weeks, monitoring the camp and handling the stove for climbers and trekkers who stopped for the night. Later on, when they were more adapted to altitude, most did the 12-mile (19-km) journey from Base Camp along the East Rongbuk Glacier to Advance Base Camp in a single day.

Upward, the landscape changes dramatically. The view widens to the many snowcapped peaks surrounding the valley, among which the glacier winds its way in rows after rows of white-blue translucent ice pinnacles. Like frozen sentinels, they flank the medial moraine, forming a natural gangway to the head of the glacier and the base of the North Col. In the sweltering midday heat, the broad stripe of broken boulders turns into a blistering stone desert amid a river of ice.

Fairytale country: Among the ice pinnacles of the East Rongbuk Glacier, with Everest in the background *(Photo © John Race)*

The walk continued past a couple of dammed lakes below the North Peak of Everest, Changtse, which are beautifully surrounded by shimmering walls of ice. The moraine, now clinging to the right side of the valley again, then enters the famous ice alley of the "trough." As it circles around the base of Changtse, the path slowly rises from the trench above the surface of the ice—and all of a sudden the huge bowl of the upper glacier opens in front of the hiker. Above it rises the sky-high, massive, triangular North Face of Everest's Northeast Shoulder, with its crown of menacing black rock teeth, the "Pinnacles." At last the crest of the moraine flattens out, and clustered beneath a cliff appeared a small village of tents: Advance Base Camp, at 21,200 feet (6,460 m).

Advance Base Camp (ABC) was in many senses a replica of Base Camp. It had many of the same facilities, including the kitchen, storage, and mess tents. At the same time, everything at ABC was smaller, higher, colder, and less hospitable. It also separated the climbers from the trekkers. Although any reasonably fit hiker could reach ABC, any stage of the route beyond required at least solid skills in handling ice ax, crampons, and fixed ropes. ABC was the climbers' Base Camp; this is where the ascent of the mountain started for real.

1922: FIRST CLIMBERS ATTEMPT THE SUMMIT

We now take for granted the well-established route up the East Rongbuk Valley to access the upper mountain. When in 1922 the second British expedition reached the mountain, they were the first to travel it in its entirety. And when the expedition became the first ever to place a camp above the North Col, they actually camped higher than anyone had *been* before on the Earth.

On May 21, 1922, George Mallory, who had returned to the mountain as climbing leader of the expedition, had hoped to reach the summit in a single push from their Camp V at 25,000 feet (7,620 m). To accompany him were Major Edward Felix Norton, thirty-eight, and Theodore Howard Somervell, a thirty-two-year-old London surgeon. Their fourth companion had been Henry Morshead, one of the surveyors of 1921, but he turned back shortly after leaving the tents, feeling unfit for the ascent. As the three climbed without supplementary oxygen, their progress was agonizingly slow—barely 400 feet (120 m) per hour—and it soon became apparent that the summit was beyond their reach. They plodded wearily up the broken crest of the North Ridge, drawing deep breaths between each step and resting every twenty or thirty minutes to recover. Upon reaching a slight recline in the ridge at 2:15 P.M., the party decided to rest and retreat. They had reached 26,640 feet (8,120 m)—the first people ever to pass the magic 8,000-meter mark.

Two hours later Mallory, Norton, and Somervell were back at Camp V, where they picked up Morshead and immediately continued their way down in order to reach the North Col before nightfall. But then the descent turned into a nightmare. Despite his daylong rest at the high camp, Morshead was feeling weak and suffered badly from frostbite. As time went on, his deterioration became more and more pronounced. His concentration faltered, his strength failed. Suddenly, when the four climbers were crossing the head of a snow couloir, Morshead slipped. Somervell and Norton were caught completely unaware and by turns were jerked off the slope. In a heartbeat, all three men were sliding toward the glacier 3,000 feet (900 m) below. Mallory, who had been in the lead, heard the sound behind him; by reflex he thrust his ice ax deep into the snow and slipped the rope around it. Hanging on like grim death, and aided by Somervell's own attempt to break the fall with his ax, he brought the three sliding climbers to a standstill. Mallory's quick reaction had saved their lives.

Daylight faded as the weary party groped their way down the rocks on the western side of the North Ridge toward the North Col. As they were navigating through the crevasses in the last part of the way, their only candle lantern burned out, and it was only by chance that they found the rope leading the remaining few yards to the tents. It was 11:30 P.M.—and even then their ordeal was not over: To their dismay, they found that the Sherpas had by mistake taken down all cooking utensils. A form of ice cream made from condensed milk, strawberry jam, and snow had to do for dinner.

Probably the first photograph of climbing on Mount Everest: The first party's porters moving up the North Ridge, May 20, 1922 *(Photo by Howard Somervell © Royal Geographical Society, London)*

The first assault ever on the world's highest mountain was over. When Mallory, Norton, Somervell, and Morshead descended the next morning to Advance Base Camp, the second assault party—George Ingle Finch and Geoffrey Bruce—were already on their way. And on their backs they carried the secret weapon: oxygen.

Right from the beginning of the 1922 expedition, there had been deeply divided opinion regarding the need for oxygen. Those who voted against it, George Mallory among them, did so mostly for aesthetic grounds—they regarded oxygen as "unsporting" because it, in effect, diminishes the altitude of the mountain and therefore the human challenge. With this argument, the 1922 Everest Expedition started a debate that dominates high-altitude climbing to this date. Those who voted for it, above all Finch, saw as the foremost aim of the expedition "to climb Mount Everest with every resource at our disposal" and therefore regarded oxygen as just another climbing aid, the same as crampons and ice axes.

By the time the expedition had reached the mountain, there were only a few members who had any faith in the oxygen equipment—and the first summit assault took place without it. Moreover, most of the ten oxygen sets that the expedition had brought along had been damaged in transit, and the design of the face masks proved impractical. Nonetheless Finch had managed to repair and redesign the apparatus, and by the time of the first summit attempt was ready to give it a final trial.

For his own attempt, Finch had found two strong allies: Geoffrey Bruce, the twenty-six-year-old nephew of expedition leader General Charles Grenville Bruce, and Tejbir Bura, a Nepalese soldier. The results of their trial of the oxygen sets were remarkable—three hours from Advance Base Camp to the North Col and fifty minutes back, still with time to take plenty of photographs! Full of confidence, they set off for another summit attempt two days later, accompanied as far as the North Col by the expedition's photographer and cameraman, John Noel—the same man whose account of his illicit journey toward Everest in 1913 had sown the seeds for the first expeditions.

As the three climbers continued up the North Ridge the next day, the oxygen was proving its worth indeed, for they were able to catch up with their twelve porters who had left an hour and a half earlier, despite carrying heavier loads! They eventually established Camp V on the very backbone of the ridge, some 500 feet (150 m) higher than the oxygenless party's Camp V. During the night, however, their luck ran out—a severe storm broke, ripping at the tiny tent and whirling the inhabitants around. Sleep was impossible. From time to time, one of the men had to crawl out into the ferocious gale to check the tent's guylines while the others clung to the flapping canvas, which was threatening to be blown off the mountain.

When the wind abated the next afternoon, Finch, Bruce, and Tejbir decided to take the chance and sit out another night. But then thirty-six hours without

THE FIRST USE OF OXYGEN ON MOUNT EVEREST

Although supplementary oxygen had been given a trial in Himalayan climbing as early as 1907, the 1922 Everest Expedition was the first to use it as a systematic aid in the ascent of a mountain.

The key figure in introducing supplementary oxygen to the expedition was George Ingle Finch (1888–1970). Born in Australia and raised in Switzerland, Finch's upbringing and background differed vastly from that of his British contemporaries. Besides being a strong climber, he also was a scientist with a creative mind whose inventions included the first down jacket used in high-altitude mountaineering. Unfortunately, Finch's unorthodox views and outspokenness made him unpopular with the establishment of the British Alpine Club and the Mount Everest Committee, so most of his skills and genius became unavailable to the early expeditions.

During a visit to Oxford, Finch had been advised to consider the usage of supplementary oxygen at high altitudes, based on experiences with Royal Air Force pilots. Finch undertook exercises in a decompression chamber, and the differences in his performance with and without oxygen convinced the Mount Everest Committee to set aside a budget for constructing a breathing apparatus to be used by the climbers.

One 1922 oxygen set consisted of a pack frame with four vertically mounted steel cylinders, air tubes, regulator valves, pressure gauges, and a face mask delivering the oxygen supply to the climber. One cylinder was capable of holding 240 liters of oxygen, stored at a pressure of 120 atmospheres. The weight of one full set with four bottles was about 32 pounds (14.5 kg). It was able to provide the climber with seven or eight hours of oxygen, depending on the chosen flow rate, 2 or 2.4 liters per minute.

Besides taking pressurized oxygen, the 1922 British expedition also experimented with "Oxylithe bags," in which oxygen was produced from a chemical reaction on sodium peroxide.

adequate sleep or food started to take their toll. The cold was numbing, they could feel the onset of frostbite, and their life resources were draining away. Suddenly Finch remembered the oxygen. He put on a mask, opened the valve—and the effect was miraculous. Warmth started to flow back into his limbs, and when Bruce and Tejbir tried this cure, it also revived them instantly. They decided to rig the oxygen in a way that they could breathe the gas during the night, and as a result slept soundly until the morning.

They set off at 6:30 A.M. on May 27, with the intention of reaching the junction between the North and Northeast Ridges, where Tejbir was to hand over his spare oxygen cylinders and return to camp. But the plan fell to pieces immediately; Tejbir collapsed from exhaustion only a short way beyond the tent. Finch and Bruce picked up Tejbir's oxygen and continued, their chances of success now greatly reduced. To add to their mishap, the relentless wind had risen again, so they were forced to leave the North Ridge and traverse out onto the North Face. After traversing for 0.5 mile (800 m), they decided to aim for the Northeast Ridge again.

They reached the Yellow Band, a conspicuously colored layer of sandy limestone stretching across the whole width of the North Face. Finch was in the lead, approaching the tip of a prominent snow triangle below the crest, when he suddenly heard Bruce crying out behind him, "I am getting no oxygen!" He climbed down just

Finch and Bruce (in front) returning to the North Col after their summit bid, May 27, 1922; note Finch's down parka and Bruce's oxygen equipment. *(Photo by John Noel © Royal Geographical Society, London)*

in time to prevent his friend from toppling over backward into the void. A connecting tube in Bruce's oxygen set had broken, and although they managed an immediate repair, they realized they would not be able to continue.

Finch and Bruce had established a new altitude record of almost 27,500 feet (8,380 m). It was even more remarkable for young Geoffrey Bruce, because probably no other climber could claim to have set an altitude record during his very first climb. On the way down, the pair reunited with Tejbir, who had fully recovered, at Camp V, and descended all the way to Advance Base Camp the same evening.

After Finch and Bruce returned from their summit bid, the expedition planned a third attempt. Although they were aware that the monsoon was about to break and snow fell regularly during the afternoons, the party tackled the North Col again on June 7. The leading rope comprised Somervell, Mallory, a porter, and Colin Crawford, a thirty-two-year-old Indian civil servant with climbing experience in the Kashmir and on Kangchenjunga. They were followed by thirteen porters, divided into three ropes.

After a brief rest some 600 feet (180 m) below the North Col, they had just resumed their ascent when they suddenly heard a muffled crack behind them, "like an explosion of untamped gunpowder." The surface of the snow buckled and broke into slabs, carrying the men with them. After what were only a few seconds that seemed like eternity, the avalanche stopped. Mallory and the others quickly extricated themselves. They were unharmed, like the first rope of four porters below them. But of the remaining nine porters there was no sign.

They had been swept over a 60-foot-high (20-m-high) cliff and buried in a yawning crevasse at the bottom. Frantically, the men started digging with their axes and bare hands. Two porters were still alive, one after being buried for forty minutes. Seven were dead. According to the wishes of the survivors, these were left in the snow that had become their grave.[3]

Jake Norton's discovery of a 1922 oxygen bottle in a frozen pond among the moraine below Advance Base Camp on March 30, 2001, marked our first encounter with the early British Everest expeditions. At the time, Norton had been unable to extract it from the ice. So he called Dave Hahn and John Race at the camp to come down to the site with their ice axes. The two managed to chop out the bottle, and Race found another lying among the moraine rubble nearby. Two days later, Hahn found a third bottle in the vicinity. Water must have seeped into this bottle through the broken

One of the oxygen bottles from 1922 on the moraine below Advanced Base Camp *(Photo © John Race)*

Oxygen bottles and crampon heel from the British 1922 Everest expedition (Photo © Jake Norton)

valve and frozen, and the pressure of the expanding ice had split the cylinder open—a visible demonstration of what ice can do even to steel! Finally, a fourth 1922 bottle was found four weeks later by Sherpa Pemba Geljen at just under 24,900 feet (7,600 m) on the North Ridge. This one was in almost pristine condition, with remnants of the original coating of white paint, an intact rubber seal, and a functioning valve.

Over the first two weeks after the first discoveries, Race, Hahn, and later also Brent Okita and Andy Politz returned several times to the area around the frozen pond. They recovered parts of wooden packing cases; countless rusted tins, some of them still with traceable imprints; and a few solid-fuel burners. Among the less-ordinary relics were a bizarre piece of wood with riveted leather straps attached to it, perhaps part of a porter's carrying basket; a hand-forged crampon heel; and several old zinc-carbon batteries, perhaps from Captain John Noel's movie camera. Scattered over the fields of scree were the remnants of the 1922 Advance Base Camp, Camp III.

At first glance the site looked like a rubbish dump, which brought up the question, what had we really found there at 21,000 feet (6,400 m) along the upper East Rongbuk Glacier? Trash or treasure? When does a piece of garbage become an archeological artifact?

On the face of it, there is little difference between, say, a rusted tin from 1922 and a rusted French gas cartridge from 1981. But it has often been rubbish, leftovers

Zinc-carbon batteries found among the remnants of the 1922 Camp III (Photo © Jochen Hemmleb)

from everyday life, that has given insights into circumstances and events of early expeditions. Food tins, for example, provided a crucial hint for Canadian anthropologist Owen Beattie in his investigation of Sir John Franklin's ill-fated expedition to the Northwest Passage in 1845. Almost 140 years later, Beattie could prove that lead from the tins' flawed soldering had poisoned Franklin's crew and ultimately caused the death of all 129 members. Incidentally, it was Beattie's combining of archeology and forensic pathology to solve a historical riddle that had greatly inspired my own quest for Mallory and Irvine.

The tins we found from 1922 did not help solve a mystery, but they gave testimony to the harshness of living on expeditions back in those days. The tins often contained only tiny quantities of food, and to sustain a whole team they must have been transported to the camps in large numbers—a far greater logistical problem than that presented by our freeze-dried, lightweight foods. It was also touching to recognize familiar brands, such as Ovaltine, some of which we had brought along ourselves.

The most telling items, however, were still the oxygen cylinders. They were a document of an event significant in mountaineering history—the first use of bottled oxygen as a climbing aid—and, at the same time, some of the oldest traces to be found on Everest. The inspiration derived from these first discoveries in 2001 set the stage for the search up high.

Part of a porter's carrying basket (or snowshoe?), found at the 1922 Camp III (Photo © Jochen Hemmleb)

HIGH-ALTITUDE ARCHEOLOGY

Although chance discoveries of relics have occurred before, the joint project of the 1999 and 2001 Mallory & Irvine Research Expeditions was only the second ever aimed specifically at looking for traces of the early Everest attempts, and the first to actually carry out its task.

With the main field area located above 24,500 feet (7,500 m), the project represented the highest archeological expedition ever conducted. At these altitudes the effects of extreme weather conditions—such as gale-force winds, extreme cold, dehydration, and lack of oxygen—combined with difficult mountain terrain often render the application of traditional archeological methods impossible. To obtain scientifically viable data under such conditions, traditional investigations need to be modified, just as they have been for underwater archeology. The two expeditions therefore have to be regarded as a work-in-progress, exploring the feasibility of certain research tasks, the experiences of which may ultimately lead to the creation of investigation techniques that can be adopted for future archeological research in similarly extreme environments.

Fieldwork: In preparation of the search on Mount Everest, we made an effort to compile the available information about the search areas. Sources included historical accounts and photographs, recent terrain descriptions, and large-scale, high-resolution aerial photos.

The actual search efforts were followed by telescope from Base Camp and some of the information relayed to the search team by radio to facilitate orientation. In 2001 we used a compact mirror-lens optic telescope (Meade ETX 90 Schmidt-Maksutov), because it combined a short tube for easy transport with a long focal length for high magnification (30x to 200x). Despite high-definition optics on a sturdy mount, viewing from Base Camp was often hampered by strong winds causing excessive vibrations and image distortion.

The equipment for the search on the mountain was chosen for its portability, ease of operation, and real-time data display. Basic measuring equipment included scale bars, tape measure, and compass, but the harsh environmental conditions often made the detailed measuring of a site awkward, if not dangerous. However, with coverage from still and video cameras that included north-oriented scale bars (or at least an object with a known size, such as an ice ax) in the field of view, satisfactory small-scale spatial information could be recorded with minimal demands on the climbers. Digital still cameras were a certain asset, because they allow checking an image on location as well as immediate analysis of images at Base Camp.

We found metal detectors useful for locating metallic objects (cameras, tins, et cetera) under snow and scree within a search site. Because their scanning range is limited to a few feet, they were not practical for any wide-field search for bodies or camps. For the latter, visual inspection by a trained search team working along a grid pattern has so far proven to be the most-effective and least-complicated method.

For recovery, artifacts were sealed in plastic bags together with sachets of silica gel to prevent damage through condensation. Special light-tight bags, originally used to protect photographic paper, were brought in case of finding ancient film, together with insulating material.

Circumstances permitting, recovered artifacts were photographed on location to record their position within the search site. Immediately after recovery, we took a set of "field photos" to document the artifacts' actual condition. Before permanent storage, we took a last set of "lab photos," for which the artifact was cleaned and positioned on a copy stand with scale bars. This last set of photographs defines the permanent and standardized documentation of every artifact. Preparation of the artifacts and photography was done by a professional archeologist (Rick Reanier, Seattle).

In the two cases where human remains were found (George Mallory and Maurice Wilson), the photographs were additionally studied by medical consultants (Donald T. Reay,

M.D., former chief medical examiner for the Seattle–King County Department of Public Health; and Lee Meyers, M.D., expedition doctor).

Office/laboratory work: At present, I am working to establish a database for all information in regard to archeological discoveries on Everest's north side, the scene of the early British and Chinese expeditions. The database encompasses the research done in 1999 and 2001, as well as discoveries made by other parties.

The compiled information includes recordings of any discovery or observation (written accounts, photographs, and films) as well as descriptions and photographs of any recovered artifacts. The location of any discovery is determined from its description, field photos (back bearings over recognizable topographical features, comparison with photographs of known locations), or GPS recordings, and its position recorded on maps and/or large-scale orthophotos.

The artifacts recovered in 2001 were stored under ideal conditions in the temperature- and humidity-controlled facilities of the Washington State Historical Society Research Center in Tacoma, Washington.

The professional curation and study of the artifacts are funded by the American Foundation for International Mountaineering Exploration and Research (AFFIMER), in collaboration with the Washington State History Museum in Tacoma. AFFIMER is dedicated to promoting public education of the world's mountainous environments by supporting scientific, cultural, and historical research projects. The organization is recognized by the Internal Revenue Service as a qualified Public Benefit Corporation and receives its funding from private contributions as well as public donations. AFFIMER, a key sponsor of both the 1999 and 2001 Mallory & Irvine Research Expeditions, has dealt with the legal and logistical aspects of the transfer of the Mallory artifacts to the Royal Geographical Society in London.

If readers of this book know of any hitherto unrecorded discovery or observation with regard to traces of the early Everest expeditions, please contact the author either by e-mail (j.hemmleb@gmx.de) or care of The Mountaineers Books.

Climb to the sun: Ascending the North Col slopes *(Photo © Jake Norton)*

Meanwhile, our Sherpas and the climbing team had found and prepared a safe route up the North Col slopes. The ice wall of the North Col is the most treacherous place on the classic route from the north, besides the summit ridge. Like a series of crested waves, broken towers of shimmering blue-gray ice cascade from the pass onto the glacier 1,200 feet (370 m) below. Especially when laden with fresh snow, the slopes are dangerously avalanche-prone, the tragedy of 1922 being just one telltale example. This year a broad, slanting ramp led past the steep, jumbled central section, which had made the climb so surprisingly demanding in 1999. Camp IV on the col was established on March 29, one of the earliest dates ever. The gate to the upper mountain was open.

GHOST FROM THE GLACIER: MAURICE WILSON

Very few relics from the early expeditions have remained in the area between Advance Base Camp and the North Col. On the snowy surface of the glacier they were slowly submerged and, as the river of ice crept downward, were transported away from their original location as if on a conveyor belt. On some occasions, however, the glacier yielded some of its cargo.

Perhaps the most famous case of such "reappearances" is that of Maurice Wilson, the eccentric British soloist who tried to climb Everest on a religious mission in 1934 and died of exhaustion below the North Col. After the discovery of his body by members of the 1935 reconnaissance, who buried it in a crevasse, Wilson seemingly refused to be put to rest—as if his indomitable spirit persevered even in death. In 1960, Chinese climbers found and reburied him, and since then

there have been regular sightings of a diminishing bundle of bones and clothing emerging from the ice below Advance Base Camp. Dr. Lee Meyers and I saw the remains still there in 1999.

In 2001, our expedition rediscovered the remnants of the Chinese 1960 "temporary camp," which in 1999 had already been found resurfacing near the base of the North Col. Together with support trekker Dick Dickerson, I excavated the site once more, adding more items to the collection brought back two years earlier. By comparing the location with photos from the 1960 Chinese expedition, we determined that the relics of the camp had traveled a distance of roughly 0.6 mile (1 km) in the past forty years. This indicated that this part of the East Rongbuk Glacier progresses some 80 feet (25 m) per year, or ¼ inch (0.7 cm) per day.

CHAPTER 6

SHORT WALK
INTO THE PAST

It was like Christmas Day and Tap Richards was Santa Claus with his pack full of goodies. One by one he pulled them out: a silvery ten-point crampon; an ice ax with a wooden shaft, its spike and ferrule missing; some pieces of fabric.

"Found this around the 1960 and 1975 Chinese Camp VI. . . . When I discovered the '75 camp, I saw two of the big blue oxygen bottles right away. . . . And I walked another twenty feet, and I found those small bottles, the same-style tents, and all kinds of stuff."

In the gravel in front of us were the fingerprints of one of the most enigmatic episodes in the history of Everest—the Chinese expeditions of the 1960s and 1970s.

For ten days after establishing Camp IV on the North Col, our Sherpas and the climbing team tried to push the route farther along the North Ridge to Camp V. The North Ridge is a 4,500-foot-high (1,350-m-high) spur forming the east border of the North Face. It leads straight up from the col toward the skyline of the Northeast Ridge, joining it in a prominent shoulder at 27,636 feet (8,423 m), a mile to the left of the summit. The lower 1,700 feet (520 m) of the North Ridge is a wide, humpbacked tongue of snow, above which the ridge becomes a rounded, irregular rock buttress. About two-thirds up the ridge, at around 25,900 feet (7,900 m), is a weakly pronounced recline, where we intended to place our Camp V.

Nowhere is the going along the North Ridge particularly difficult or steep, but there is one big enemy, the wind. When it screams across the buttress at up to 100 miles per hour (160 km per hour), ripping the snow off in streaming banners of spindrift, it can ground climbers for days or even weeks. From his various Everest trips, Dave Hahn had some tall stories of how moving up the ridge could then become like scrambling into a jet engine, with the wind blowing people off their feet or

NORTH RIDGE ARCHEOLOGY

Nothing demonstrates the time capsule-like character of Everest's North Face better than the 1,000-foot-high (300-m-high) stretch of the North Ridge above 24,900 feet (7,590 m), between the top of the snow crest and the first recline.

Since the early British attempts, expeditions have placed their Camp V along this section of the ridge. During the British pre–World War II expeditions, the camp was placed progressively higher with time; the 1922 Camp V was lowest and the 1938 Camp V was highest. All in all, there were five different Camp V sites used during these early expeditions, two in 1922, and one each in 1924, 1933, and 1938. Higher up, but also along the crest of the North Ridge, were the 1924 and 1938 Camp VIs.

Within a relatively small area, therefore, the North Ridge offers a true sightseeing trip through history, with each historic campsite and its artifacts representing stages in the development of equipment for high-altitude climbing.

Because the main search areas of the 2001 Mallory & Irvine Research Expedition were situated higher up the mountain, logistics and time constraints prevented a systematic investigation of the Camp V sites along the North Ridge. Dave Hahn attempted to locate the lower 1922 camp by traversing left from the top of the snow crest, but abandoned his effort due to high winds and the awkwardness of the terrain. Other expeditions, however, have managed to rediscover some of the sites in recent years.

In 1960, Chinese climbers found an old campsite a short distance above their Camp V at 25,560 feet (7,790 m). The site contained remnants of an old tent, tent poles, a green sleeping bag, a stove board, candles, and chocolate bars. The Chinese brought back a functioning oxygen set consisting of a stocky steel cylinder, the breathing apparatus, and the pack frame. This was later identified as the set left behind by Peter Lloyd in 1938. The camp was visited again in 1997 by a commercial expedition, which still found the tent with wooden poles and pegs, some food tins, and a brass pocket knife.

In 1984, David Hambly of the American Ultima Thule Expedition found a wooden-handled ice ax and some food tins on tent platforms at about 25,600 feet (7,800 m). The head of the ax bears a stamp of the Austrian manufacturer "A. Horeschowsky, Wien," which is known to have equipped the 1933 expedition.

Also in 1984, Donald Goodman wandered from the present-day Camp VI over to the scree shoulder at the top of the North Ridge, where he came across the remnants of the 1938 Camp VI. Goodman found a tattered tent frozen to the ground, from which he recovered an aluminum thermos flask.

All these discoveries underline how many relics of the early expeditions have actually remained on the upper slopes of Everest's North Face, and that they can still be found after several decades.

---

forcing them into all sorts of weird performances worthy of Monty Python's "Ministry of Silly Walks."

Twice the wind drove our team back from the top of the snow. Not willing for the group to waste more time and strength, Eric Simonson decided to send five additional Sherpas to the col. When the wind abated the next morning, April 9, they took no chances. By 10:00 A.M. Tap Richards, Jake Norton, Andy Politz, Brent Okita, and the eleven Sherpas had already reached the first rocks of the North Ridge, where they dumped their loads. From there they fixed ropes all the way to 25,600 feet (7,800 m). This was still some 200 feet (60 m) or so below the intended spot, a larger shelf where the ridge reclines briefly. In fact, it is about the only place on the

North Ridge where four tents can be pitched next to each other. The following day, Ang Chhiring "Kami" and seven of his colleagues finally succeeded in establishing Camp V by carrying up the stashed loads and fixing ropes the rest of the way.

Beyond Camp V the route veers to the right, onto the North Face, and up to Camp VI. At 26,900 feet (8,200 m) the slope starts to relent into a vast, tilted expanse of scree and snow, 0.3 mile (500 m) long and 300 yards (270 m) wide. This is the somewhat misnamed Snow Terrace. After a fresh snowfall, it looks like a draped curtain hanging across the upper North Face from the lower edge of the Yellow Band, with a fold running diagonally through its center. This is the ill-defined rib, a key reference point in the search for Mallory and Irvine. We had found Mallory's body to the right of the rib's lower end in 1999. Now, on a clear and still afternoon, we could even see his burial mound through the telescope at Base Camp. And somewhere among these slopes still lay, perhaps, the solution to the mystery of his and Irvine's final climb.

Our plan was to follow the trail of the early British expeditions along the North Ridge and North Face, but we knew we would inevitably also follow another trail—that of the Chinese expeditions of the 1960s and 1970s—because on one day in May 1975, these two trails had intersected.

The North Ridge and North Face of Mount Everest from Camp IV on the North Col
(Photo © Jake Norton)

On May 5, 1975, two Chinese climbers, Wang Hongbao and Zhang Junyan, were resting in their tent at Camp VI on the North Face at around 26,900 feet (8,200 m). In the morning, their group climbing leader, Chen Tianliang, had left the camp together with a Tibetan porter for Camp VII in search of a missing climber. Wu Zongyue had disappeared somewhere between the camps the day before and so far had not turned up. At one point during the day, Wang crawled out of the tent "to go for a walk," while Zhang stayed in his sleeping bag. Twenty minutes later Wang came back. He did not say anything, but a couple of days later, when he and Zhang descended, Wang revealed that during his walk from Camp VI he had found the body of a foreign mountaineer.

Four years later, in autumn 1979, Wang returned to Everest with a Japanese reconnaissance expedition. On October 11, he hiked up to Camp III together with a Japanese climber, Ryoten Hasegawa. Although neither spoke the other's language, they had managed to string a conversation along through gestures and characters etched in the snow. Hasegawa was interested in the story of Maurice Wilson, who had died on Everest in 1934. The Chinese climbers had spotted his body near Camp III on several occasions, and Hasegawa asked Wang about it. "Yes," Wang replied, he had seen Wilson's body before (during a reconnaissance in 1965). But then Wang pointed up to the Northeast Ridge, saying, "Eight thousand, one hundred meter . . . Engleese" and put his hands together against his cheek in a gesture of sleeping. Then he opened his mouth, pecked his cheek slightly with his finger, and whirled it. He also picked at his clothing, moved his fingers to his mouth, and blew against them. Hasegawa took this as indication that the body's mouth was agape, its cheek sunken or pecked by birds, and that the body's clothing was in tatters, flapping in the wind.

A sleeping (dead?) "Engleese" (Englishman?) at 8,100 meters (26,575 feet)? To make sure he had not misunderstood, Hasegawa etched some characters in the snow, "8,100 m—dead English body," and Wang gave a big nod. Hasegawa realized the implications of what he had just heard. Only two climbers had died above 8,100 meters before 1975—the "English dead" could only be Mallory or Irvine! Hasegawa felt he would need to talk to Wang again later, asking for more details.[1]

It was not going to happen. The very next day, Hasegawa, Wang, and two other Chinese climbers, Nima Zhaxi (or Nima Tashi) and Luo Lang, were ascending to the North Col when an avalanche swept them away. Hasegawa arrested himself on the edge of the slope, escaping with five broken ribs, but the three Chinese climbers fell into a crevasse. All were killed.

Whom had Wang found, Mallory or Irvine? In 1933, Irvine's ice ax had been discovered near the crest of the Northeast Ridge, above and to the southwest of the Chinese Camp VI. Therefore a body somewhere near the Chinese camp was most likely Irvine's. But it was Mallory our expedition found below the ice-ax site in 1999.

Mallory's posture, facedown in the gravel, would not have allowed Wang to see a hole in the cheek. Only the clothing on Mallory's back was shorn away by the wind, demonstrating that the body had rested in the same position, unmoved, throughout the years. Later inspection also showed that Mallory's cheeks were undamaged anyway. Also, the 1999 search team felt that the body's location was too far away from the area of the Chinese camp to have been discovered within twenty minutes, the time Wang had been away from his tent.

Yet time estimations at altitude can easily be erroneous, and the 1999 team had not found the actual 1975 Chinese Camp VI to confirm our estimates of its distance from the body. Jake Norton's discovery of a 1975 oxygen bottle had merely put the searchers in the vicinity, not in the camp itself.

Our 2001 expedition continued to operate on the belief that Wang had found Irvine and that Irvine's body was still up there somewhere on the North Face, in the vicinity of the Chinese camp. Others were not convinced. In order to find out the true identity of the "English dead," we needed to find the 1975 Chinese Camp VI—and put ourselves in Wang Hongbao's footsteps.

The first search team of Dave Hahn, Andy Politz, and Tap Richards left Camp V at 6:00 A.M. on April 24, 2001. The day before, two Sherpas had completed the route to Camp VI, but the climbing was still taxing because there were yet no well-trodden steps, and the reliability of the fixed ropes was untested. The searchers were the first to tread the upper slopes of the North Face while the majority of climbers waited below.

Two hours later, Hahn, Politz, and Richards wrestled with the usual high winds on the North Ridge, but were hoping for better conditions on the face, on which they were about to traverse. From Base Camp, we first saw them through the telescope at 9:45 A.M., three black dots moving over a snowfield to the start of a pronounced ledge leading to the right, into the gully stretching upward to Camp VI. We could see them clearly at 80x magnification, even though they were 11 miles (17 km) away.

When they were two-thirds up the gully, at around 11:00 A.M., something unexpected happened. We watched one climber—it turned out to be Richards—leaving the fixed ropes and climbing to the right, along a fairly prominent ledge system, out onto the ill-defined rib. After walking his solitary way for about 150 yards (140 m), he finally came on the air. "Can you see me through the telescope?"

"If you are the one doing that great detour to the right, then we can," I answered.

This was followed by a tantalizing reply, "Here's the 1975 Camp VI!" Richards had finally found the very camp from where Wang Hongbao had come across his "English dead."

"The first thing I saw," Richards remembered, "were pieces of white tent

The debris of the
1975 Chinese Camp VI
(Photo © Tap Richards)

Below:

1960 Chinese oxygen
bottle. Note German
inscription "Sauerstoff"
(oxygen) and date 11.59.
*(Photo/video image
© Dave Hahn)*

fabric, which immediately reminded me of the Chinese camp we
had found in 1999 below the North Col. Then I looked down
below me and saw an aluminum tripod lying on the rocks. Next
I found an old-style crampon and, after walking for a few more
minutes, two big blue 1975 oxygen bottles. So I figured this is
it." But the 1975 expedition was not the only one to have left
traces in the area. Less than 30 feet (10 m) away lay an old oxygen
set with mask, regulators, and a stocky blue bottle. We had seen
identical bottles in a copy of the 1960 Chinese expedition film,
which I had obtained from the BBC a few years ago and brought
with me. The 1960 team, which claimed the first ascent of Everest
from the north had come this way, too (see "1960: The Chinese
Go for the Prize," in Chapter 9, The Invisible Summit).

COLOR-CODED FINGERPRINTS—THE CHINESE OXYGEN SETS

During the 1999 and 2001 Mallory & Irvine Research Expeditions, our team discovered several campsites and other equipment from the Chinese expeditions of the 1960s and 1970s. Once the relics had been identified as Chinese, it became apparent how widely distributed they were across the upper mountain. This brought up the difficulty of how to distinguish one expedition's camp from the other, or how to date each camp.

A vital key to the task proved to be the various oxygen bottles the Chinese expeditions had used. Up to Camp VI, the 1960 expedition had used short, stocky steel cylinders with rounded ends. They were manufactured by a German company, Dräger. Each cylinder held 400 liters of oxygen stored at 200 atmospheres. Two or three of these were mounted horizontally in a pack frame, which also held an array of valves and regulators. Their bright blue color distinguishes them from the dark British cylinders, which were slightly larger but similar in shape.

Above Camp VI the 1960 Chinese expedition used a different type of bottle, a long aluminum-alloy cylinder with a capped end, wrapped with wire for reinforcement. Each of these bottles, made in France, held between 700 and 900 liters of oxygen stored at 180 to 230 atmospheres. This had been the standard oxygen bottle for high-altitude climbing during the mid-1950s to late 1970s, and the 1975 Chinese expedition had used this type in abundance. With only this type present at a camp, a distinction becomes more difficult. Sometimes it can be made by color. The 1960 expedition's bottles were often gray or unpainted, whereas the bottles used in 1975 were painted blue—although the 1960 team had also used a number of blue French bottles.

Knowledge of the differences in design, shape, and color of the various oxygen sets used by the Chinese helped our expedition to determine conclusively the correct positions and altitudes of the 1960 and 1975 Chinese Camps V and VI, which had so far been known only insufficiently. This in turn enabled us to reconstruct for the first time the route these expeditions had taken on the upper mountain, offering a fresh perspective on Wang Hongbao's find of an "English dead" in 1975 and other discoveries the Chinese may or may not have made during their ascents of Mount Everest.

As Richards climbed the remaining way through some blocky terrain to the rounded crest of the ill-defined rib, he tried to imagine how Wang Hongbao would have thought. "He could have walked everywhere from this point, but to me the most likely direction clearly seemed 'up.' So I began switchbacking up the rib."

Driven on by the belief that the discovery of Sandy Irvine—and, with it, possibly the solution to the mystery of Mount Everest's first ascent—might be less than twenty minutes away, Richards never stopped. He had left his pack behind at the fixed ropes and was climbing without oxygen. As he crisscrossed up the crest and right side of the rib, Richards found that the Chinese had left a virtual trail of equipment leading out of their camp. First he came across another tent, then more crampons and oxygen bottles, strewn along the slope all the way up to the point where, two years earlier, Jake Norton had found another 1975 bottle. All along the way, Richards kept looking for places where Wang could have walked during his twenty-minute stroll. But only when he linked up with the higher 1999 search route did he see an obvious ramp leading over into the basin to the right of the rib.

Brent Okita climbs toward the Yellow Band above Camp IV. *(Photo © Jake Norton)*

At this point Hahn and Politz reached our Camp VI. The modern-day Camp VI is located halfway between the North Ridge and the ill-defined rib, at 26,900 feet (8,200 m). There is another site farther uphill, near the head of the rib at 27,200 feet (8,290 m), but it is less used because it adds an additional hour of climbing to the ascent from Camp V.

From the crest of the rib, Richards could see his partners moving around the camp. His radio batteries were dead and he had left behind any spares with his pack, so he shouted and waved for Hahn and Politz to join him. Together, the three probed the shelves around the head of the rib up to the higher Camp VI site, which was marked by a mess of shredded tents and broken tent poles. Soon after, Politz headed back in the direction of the North Ridge with the aim of searching for the 1924 British Camp VI (see "1924: A Strong Team Arrives with High Hopes" in Chapter 7, Last Camp), while Richards and Hahn descended the southwestern part of the snow terrace toward the place where Mallory lay.

At one point we held our breath when we saw Richards crouching for at least fifteen minutes beside a large boulder on the right flank of the rib. Had he found Irvine and was now investigating the body for a camera? No. Richards had merely stopped to take a rest and survey the surrounding terrain. Meanwhile, Hahn had come down the slopes farther to the west, and we saw the two converging briefly on the snow above Mallory.

After that they separated again, with Hahn climbing back up the basin and Richards retracing his steps all the way back east to the fixed ropes to retrieve his pack. As Richards recrossed the chute between Mallory and the ill-defined rib, he found a poignant memento of 1999: a piece of Mallory's brown sweater frozen in the snow, which the wind must have carried away from the grave. Richards found a ramp leading back over the rib, which brought him onto a slabby ledge below the Chinese camps. Shortly before reaching the gully leading to our Camp VI, he found at the base of a huge square rock a second Chinese campsite, marked again by a white tent and oxygen bottles.

When Dave Hahn returned to Camp VI that evening, we heard that he had discovered a modern crampon and boot only 30 or 40 feet (10 to 12 m) away from Mallory's grave. Two days later, Richards found a broken ski pole nearby. The equipment belonged to a Danish climber who had fallen from the Yellow Band the year before—a grim reminder that the slope had lost little of its danger in the decades since it had claimed Mallory's life.

Camp VI (*Photo © Mike Otis*)

The next afternoon, Richards and Politz returned again to the search. Traversing the head of the basin, they came across the crumpled corpse of Wu Zongyue, the Chinese climber who had died in a fall from the ridge in 1975. Richards had already seen his remains two years before, identifying him by his old-style crampons and red, blue, and white clothing.

The two climbers finally arrived at a rocky tongue stretching down the slope from the base of the Yellow Band. As they searched the broken ledges, Richards and Politz suddenly saw a massive, dark-gray storm cloud rapidly approaching the mountain. "I was amazed at how fast it moved," recalled Richards. "It was really frightening. Andy and I just looked at each other and said, 'Let's get the hell out of here!'" To cover some more ground, they took a higher line than they had when traversing into the basin and hurried back to the tents. Fortunately, apart from a few flurries of snow, the storm never materialized.

DEAD BODIES ON MOUNT EVEREST

During our team's searches of the upper North Face in 1999 and 2001, we not only found Mallory's body, but also came across four other victims from more recent times.

Such grisly encounters have become regular occurrences over the last decade. With the increased number of expeditions, the death toll on Mount Everest has also risen. As of spring 2001, 171 people have died on the mountain, including five women. Before the 1990s, a majority of fatalities occurred in the Khumbu Icefall on Everest's southern ascent route or on the North Col and were caused by avalanches, collapsing seracs (ice towers), or falls into crevasses. Nowadays, proportionally more climbers die up high, either of exhaustion or in falls during the descent from the summit. Although some victims have never been found, many remain on the upper slopes of the Southeast and Northeast Ridges, the two most-frequented routes.

The decisions and difficulties that our search teams faced while encountering some of these victims brought up some controversial issues regarding the treatment of dead bodies on Mount Everest (and other mountains). Can bodies be recovered or receive a proper burial? If so, by whom and how? If not, why did Mallory qualify for special treatment?

Some of the victims who died on the lower mountain have been brought down for cremation, burial, or, in a few cases, conveyance to their home countries. By contrast, bringing down corpses from high altitude is mostly considered impossible. Only in very few cases have bodies been recovered from the elevation of a high camp, around 26,000 feet (7,920 m) or above—and these all have been on Everest's South Side, where the predominantly snowy terrain makes transport less difficult than on the rocky North Side. Still, any such effort essentially required a separately organized expedition.

Because any recovery is a logistically complex and costly affair, members of commercial expeditions are often asked to sign a "body disposal form," in which they determine what will happen to their bodies if they die on the mountain. Thus a recovery is attempted only upon the climber's own wish.

A proper burial on the mountain can be equally problematic, as was exemplified by Mallory's case. It took five men three-quarters of an hour to cover the body with rocks, which they first had to pry up from the frozen ground or chop off from larger boulders. The work was exhausting, time-consuming, and risky, done on a steep slope threatened from above by rockfall.

Our search team was looking specifically for Mallory and Irvine, and had been asked to bury their remains if found. The burial was one of the expedition's agreed-upon tasks. There was neither time nor manpower available to perform a similar service for the other victims that the search team had incidentally come across. The latter is probably true for most cases, because planned searches are an exception and most victims are found more or less by chance.

As a least act of piety, climbers passing dead bodies often try to conceal them or move them away from the route, out of sight. In extreme circumstances, this includes throwing a corpse down the mountain. Horrifying and disrespectful as this might seem, it is often the only way to put it to rest forever—and arguably more respectful than leaving a body to become a landmark on a well-traveled route.

On day three of the search, April 26, all climbers returned to the Chinese Camp VI for a final investigation. First they found a broken, wooden-handled ice ax. The rusted head bore a stamp, "11-58," which put it squarely in the time period of the 1960 Chinese ascent. Then they came across a "ribbon basket," a survey target made of two red-painted aluminum discs connected by a dozen red nylon ribbons. It belonged to the tripod Richards had found two days earlier and was identical to the

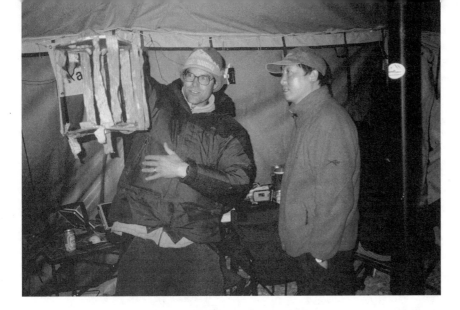

survey tripod that the 1975 Chinese expedition had erected on the summit. All in all, there were at least three established tent platforms and a number of usable, albeit sloping ledges distributed over an area the size of an Olympic swimming pool.

Throughout the search Politz, normally a man of indefatigable strength, felt cold and exhausted—until he found he had not switched on his oxygen all morning. Together with Hahn he remained in the vicinity of the Chinese camps while Richards decided to have a last look at the slopes above Mallory's body for signs of Sandy Irvine.

Survey target found at the 1975 Chinese Camp VI site. An identical survey target was erected on the summit by the 1975 Chinese expedition. (Photo © Jochen Hemmleb)

Ice ax, oxygen set, and marker wand from the 1960 Chinese expedition (Photo © Jake Norton)

Chinese climbing equipment (piton hammer, rock pitons, crampon, and ice ax) recovered during the 2001 research expedition *(Photo © Andy Politz)*

Below the Chinese 1960 and 1975 camps the ill-defined rib broadened, forming almost a little knoll. It was a spectacular viewpoint, overlooking the whole basin to the right of the rib. Getting into the basin from there, however, proved to be difficult. "There were a few precarious rock steps on that downsloping traverse, and it really did not seem like the natural place where somebody would walk," Richards observed. He followed a line along the ledges just above the point where the slope breaks off into the North Face, which led him right below Mallory's grave. "I just spent a few seconds with George. [The] 1999 [expedition] was a thing of the past, so I did not want to disturb him with my presence again."

As Richards cramponed up the 40-degree snow slope above, which was as crisp as Styrofoam, he tried to picture how a fall would take place under these conditions. "If someone had fallen from higher up, with time to accelerate, he would have gone past Mallory's location at 80 miles per hour," Richards theorized. For Mallory to have stopped at his resting place, Richards felt more and more convinced that the fatal fall must have occurred from low down, perhaps even below the Yellow Band. Politz, who was to cross the same slope later that day, agreed and pointed out how easily a slip could have happened to an exhausted party on this kind of snow, especially when wearing only hobnailed boots.

Richards continued upward. Below the 1999 search route, he noticed some big ledges and rock steps on the right flank of the ill-defined rib, "where somebody perhaps would curl up for the evening if they were exhausted or injured." A few technical moves took him through these, but he found nothing. Having spent a long

View across the Mallory basin from the crest of the ill-defined rib *(Photo © Tap Richards)*

time at high altitude and having covered a lot of ground, Richards now felt his search was finished. After a brief rest, he headed down, bound for Advance Base Camp. The others opted for staying one more night.

"When I heard the radio calls between Base Camp and Dave and Andy, still up there, it struck me what an amazing few days it had been," said Richards later of his feelings as he descended alone. "Finding all these things, such as picking up a crampon or discovering a tent, and being able to walk right into the old Chinese camps—this really brought a sense of accomplishment to me and about the team. This was so much more than just walking around on the roof of the world. There was real research done here!"

That afternoon, Dave Hahn and Andy Politz stuck it out to the limit. First they did a high reconnaissance along the base of the Yellow Band, investigating some of the narrow gullies that Mallory and Irvine might have descended or fallen from. Then they scoured once more the upper 300 feet (90 m) of the basin, all the way down to the level of our Camp VI. By the time the sun had dropped below the horizon, Politz and Hahn were still out there on the North Face, searching. The image of the two lonely figures walking between the snow-speckled rocks in the pinkish-gray twilight had a coldness to it that even seemed to creep through the telescope at Base Camp. They were moving in a world far removed from ours down below, a world devoid of warmth and life. Finally, around 7:30 P.M., Politz and Hahn called it a day and picked their way along the ledges back to Camp VI. Fifteen minutes later it was dark.

Three search days had passed. Among them, Hahn, Politz, and Richards had covered eight or nine times the area of the 1999 search. Yet the mountain had not yielded a single trace of Sandy Irvine or other significant clues to the 1924 expedition.

Had we come any closer to solving the mystery of Wang Hongbao's "English dead"? It was rather surprising for us to have found the 1975 Chinese Camp VI at 26,800 feet (8,170 m), some 100 feet (30 m) lower and slightly farther to the east than predicted from photographs. This puts the camp 65 feet (20 m) above and some 150 yards (140 m) to the east of Mallory's location. With the camp so close, there was suddenly the possibility that Wang had indeed found Mallory during a short walk from there, as Tom Holzel, the pioneer of the search for Mallory and Irvine, had maintained.

However, to have done so, Wang would have had to climb downhill into the steep basin west of the ill-defined rib. There would have been no particular reason for Wang to do so, except perhaps for a tentative search for his missing comrade, Wu. And there also remains the unresolved conflict between Wang seeing damage to the body's face, but Mallory being found facedown in the gravel, where any such damage could not be seen.

Thin air snooping: Andy Politz investigating
a gully at the base of the Yellow Band
(Video images © Dave Hahn)

Yet if Wang had encountered the body of Irvine, where was it? There was more snow on the upper North Face in 2001 than had been there two years earlier, and we thought there was a chance that Irvine's body was buried too deeply and the search team had simply missed it.

Tap Richards searching the nooks
and crannies of the North Ridge
(Photo © Andy Politz)

As for the story of the Chinese expeditions and the various campsites discovered by our team, we later found out that the second camp Richards had come across on April 24 was the 1960 Camp VI. Its altitude was 26,640 feet (8,120 m), which is very close to the 8,100 meters the Chinese had given in their accounts.

As historian, for me the discovery of the 1960 Camp VI filled not only an important gap in the story—it also came as a relief. Although more recent Chinese accounts have been very candid about any discoveries their expeditions had made on Everest, there was still a lingering suspicion that some information could have been suppressed. This concerned especially evidence from the Mallory and Irvine climb, because it could rob the Chinese of their claim for the first ascent of Everest from the north. Until Richards's discovery, no one had known the exact route the Chinese had taken on the upper part of the mountain in 1960. If they had followed the entire crest of the North Ridge, as the British had done, they could have come across the relics of the 1924 Camp VI, Mallory and Irvine's last camp, without mentioning this in their reports.

Now we knew that they probably had not. From the position of their Camp VI, the 1960 Chinese expedition must have left the North Ridge above Camp V and traversed all the way to the ill-defined rib, which in turn they must have climbed for its full length to the base of the Yellow Band. This was exactly the route first explored by the 1933 British expedition as a shortcut to the upper Northeast Ridge. The Chinese must have studied the accounts of their predecessors very well.

CHAPTER 7

LAST CAMP

It was a pathetic little collection of items that Brent Okita and Jake Norton brought back from the mountain and handed over to me for photography. Tiny bits and pieces: a mitten, some leather straps, matches, a few chunks of solid fuel, a tin, a half-frozen lump of olive-colored cotton. I carefully scraped away the ice and chips of rock from the last item and unrolled the wet fabric. It was a sock. There was a name tag on the calf. I looked closer, blinked hard—then rushed out of the mess tent.

"Hey, Jake, next time don't leave your old socks lying about on the North Ridge!"

His tent door zipped open and a pair of sleepy eyes stared at me, confused. "Huh?"

"Well, the sock you found at the 1924 Camp VI has a laundry label on it that says 'Norton'!"

The sock was from 1924 expedition leader Edward Felix Norton, who happened to share a surname with Jake but was no relation. On June 4, 1924, he and Howard Somervell had started from this camp on their historic climb to 28,000 feet (8,535 m) without oxygen. It was the camp where, three days later, Mallory and Irvine had spent their last night before they disappeared.

Andy Politz was frustrated and angry. For the better part of the afternoon on April 24, 2001, he had been scurrying back and forth between our Camp VI and the North Ridge, traversing ledges, scrambling over walls, and peeking behind boulders. Nothing. Now he was trapped above a vertical cliff band, in an untrodden part of Everest's North Face, far away from the security of any fixed ropes. The comments from that historian down at Base Camp were not of much use either. Each unnerving call was forcing him to seek a secure stand, remove the oxygen mask from his face, and fumble the radio out of its pocket—only to receive some vague directions that got him nowhere. Damn! If looking for the bodies of Mallory and Irvine had been tricky, searching for their last camp was even more so.

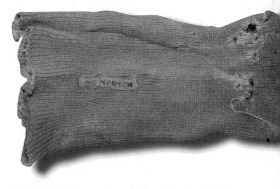

Colonel E. F. Norton's sock, found at the 1924 Camp VI site *(Photo © Jochen Hemmleb)*

Thoughts of that place evoked images of mystery and seclusion: a lonely tent where two men had spent their last night on Earth. . . . What had Mallory and Irvine been doing during those final hours? What had been their feelings and thoughts on the eve of the summit day? Would they have left any clues to their possible fate? It was believed that no one had visited this mystery-shrouded camp for sixty-three years, and no one knew exactly where it was.

We wanted to find Mallory and Irvine's last camp, the 1924 Camp VI, for two reasons. First, although the camp had been visited three times after the climbers' disappearance (by Odell in 1924, in 1933, and 1938), there was still a chance that some clues had been overlooked, such as a written note or a telling piece of equipment. Second, we hoped to recover the oxygen cylinders and parts of the oxygen apparatus known to have been left behind at the site. The apparatus could reveal any repair work or other indications of malfunction, which might have hindered Mallory and Irvine's progress. From the number of oxygen cylinders left at the site, we could deduce how many the pair had taken on their final climb. But for any of these tasks, we needed to find the camp first.

No photographs had ever been taken of the 1924 Camp VI, and the best information we had for guessing its possible position were some descriptions from 1933, when the next British Everest expedition had discovered the remains. Frank Smythe, one of the climbers who had passed through the location, wrote, "We were climbing along the [North] ridge at about 26,500 feet. . . . A little higher the ridge flattened out. A few yards to the west was a shallow hollow, really the head of an ill-defined gully. . . . Here lay a little tangle of green canvas and tent poles—the highest camp of 1924."[1]

On pictures of the North Ridge, we had made out a spot where "the ridge flattened out," a prominent, wide notch about level with our Camp VI. To the west of this, the aerial photographs showed indeed an "ill-defined gully." When the clouds finally parted and we could see Politz again, I guided him over the radio to the snow-filled crevice. Politz moved into the gully. When Simonson contacted him fifteen minutes later, Politz's reply raised everybody's eyebrows. "I found an old sock and a mitten, which I had to excavate. . . . " Had he found the camp at last? Despite our excitement—"socks and mittens don't just grow up there!" Simonson commented dryly—Politz himself was less sure. Although he dug deeper in the snow and gravel, he did not discover anything further. And the cleft in which he stood did not look like a suitable campsite at all.

The next morning Politz returned to the site, together with Dave Hahn and Tap Richards. The weather was marginal, with high clouds, the occasional snow squall, and a biting, cold wind. At first the men spent more time seeking shelter and warmth rather than artifacts.

It soon became clear that the cleft Politz had investigated the previous afternoon was a false lead. Even when the men descended the gully for some hundred feet until it was blocked by a steep rock step, they found nothing. They then traversed over into the wide notch on the crest of the North Ridge. It was a spectacularly exposed place. From where they stood, they could look over into the crazy maze of rock towers that forms the Pinnacles of the Northeast Shoulder, and straight down the vertiginous funnel of the North Couloir to Advance Base Camp, 6,000 feet (1,800 m) below.

From a massive, pyramid-shaped tower bordering the notch on the left, the North Ridge dropped away in a wave of big, blocky rocks. As the three climbers started their descent into the flanks of the ridge, they were surprised to find new-looking fixed ropes and carabiners. There had been no specifically recorded ascent of the entire North Ridge in recent years—so who had left them? And when?[2]

Steering their way through the boulders, slabs, and patches of snow, the men searched for any signs of an old camp, without success. Over increasingly steep terrain, they edged downward. Hahn soon found the going too insecure and retreated back to our Camp VI. Politz and Richards continued for another 100 feet (30 m) before they were stopped by a near-vertical 15-foot (5-m) wall, which they did not dare descend without protection. Their search was over. There were no traces of the 1924 Camp VI. The whereabouts of Mallory and Irvine's last camp, like that of Irvine himself, remained a mystery.

1924: A STRONG TEAM ARRIVES WITH HIGH HOPES

"If you put us up a camp at 27,000 feet and we reach the top, your names shall appear in letters of gold in the book that will be written to describe the achievement,"[3] Edward Norton had promised the porters in 1924. Strange motivation this might be, but in his emphasis Norton had a point: At the time, few had reached such altitudes, let alone slept there. Establishing so high a camp would be a tremendous feat in itself—and crucial for reaching the summit.

The 1924 Everest expedition was a strong team with high hopes of success. Again led by General Charles Bruce, its core was formed by the climbers who had been high on the mountain in 1922: George Mallory, Edward Norton, Howard Somervell, and Geoffrey Bruce. The notable exception was George Ingle Finch, whose unpopularity with the Mount Everest Committee had finally led to an irreconcilable rift. The climbing team was further strengthened by Noel Odell, a geologist with solid climbing experience and two expeditions to Spitsbergen in the Arctic to his credit; and Bentley Beetham, a schoolmaster, photographer, and climbing companion of Somervell. Other members were transport officer Edward Shebbeare; medical officer and naturalist Richard Hingston; climber and surveyor John de Vere Hazard; the expedition's cinematographer, John Noel; and lastly a twenty-two-year-old Oxford student whose name would be forever linked to Mallory's—Andrew "Sandy" Irvine.

Although he had shown a remarkable performance on one of the Spitsbergen expeditions with Odell, which was the main reason behind his invitation to the Everest expedition, Irvine's mountaineering experience was limited. General Bruce called him "the experiment"—and the question why Mallory chose him as partner for the final climb when more experienced climbers had been available has puzzled historians for decades. Explanations were far-reaching, even to the point of speculating that Mallory and Irvine had been "more than just friends."[4]

However, the biography of Irvine, written by his grandniece, Julie Summers, paints a very different picture of the young man. He was a trained athlete and possessed an adventurous, daring spirit. Medical tests before the final climb had rated him second-fittest after Geoffrey Bruce, and his determination to reach the summit was more than a close match to Mallory's. Rather than being an inexperienced novice, he comes across as an integral member of the team, who fully justified his participation by showing remarkable perseverance and exceptional engineering skills as the expedition's "Mr. Fix-it"—especially with regard to the oxygen apparatus. "The pairing seemed an ideal match," wrote Mallory's latest biographer, Peter Gillman, "Mallory the strategist and dreamer, Irvine the practical, down-to-earth partner who took care of the detail."[5]

The expedition got off to a difficult start. Within two weeks after their departure from Darjeeling, General Bruce was struck down by a recurrent bout of malaria. He handed over the expedition's leadership to Norton and returned to India. Two other members' health was also impaired; Beetham was suffering from dysentery, and Mallory had suspected appendicitis but recovered soon. Irvine was also fighting problems, yet of a very different kind: the oxygen sets.

A third of the expedition's ninety oxygen cylinders had leaked and were empty by the time they reached Shekar Dzong, and the apparatus itself was full of faults. In the weeks to come, Sandy Irvine single-handedly invented and built an improved and lightened version—a "much more certain as well as more convenient instrument," according to Mallory.

The party arrived at Base Camp on April 28, and by May 2 the first two camps had been placed along the East Rongbuk Glacier. Plan had it that two groups of porters together with a team of climbers should establish the remaining camps up to the North Col. But then things started falling apart.

For almost two weeks the mountain was battered by violent blizzards. Climbers and porters became stranded at Camp III, which became a freezing hell, and several attempts to relieve them failed in the abominable conditions. Loads were abandoned en route as parties fled from the fierce weather. The chain of transport, essential for further progress up the mountain, collapsed. By May 12, everybody had withdrawn again to Base Camp, where doctors Hingston and Somervell had their hands full. Two men were in a particularly bad state. Shamsher, a Gurkha soldier, had a blood

THE 1924 OXYGEN SETS

Originally, the 1924 oxygen sets should have been similar in design to the 1922 sets (see "1922: First Climbers Attempt the Summit" in Chapter 5, Trash and Treasures). However, in 1923 Howard Somervell tested the apparatus on a training climb of the Eiger in Switzerland. Afterward he complained about the unbalancing effects of a fully charged set, especially when climbing rock. He suggested the usage of three larger cylinders instead of the usual four, which had been smaller.

Each of the new bottles had a capacity of 535 liters of oxygen, stored at a pressure of 120 atmospheres. The apparatus could be set to deliver oxygen at two flow rates, 1.5 or 2.2 liters per minute. A fully charged set with three cylinders weighed 33 pounds (15 kg) and would provide an oxygen supply of twelve to sixteen and a half hours (four to five and a half hours per bottle), depending on flow rate.

In the original new design, the three bottles were mounted upright into a pack frame, valves on top. An arm of metal tubing reached over the climber's left shoulder, supporting the gauges and regulators in front of his chest.

Irvine redesigned the apparatus to have the cylinders inverted and most of the valves, gauges, and regulators mounted below. The awkward metal tubing was removed, and the oxygen instead flowed through a rubber tube passing underneath the climber's right arm. A gauge and regulator were inserted into the rubber tube and clamped to the climber's jacket at about waist level. The modified version of the oxygen set weighed 28 pounds (12.7 kg) with three cylinders, 20 pounds (9 kg) with two.

---

clot in his brain; and the cobbler, Manbahadur, had his feet frostbitten up to the ankles. Both died soon after.

A week later the ascent was resumed and all camps reoccupied. On May 20, Mallory and Norton, followed by Odell and Lhakpa Tsering, finally pushed the route to the North Col. They avoided the avalanche-prone slopes of the 1922 disaster and found a more direct line, which included a spectacular 200-foot (60-m) ice chimney, a cleft cutting through a vertical section of the glacial wall. The col was stocked with supplies the next day, and Hazard with twelve porters stayed there to set up Camp IV.

It snowed all night and until the following afternoon. There was no hope of establishing Camp V on the North Ridge, and Hazard eventually evacuated the col. But when he arrived back at Camp III, only eight porters were with him. Four had refused to descend the dangerous slopes and were now stranded at Camp IV. They needed to be rescued.

The task fell to the strongest climbers—Mallory, Norton, and Somervell. To their luck, the weather was fine the next morning and the snow less dangerous than feared, though waist deep in places. The last pitch to Camp IV was the most difficult, a delicate traverse over a steep, avalanche-prone slope. Somervell led the pitch on a 200-foot (60-m) rope. Thirty feet (10 m) before reaching the waiting porters, the rope ran out. The men had to make their way across the gap unassisted. Just as the last two porters decided to come down, the snow beneath their feet gave way— but miraculously, the slide stopped after 30 feet. Somervell untied from the rope, passed it around his ice ax, and lowered himself one-handed from the free end until he could grasp the frightened men by their collars and drag them to safety. The whole party was not back at Camp III until 7:30 P.M., and in the morning once again a general retreat to Base Camp was ordered.

The trials of the storm and the rescue had severely sapped the strength of climbers as well as porters. In an emergency plan, any summit attempts with oxygen were ditched—because at present there were not enough men available to carry all the bottles—and instead two teams of two climbers each were to try for the top without oxygen.

The first team of Mallory and Geoffrey Bruce was to establish Camps V and VI before attempting the summit, followed a day later by Norton and Somervell.

The first party set out from the North Col on June 1. When Norton and Somervell pushed up the North Ridge in the battering wind the next day, to their consternation they saw Mallory's party coming down.

The ferocious gusts kept conversation short, but Norton and Somervell understood that a similar wind had stopped half the porters in their tracks at 25,000 feet (7,620 m) the previous day. Mallory, Bruce, and the other four Sherpas had pushed on for another 300 feet (90 m) to the site of Camp V. While Mallory had organized the camp, Bruce and Lobsang Sherpa had returned twice to fetch the abandoned loads. The effort had strained Bruce's heart. The next morning, none of the porters could be stirred into going higher and the whole party had turned to descend.

On the face of it, the causes of their retreat seemed obvious. But historians Audrey Salkeld and Tom Holzel have suggested a deeper reason. Mallory had probably realized that under the prevailing conditions and without oxygen, he stood nil chance of getting to the top. So rather than wasting all his remaining energy on a forlorn hope, he bailed out early—to recuperate and to reconsider.[6]

Norton and Somervell, together with four porters, continued to Camp V, where they spent the remaining day resting and cooking. The camp's two tents were pitched one above the other on platforms on the sheltered eastern side of the North Ridge. When Norton visited the porters later that afternoon, he discovered that stones from the upper platform had dislodged and struck their tent, injuring two of the men—a grim prospect for the planned ascent to Camp VI the next day.

The following morning, it took Norton four hours and all of his persuasion to get the porters to rise. Finally, three of them were ready to go—Narbu Yishe, Llakpa Chede, and Semchumbi. It must have looked an unequal party that started toiling up the ridge at 9:00 A.M. While Norton and two porters forged ahead, Somervell and Semchumbi lagged behind, one coughing, his throat parched by the cold and dry air, the other limping from a nasty cut in his knee. After more than three hours, Norton and Somervell noticed to their immense satisfaction that they were passing the highest point reached by them and Mallory in 1922. To that day, it had been the highest point reached by human beings without artificial oxygen. Now they were going to sleep even higher than that. At 1:30 P.M., however, Semchumbi could carry on no farther, and Norton called for a halt.

"I selected a site for our tent, a narrow cleft in the rocks facing north and affording the suggestion—it was little more—of some shelter from the north-west wind. Here I set the two leading porters to scrape and pile the loose stones forming the floor of the cleft into the usual platform for a tent."[7]

With the 1924 Camp VI becoming the proverbial needle in the haystack, we needed to revise our plan of action. While our search team returned to their camp, Eric Simonson and I at Base Camp decided on a brainstorming session. We had brought with us several books on the 1924 expedition, including Edward Norton's classic account, *The Fight for Everest.* Would we find some hidden clue to the camp's location in there, some helpful detail we had missed so far? We started leafing through the pages.

A first contradiction: A diagram showed the 1924 Camp VI at the pyramid-shaped rock tower on the North Ridge, which we knew to be at 26,900 feet (8,200 m)—but the altitude of the camp was given as only 26,700 feet (8,140 m). To add to the confusion, there was also speculation that Mallory had moved the camp *higher,* to about 27,000 feet (8,230 m), prior to his last attempt.[8]

We found another contradiction: After his visits to Camp VI in search of Mallory and Irvine, Noel Odell had written that the camp "was in a concealed position" and not easy to find in bad weather. Norton felt bound to disagree with this, saying the camp was "on the very backbone of the ridge, just below the point where the steepest part of the upper Arête [North Ridge] alters its character and becomes a gently rounded hump." Now here was a clue. The camp was *below* the point where "the ridge flattened out," as Smythe had put it. Had our search team looked too high?

In what was probably one of the highest history classes ever, Simonson read the various passages over the radio to the climbers at Camp VI. A deep sense of nostalgia filled the air, and all camps listened to these classic words of mountain literature. For a moment it seemed as if the pioneers—Norton, Odell, Captain Noel—had returned and were talking to us.

In the afternoon, while Richards and Politz resumed the search for Sandy Irvine (see Chapter 6, Short Walk into the Past), Hahn made a solitary excursion partway down the North Ridge, again without success. It was a supreme effort on his part, and an unforgettable sight for the watchers at Base Camp. The ridge glowed golden and copper in the low afternoon sun. Among the sea of broken slabs, Hahn, a tiny figure clad in bright red and purple, slowly and steadily moved upward over what was obviously some steep and technical terrain. Finally, in the fading light, he took the last steps to the tents at our Camp VI.

Lower down the mountain, the second search team of Brent Okita and Jake Norton was already in position. John Race had originally planned to join them, but a painful high-altitude cough confined him to Advance Base Camp. On April 27, the two climbed from the North Col to Camp V. The unsuccessful efforts by the first search team to find the 1924 Camp VI meant a major change in plans for the next day. Instead of first passing through our Camp VI, Okita and Norton would search for the 1924 high camp from below.

This entailed leaving today's "normal route," which traverses out onto the North Face from above Camp V, and instead following the route of the early British expeditions along the crest of the North Ridge. Although the stretches of fixed ropes found by the first search team indicated that the ridge had been climbed at least in parts in recent years, Okita and Norton were likely to do the first repeated ascent of the entire ridge between Camps V and VI since Bill Tilman and Peter Lloyd, the last British pair who climbed the route before World War II, in 1938.

At 7:00 A.M. on April 28, Okita and Norton took the first steps of retracing this historic route. Above Camp V, the North Ridge rises as a broad whaleback of broken, jagged boulders, getting progressively narrower until culminating in a lofty tip some 1,200 feet (370 m) above. Even from Base Camp we could sense the aesthetic beauty and technical difficulty of the line—a slender spur between the shadowy dark-brown slopes of the North Face on the right and the glistening white

Looking down from the crest of the North Ridge to the East Rongbuk Glacier. Advanced Base Camp is on the moraine running along the base of the ridge coming in from the left (Photo © Brent Okita)

runnels of the North Couloir on the left. The crest was interspersed with crags and short snow ridges, offering varied and entertaining climbing.

The higher Okita and Norton moved, the greater their respect for the pioneers became. "The climbers on those early trips were very adept at their craft," acknowledged Okita. "Not only did they have to be solid climbers in this terrain, but they had to lead and guide their porters through this same area. And although much has been made of how inadequate these early pioneers' equipment was for handling the demands of Everest, the low volume of their wool outfits and hobnailed boots were especially well matched to the type of climbing we encountered here. By contrast, clad in our big down suits, double boots with crampons, and cumbersome oxygen masks, we felt like the Michelin Man, that French cartoon figure with its bulky car-tire arms and legs. . . . Tears in our down suits reflected some nervous moves where we'd leaned just a little too close to the rock."[9]

At 10:00 A.M., Okita and Norton came into view from Base Camp. They were at about 26,400 feet (8,050 m), climbing a thin stripe of snow to the right of the ridge. After negotiating an awkward rock step, they briefly rested on a snow crest before moving onto a scree slope. At this point, they could look up into an ill-defined gully some 100 feet (30 m) above. From Base Camp, this had appeared as one of a few locations of fair promise; below "precipitous rocks" and with "a steep snow-patch plastered on a bluff of rocks above," as Odell had written. Yet when Okita and Norton entered the recess, we could see them staying in it for only a few minutes before continuing their way up the crest. They had found nothing.

Now there remained only one other possible spot before they would link up with the area already investigated by the first search team a few days earlier: a rock bluff on the ridge with a shallow hollow and snow patch beneath. Either this would be the location, or the 1924 Camp VI was nowhere to be found. Ten minutes later, at 10:55 A.M., Okita and Norton traversed into the hollow. There was a bit of wood sticking out of the rubble ahead. Seconds later, the radio at Base Camp crackled to life and Okita's voice came on the air.

"Jochen, do you copy North Ridge?"

"Yes, I copy you," I replied.

Okita's answer was swift and simple: "Got it!"

1924: NORTON SETS A RECORD

When Edward Norton awoke at Camp VI on the morning of June 4, 1924, he was greeted by an unpleasant surprise. During the night, one of the thermos flasks he had filled with tea the previous evening had leaked and emptied its contents into his sleeping bag. He and Somervell had intended to leave at 5:30 A.M., but now more than an hour was lost by the long and cumbersome process of melting snow over their solid-fuel stoves to replace the lost liquids.

View across the Yellow Band toward the Great Couloir, June 4, 1924
(Photo by Howard Somervell © Royal Geographical Society, London)

They were finally off by 6:40 A.M. To them, the jagged skyline of the Northeast Ridge looked too difficult a way, so they headed diagonally upward in the direction of a massive gash cutting through the whole flank of the mountain from below the final pyramid. By way of this gash—later named the Great or Norton Couloir—they hoped to access the northwestern slopes of the summit cone, where the ground looked easier again.

After an hour, Norton and Somervell reached the bottom edge of the Yellow Band. Although the strata of the rock dipped outward, the stepped ledges offered a convenient way and the men steadily clambered over shelf after shelf, slowly gaining height.

Quite suddenly, at about 27,500 feet (8,400 m), the effects of altitude took their toll. They had been taking three or four breaths to each step, but both men were now forced to take ten or more. Norton never managed to take thirteen steps before having to pause and pant, elbow on bent knee. His brain suffered from the lack of oxygen and he started seeing double. He had already taken off his goggles, because he felt they interfered with his vision—a mistake that was to render him snow-blind for two days after the climb. Somervell, on the other hand, had to cough constantly, still plagued by his painful throat. They struggled to the top of the Yellow Band, where Somervell eventually succumbed to his throat trouble. He sat down on a ledge and urged his companion to go on alone.

Norton continued over the increasingly steeper slabs, which sloped and overlapped like tiles on a roof. Once in the couloir, he found it full of powder snow into which he sank to the knees or even to the waist.

> Beyond the couloir the going got steadily worse; I found myself stepping from tile to tile, as it were, each tile sloping smoothly and steeply outward; I began to feel that I was too much dependent on the mere friction of a boot nail on the slabs. It was not exactly difficult going, but it was a dangerous place for a single unroped climber, as one slip would have sent me in all probability to the bottom of the mountain.[10]

In the hour since he had left Somervell, Norton had been able to gain a mere 100 feet (30 m) in altitude. There was no way he could cover the remaining 900 feet (275 m) to the summit and return to Camp VI before nightfall; and being benighted without adequate shelter would mean certain death. He turned around. There was no disappointment, only an overwhelming relief that the "up" was over. Norton had reached 28,125 feet (8,572 m), a record for climbing without oxygen that was to stand for more than half a century.

When he rejoined Somervell, Norton was so done in that he had to ask for the aid of a rope to help him back over a patch of snow he had previously crossed without trouble. And soon after they started down at 2:00 P.M., Somervell's ice ax slipped from his exhausted grip and disappeared into the void—an ample warning about the steepness of the flank. Both weary men were, in the words of Somervell, "the very epitome of human limitations."

After a brief stop at Camp VI to collect half a tent pole as replacement for the lost ice ax, the two continued down as evening approached. At one point Somervell almost suffocated when a particularly heavy fit of coughing dislodged the mucous in his throat and he could breathe neither in nor out. Fainting, he pressed his chest in a last desperate effort—and the obstruction came up. Though the pain was intense, he could breathe more freely than he had done for days and soon caught up with his partner again. At 9:00 P.M., more than fourteen hours after setting out, Norton and Somervell stumbled into the welcoming arms of Mallory and Odell, who had come to meet them above the North Col with oxygen in case of emergency. But all the men wished for was drink. Lots of drink.

Despite the climbing difficulties they had encountered, both men in retrospect attributed their failure to sheer physical exhaustion on an otherwise perfect day. Somervell wrote, "We have no excuse—we have been beaten in a fair fight; beaten by the height of the mountain, and by our own shortness of breath."[11]

That night, Mallory announced that he would make another summit attempt—with Irvine, and with oxygen.

When Brent Okita and Jake Norton reached the site of the 1924 Camp VI on April 28, 2001, they could see almost nothing. Seventy-seven years of erosion had covered the camp in a thick layer of frozen gravel, completely filling up the platform where the tent had been pitched. A few wooden tent poles protruded and a few pieces of faded green tent fabric with some guylines stuck out from underneath a couple of larger boulders. It looked as if the shifting masses of rock debris had engulfed the tent and dragged it down the slope, spilling out the contents.

The men looked around and picked a handful of smaller items from the talus: a mitten, made of the same yellow-green wool as a glove found with Mallory in 1999; an olive-colored sock, later identified as Edward Norton's; two leather straps, one apparently from a pack frame, the other from a small leather case; matches, a few chunks of solid fuel, a diffuser from an electric torch, and a tin of "Acid Drops." When we opened the tin at Base Camp, it was found to contain black tea leaves—still fragrant after almost eighty years! Another investigation of the site in late May revealed more tent poles, two empty food tins, an aluminum tablespoon, and a piece of red rubber tubing, most likely from an oxygen set.

But any items of relevance to the mystery of Mallory and Irvine's last climb—such as oxygen bottles, parts of the oxygen apparatus, or notes left in the tent—seemed beyond recovery. They had either been swept away by rockslides or were deeply

"Acid Drops" tin, found at the 1924 Camp VI site. The tin actually contained black tea. *(Photo © Jochen Hemmleb)*

Ready for brewing: 77-year-old tea leaves *(Photo © Jake Norton)*

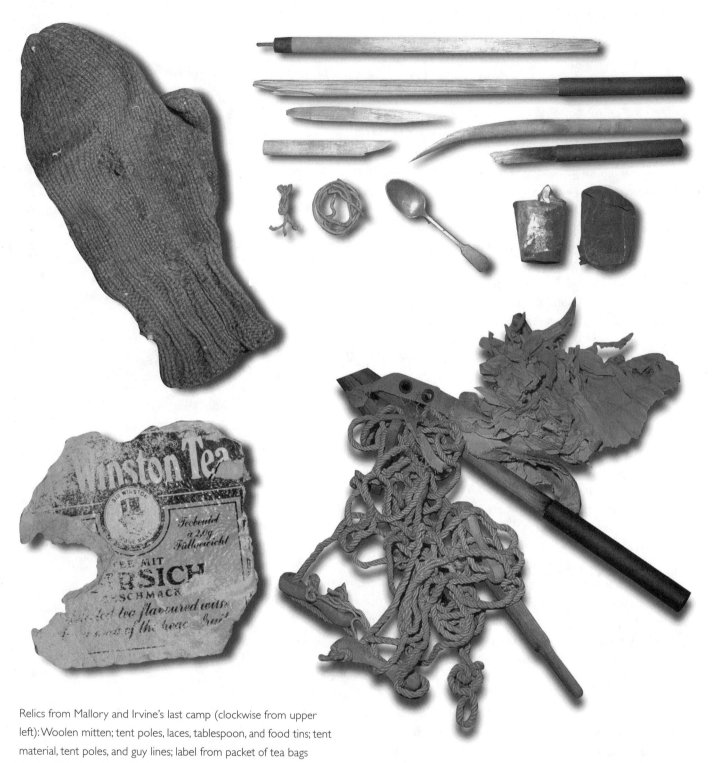

Relics from Mallory and Irvine's last camp (clockwise from upper left): Woolen mitten; tent poles, laces, tablespoon, and food tins; tent material, tent poles, and guy lines; label from packet of tea bags *(Photos © Jochen Hemmleb, Jake Norton [lower right])*

Mount Everest North Ridge (right) and the summit from Advanced Base Camp *(Photo © John Race)*

Camp VI on the
upper North Face
(Photo © Mike Otis)

Camp V on the North Ridge
(Photo © Brent Okita)

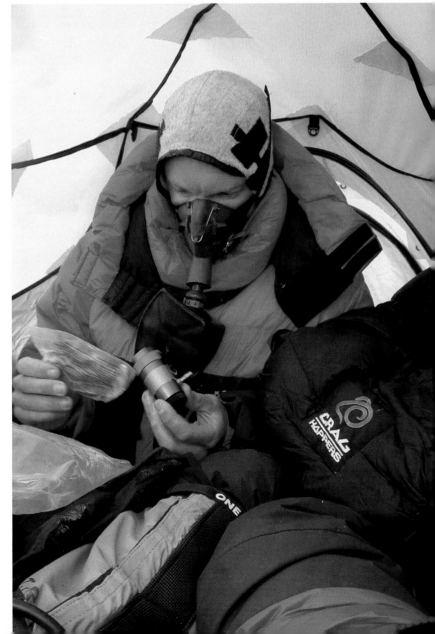

Tap Richards using
oxygen at Camp VI
(Photo © Andy Politz)

Climbing at
26,000 feet on
Everest's North
Ridge between
Camps V and VI,
summit above
(Photo © Andy Politz)

Jake Norton
holding a tent pole
from the 1924
Camp VI, Mallory and
Irvine's last camp
(Photo © Brent Okita)

Climbing the Second Step
on Everest's Northeast Ridge
(Photo © Mike Otis)

Climber at the Mushroom Rock, 28,120 feet,
on Everest's Northeast Ridge *(Photo © Mike Otis)*

Dawn on the Northeast Ridge
(Photo © Mike Otis)

Safe, almost. Dave Hahn (front) and Phurba (back) leading Jaime Vinals back to the Mushroom Rock after rescuing him from 28,500 feet on the Northeast Ridge. *(Photo © Andy Politz)*

Tap Richards and Jason Tanguay safeguarding Andy Lapkass on the traverse from the Mushroom Rock back to the First Step. Note Lobsang coming up the ledge at lower left. *(Photo © Andy Politz)*

The end: The rescue
team descending the
Second Step
(Photo © Andy Politz)

encased in the concrete-hard rubble. Any attempt at salvage would probably require several days at the site, including lengthy procedures such as thawing the ground with hot water. Okita and Norton hesitated at prying loose some of the bigger rocks, because the chute below the site pointed directly at the route, where several people could already be seen coming up the fixed ropes.

One significant aspect emerged through the discovery in 2001 of Mallory and Irvine's last camp, though; the 1924 Camp VI was found by our expedition some 200 feet (60 m) lower than previously assumed, at around 26,700 feet (8,140 m). Mallory clearly had not moved it any higher. This low position would have added about one hour to Mallory and Irvine's climb in comparison to today's expeditions, half of it over fairly technical terrain.

But this aspect is not necessarily interpreted to Mallory and Irvine's disadvantage. We know that they had discarded their first empty oxygen cylinder—the famous bottle "No. 9"—about 200 yards (180 m) from the First Step, at 27,800 feet (8,475 m), where we recovered it in 1999. The lower position of Camp VI therefore means they had actually covered a greater distance within the time the bottle had lasted. Covering more ground in a given amount of time in turn means Mallory and Irvine had climbed *faster* than previously assumed, between 200 and 275 feet (60 and 85 m) per hour. Little is known beyond this first stage of their ascent.

After ninety minutes at the site, Okita and Norton finished their investigation. They climbed a short chimney and circled around the pointed rock tower, or gendarme, above the camp. This brought them to a pedestal above a steep wall, from where a feasible line over crags and ledges led along the western flank of the ridge to our Camp VI. This was the way the first search team had come—they had missed the 1924 camp by 30 feet (10 m)!

From their stance, Okita and Norton looked again at the campsite just below them, and then gazed across the North Face. They could see the ill-defined rib, only 300 yards (270 m) away. Beyond it lay Mallory in his grave. To him, salvation must have seemed so close.

1924: MALLORY AND IRVINE VANISH IN THE MISTS

Mallory and Irvine's final climb has become part of mountaineering history and legend, their story told in countless books and articles. The facts are briefly as follows:

The pair left the North Col for Camp V at 8:40 A.M. on June 6, 1924, accompanied by eight porters. They were using oxygen and, according to the returning porters, had "traveled well."[12]

From notes found with Mallory's body in 1999 we know that behind his and Irvine's last climb had stood an elaborate plan. Mallory had meticulously calculated the food and equipment already stashed at the higher camps, so the porters could carry more oxygen instead. By also deciding to use practically no oxygen up to

Searching the 1924 Camp VI site
(Photo © Brent Okita)

Camp VI himself, he wanted to ensure that a maximum number of oxygen cylinders would be available for the summit day[13]—because in oxygen Mallory now saw his last chance for success. Some bottles were already at the North Col, and Irvine wrote in his diary that they had selected some more from a dump above Camp III. On the envelope of a letter he had with him, Mallory noted the numbers and filling pressures of five bottles, so they knew how long each bottle would last.

From Camp V, Mallory sent down an optimistic note, "There is no wind here, and things look hopeful."[14]

The next day, June 7, Mallory and Irvine continued to Camp VI. Their four remaining porters returned to the North Col in the late afternoon, reporting that the pair had been "going exceedingly strong with oxygen."[15]

The porters also brought down two written notes from Mallory. One was to Odell, who was climbing one day behind in support of the climbers. It contained instructions for Odell's own ascent to Camp VI and confirmed that Mallory had indeed used little oxygen to this point—"90 atmospheres for the two days," just three-quarters of a full bottle.

Dear Odell,

We're awfully sorry to have left things in such a mess—our Unna Cooker rolled down the slope at the last moment. Be sure of getting back to IV to-morrow in time to evacuate before dark as I hope to.

In the tent I must have left a compass—for the Lord's sake rescue it: we are without.

To here on 90 atmospheres for the two days—so we'll probably go on 2 cylinders—but it's a bloody load for climbing.

Perfect weather for the job!

Yours ever,
G. Mallory[16]

The other note was addressed to the expedition's photographer, Captain John Noel, who wanted to film the summit assault from above Camp III. When Mallory noted the time that Noel should start looking out for him and Irvine, he mistakenly referred to 8:00 P.M.; he clearly had meant to write 8:00 A.M.

Dear Noel,

We'll probably start early to-morrow (8th) in order to have clear weather. It won't be too early to start looking out for us either crossing the rock band under the pyramid or going up skyline at 8.0 P.M.

Yours ever,
G. Mallory[17]

These were the last words anyone would receive from the two men at Camp VI.

Sometime in the morning of June 8, 1924, Mallory and Irvine left Camp VI for their final climb toward the summit. The earlier morning had been clear and not unduly cold, although later, banks of mist obstructed the view of the upper mountain from below.

Noel Odell, who was climbing in support of the pair one day behind, had left for Camp VI that morning with the intention of doing a geological survey of the North Face en route. At around 26,250 feet (8,000 m), he topped a small crag. It was 12:50 P.M.

There was a sudden clearing in the atmosphere, and the entire summit ridge and final peak of Everest were unveiled. My eyes became fixed on one tiny black spot silhouetted on a small snow-crest beneath a rock-step in the ridge; the black spot moved. Another black spot became apparent and moved up to join the other on the crest. The first then approached the great rock-step and shortly emerged at the top; the second did likewise. Then the whole fascinating vision vanished, enveloped in cloud once more.[18]

It was the last time Mallory and Irvine were seen alive.

Odell continued and reached Camp VI after another hour, just as a snow squall started. As he sought shelter in the tent, he found inside Mallory and Irvine's sleeping bags, spare clothes, scraps of food, oxygen cylinders, and parts of the oxygen apparatus. Outside he had already seen more parts and carrying frames, which made him wonder whether these were signs of repair work and possible difficulties with the oxygen sets.

While he waited, he worried about Mallory and Irvine missing the camp in the blizzard if they had abandoned their attempt and were already on the way back. So Odell braved the driving sleet and started climbing in the direction of the summit, whistling and shouting to attract the party's attention. But they were nowhere within earshot. After 200 feet (60 m), Odell found conditions so trying that he hid behind a boulder and within an hour turned around. As soon as he arrived back at Camp VI, the snow squall blew over and the upper mountain was bathed in sunshine. There was no sign of Mallory and Irvine.

As instructed, Odell placed Mallory's compass in the tent, and by 4:30 P.M. started his way down. After a true helter-skelter descent, glissading much of the way, he was back with Hazard at Camp IV less than two and a half hours later! During the night a pale crescent moon rose, and the men kept a watch on the mountain for lights or distress signals. The mountain remained dark.

Driven on by concern for his friends, Odell headed back up the mountain at noon the next day, and after a night at Camp V, reached Camp VI again around

Northeast Ridge

Mallory & Irvine oxygen bottle, found 1991
(27,800 feet/8,475 m)

Irvine's ice ax, found 1933
(27,730 feet/8,450 m)

Mallory & Irvine mitten, found 2001
(27,690 feet/8,440 m)

FIRST STEP · SECOND STEP · THIRD STEP

Somervell's high point

Yellow Band

Great (Norton) Couloir

1924 Camp VI

North Couloir

Mallory's body

North Ridge

(Photo © Jake Norton)

The 1920s

1922

——	Mallory, Norton, & Somervell
------	Finch & Bruce
············	Finch & Bruce descent route
×	Highest point reached in 1922 (Finch & Bruce) 27,500 feet/8,380 m

1924

——	Norton & Somervell
------	Mallory & Irvine (known) to 27,800 feet (last trace found)
············	Mallory & Irvine (uncertain) to 28,500 feet (highest possible last sighting)
×	Highest point reached in 1924 (Norton) 28,125 feet/8,572 m

midday on June 10. The tent was empty; everything looked the same as he had left it. His hopes were dashed. Once more he went off along Mallory and Irvine's probable path, but after more than an hour of scrambling around the desolate, windswept landscape, he finally realized the futility of his solitary search and gave up. Spreading two sleeping bags on a patch of snow in the form of a T, he signaled to the North Col "no traces found." With heavy heart, Odell retrieved Mallory's compass and an oxygen set he had taken up, the legacy of his close companion Sandy Irvine's workmanship.

"Closing up the tent and leaving its other contents as my friends had left them, I glanced up at the mighty summit above me, which ever and anon deigned to reveal its cloud-wreathed features. It seemed to look down with cold indifference on me, mere puny man, and howl derision in wind-gusts at my petition to yield up its secret—this mystery of my friends."[19]

MALLORY AND IRVINE— THE PUZZLES

Over the days and weeks after June 8, 1924, the snow and wind erased Mallory and Irvine's final steps on the Northeast Ridge—and with them a simple answer to Noel Odell's "mystery of my friends." Had they reached the summit? How did they die?

In the decades after, the mountain revealed pieces of the various puzzles surrounding Mallory and Irvine's last climb. But the picture emerging from the pieces remains incomplete, because the pieces fit in only some parts—in others, they do not fit.

PUZZLE #1: When did Mallory and Irvine leave Camp VI? In his last note to Captain John Noel, Mallory stated the intent to "start early to-morrow." But what could "early" have meant? Although a predawn start had certainly been in their minds, none of the climbers from the early expeditions had managed to leave Camp VI earlier than 5:40 A.M. With one exception (in 1938), none of these climbers used oxygen, which made them feel even more strongly the debilitating effects of cold and altitude.

THE PIECES: When Odell arrived at Camp VI, he saw oxygen cylinders as well as parts of the oxygen apparatus and of the pack frames strewn around the site. Odell also found magnesium flares inside the tent, and the 1933 expedition discovered a candle lantern and electric flashlight at the site.

From these clues, researchers reconstructed a straightforward scenario. Mallory and Irvine were delayed by a necessary repair of the oxygen sets—for so long that they departed when it was already daylight and left behind all their light sources.

Alternatively, Mallory and Irvine could have used oxygen for sleeping, as Finch had done in 1922. For this, they likely would have unscrewed the bottles and regulators from the bulky pack frames to save space in the tiny tent. As far as the lighting equipment is concerned, it is by no means certain that the items found at Camp VI were all they had. They could have used some light sources that morning and stashed them later en route.

As of 2001, the picture emerging from the puzzle hints at a start *no sooner* than sunrise, which was around 5:00 A.M. on June 8, 1924. But because the morning was clear and not unduly cold, and with the aid of oxygen, a start *no later* than sunrise seems equally possible.

PUZZLE #2: What camera or cameras did Mallory and Irvine carry? When looking for ways to solve the mystery of Mallory and Irvine's summit climb, attention has focused mainly on any camera they had carried and the pictures it might possibly still contain. Many accounts speak of only one camera—in fact, there might have been more.

THE PIECES: Descendants of Howard Somervell believed that he lent Mallory his camera—a Vest Pocket Kodak (VPK)—for the summit bid. Mallory had forgotten his own in one of the lower camps, where it was found later and returned to his son. Irvine, the more prolific photographer of the two, possessed his own still camera. His diary entry of June 4, 1924, revealed he had also borrowed a small movie camera from John Noel before the climb.

The logbook at the 1924 expedition's Camp IV on the North Col recorded that "Noel's ciné camera" was taken down to Camp III on June 10. It is unclear whether this referred to the camera borrowed by Irvine or one possibly left behind by Noel himself: He had visited the North Col with four porters three days earlier.

No camera was found with Mallory's body when it was discovered in 1999. If he had brought Somervell's camera along, perhaps it was lost in the fatal fall or he had handed it over to Irvine at some stage during the climb. Theoretically, all of this could leave a maximum of three cameras with Irvine (his own, Somervell's Kodak, and Noel's movie camera)—waiting to be recovered.

PUZZLE #3: How much oxygen did Mallory and Irvine use? Besides any cameras, there is another item Mallory and Irvine carried that could equally provide clues about the progress they made and the altitude they reached on summit day—their oxygen sets. Each oxygen bottle had a known duration, determined by its capacity and the flow rate at which the apparatus was set. Therefore an oxygen bottle found along a climber's route can yield the time the climber had taken between the point where he started using the bottle and the place where he discarded it when it was empty. This is assuming the climber had used oxygen continuously and at a constant flow rate.

THE PIECES: From the last documented conversation between Mallory and Edward Norton, Mallory had originally planned for a full-scale attempt with oxygen. By using most of his porter capacity to carry oxygen and using only little of the supply himself up to Camp VI, he tried to save as many oxygen bottles as possible for the summit day.

A list of provisions for the summit attempt, found with Mallory's body in 1999, noted six spare cylinders in the porters' load. In addition, the last picture of Mallory and Irvine setting out from the North Col shows Irvine carrying two bottles himself, and Mallory at least one.

According to Mallory's last note to Odell, he had used only three-quarters of a full bottle during the two days of climbing to Camp VI—little oxygen indeed. If Irvine had used the same quantity, this would have left the pair with one or two full bottles plus the six cylinders from the porters' load—seven or eight full cylinders, enough for an attempt with the full supply of three cylinders per climber. To this point, everything tallies with Mallory's original plan.

But their low oxygen consumption and good going to Camp VI could certainly have given rise to a different idea: Perhaps they could attempt the summit with less oxygen: "probably . . . two cylinders," as Mallory wrote.

The decision Mallory and Irvine faced that evening was an important one. Would the advantage of more oxygen from a third cylinder outweigh the "bloody load" of the oxygen sets, which was a notable 20 pounds (9 kg) already with two cylinders?

At this point we know how much oxygen Mallory and Irvine *probably* took (two cylinders each) and how much they *could have* taken (three cylinders each).

One of Mallory and Irvine's oxygen bottles was found close to the first step in 1991, from where our search team recovered it eight years later. It was most likely the first bottle one of them had used. Given the bottle's known capacity and the possible flow rates, it indicated that the climber had taken between four and five and a half hours to reach this point from Camp VI. Incidentally, having used one bottle over this distance suggests he (and presumably his partner) had made good progress, which in turn suggests the oxygen sets had been functioning.

The remaining bottles they had carried, as well as the apparatus and pack frames, are still missing. If these are found farther along the route, they could help in reconstructing Mallory and Irvine's progress above this point and eventually determine the pair's chances to have reached the summit.

PUZZLE #4: Which route did Mallory and Irvine choose? Mallory left this question unresolved when he instructed cinematographer John Noel "to start looking out for us *either* crossing the rockband under the pyramid *or* going up skyline at 8 [o'clock]" (italics added). On the face of it, "going up skyline" means just that, climbing along the crest of the Northeast Ridge above Camp VI, which is nowadays reached some 400 yards (360 m) before the First Step. By also mentioning "crossing the rockband under the pyramid," Mallory seemed to indicate that he had not totally ruled out Norton's route as an alternative to the ridge—so he could not say whether the next morning he and Irvine would be moving across the Yellow Band or emerging atop the ridge crest. Expecting an early start and using oxygen, it was not unreasonable for Mallory to assume he could attain either goal from Camp VI by 8:00 A.M.

THE PIECES: The oxygen bottle recovered from the Northeast Ridge in 1999 showed that the pair had indeed chosen the crest of the ridge as their line of ascent— at least to the point where they discarded the oxygen bottle, close to the First Step.

To this day, no higher traces of Mallory and Irvine have been found. The oxygen bottle thus marks the *least* altitude the pair (or one of them) had reached, 27,800 feet (8,475 m). Based on solid evidence alone, we have as yet no knowledge of their route above this point. They could have continued over the First Step and along the ridge or traversed below the step and toward the Great (Norton) Couloir.

PUZZLE #5: Where were Mallory and Irvine last seen? At 12:50 P.M., on June 8, 1924, Noel Odell saw Mallory and Irvine for the last time as they were moving along the upper Northeast Ridge. But did he really see them? And if so, where exactly did he see them?

THE PIECES: Throughout his life, Odell was adamant that he had seen two moving figures, taking the strongest objection against any suggestions that he had hallucinated or been deceived by an optical illusion. On this, Dave Hahn once commented, "What Odell described—the climb of a significant rock step—must

The First Step as seen along Odell's line of sighting; note climber on snow patch. *(Telephoto taken from above ABC © Jochen Hemmleb)*

The Second Step as seen along Odell's line of sighting *(Telephoto taken from above ABC © Jochen Hemmleb)*

The Third Step as seen along Odell's line of sighting; note two climbers nearing the base of the step. *(Telephoto taken from above ABC © Jochen Hemmleb)*

have lasted at least ten or fifteen minutes. By then he would have realized if he'd been tricked somehow."

Unfortunately, Odell was less sure about *where* he saw the two figures. Odell's initial impression, recorded in his diary less than four days after the event, was that Mallory and Irvine were "nearing the base of the final pyramid." In an account for the British *Alpine Journal* in November 1924, he became more precise and placed them at 28,230 feet (8,605 m), then the accepted figure for the top of the Second

Step. In the same account, he termed the location "the last step but one from the base of the final pyramid." It indicated his awareness of another steplike feature above, later known as the Third Step. The First Step entered the debate with Odell's doubts about his initial impression, which he first expressed in Norton's expedition book, *The Fight for Everest*, published in 1925.

The least we can conclude then is that he saw *someone*—Mallory and Irvine—climbing *something* on the upper Northeast Ridge. His reference to a "great rock-step" or "prominent rock-step" strongly suggests that he saw them on either the First, Second, or Third Step.

There are strong doubts among the climbing community that Mallory and Irvine could have climbed the Second Step (see Puzzle #6 on page 123), the most prominent and most difficult of the three. The logical place for Odell's sighting would therefore have been the First Step. But if the pair had been going well that morning, as the location of their discarded oxygen bottle suggests, why had they been on the First Step as late as 12:50 P.M.? In this case, a delay of at least two hours would have to be accounted for and explained.

Furthermore, Odell described the climbers moving over a snow crest or slope, then surmounting a short rocky section before emerging on top of the rock step. There is a pronounced snow patch below the First Step, but any route from this point forward either bypasses the true top of the First Step or avoids the step altogether.

So was it the Second Step, after all, where Odell had last seen the pair?

If Mallory and Irvine had been going well, the Second Step would have fit the time frame better than the First. Could they somehow have climbed the crux? Even if they had—perhaps aided by unknown factors such as a higher snow cover or rock features that have been altered by erosion since then—Odell described no belay or the climbers assisting each other, as one would expect on a pitch of such difficulty. Also, the snow patch beneath the crux is comparatively small and, due to its northern exposure, in the shadows for most of the day—not an obvious place to spot two ascending climbers.

What about the Third Step?

It should be pondered heavily why Odell, if he was somehow mistaken, happened to provide a description that matches this particular feature of the Northeast Ridge with almost step-by-step accuracy. At the foot of the Third Step is a snow crest or slope, which is followed by a rocky section sufficiently easy to be climbed within a couple of minutes—and if the Third Step is tackled along the crest, as most parties do nowadays, climbers do pass over the true top of the step.

Andy Politz, who purposely watched the ridge from the vicinity of Odell's viewpoint in 1999, is convinced that Odell meant the Third Step (see Chapter 2, Tracking Down Mallory's Spirit). Politz also noted that from Odell's viewpoint, the three steps are clearly separated, ruling out any confusion—especially if Odell had seen the "whole summit ridge unveiled," as he had maintained throughout his accounts.

Factors that weigh against the Third Step is the time element. To have climbed that far along the ridge by 12:50 P.M., Mallory and Irvine would have to have made a very early start (before sunrise), even if we assume the best possible circumstances for their ascent, such as continuing good weather up high and no routefinding difficulties. Climbing for so long would most likely have put them beyond the duration of two oxygen cylinders per climber. A sighting at the Third Step, if true, therefore has to carry the additional implication that Mallory and Irvine had used a third cylinder each.

PUZZLE #6: Could Mallory and Irvine have climbed the Second Step? The Second Step forms the most difficult part of the upper Northeast Ridge. The feature, some 100 feet (30 m) high, is comprised of steep, brittle rock, the crux being a 16-foot (5-m) perpendicular slab in the upper part, which is split vertically by three wide cracks. The Chinese expedition of 1975 equipped this pitch with an aluminum ladder.

THE PIECES: In 1999, Conrad Anker nearly free-climbed the crux of the Second Step—that is, without using the Chinese ladder, just as Mallory and Irvine would have to have done. He found the corner crack on the left to be the only feasible way, because the rock was too brittle elsewhere. Initially Anker rated the pitch 5.8, but later revised the grading to 5.10—a technical difficulty beyond the standards of Mallory's days. Anker considered it improbable that Mallory and Irvine could have surmounted the obstacle in 1924.

In 1960, however, the first Chinese expedition scaled the Second Step without a ladder by using a shoulder stand on the crux. They showed that climbers less experienced than Mallory *could* overcome the pitch, albeit requiring a total of three hours and many attempts. The Chinese also had the aid of pitons, which the 1924 expedition did not have.

In 1991, Andy Politz checked some of the climbing moves in the corner crack (although he did not free-climb it) and felt it was in the 5.7 to 5.8 range. After repeating some of Mallory's routes in Wales (see Chapter 2, Tracking Down Mallory's Spirit), he was convinced that Mallory had been fully capable of climbing something as difficult as the Second Step crux—especially given the added demands of his routes at the time, such as inadequate protection and loose rock.

All other climbers who surmounted the Second Step had used the Chinese ladder. Their opinions on Mallory and Irvine's chances to have climbed it have to be taken as educated guesses. A majority believes the pair could not have climbed it in 1924; some still think it possible.

It is curious to note that of the few who tried to grade the pitch after looking at it, all gave an estimation between Politz's and Anker's. The Catalans in 1985 and Briton Jon Tinker in 1993 thought the crux was around 5.7; American Bob Sloezen, who had climbed the Second Step three times, estimated it was around 5.10. Those who gave a lower rating generally thought it possible for Mallory and Irvine to have climbed the step in 1924; those who gave a higher rating all considered it unlikely.

At present, the answer to the question of whether Mallory and Irvine could have climbed the Second Step is a matter of weighing the differing opinions as well as the factors influencing them. A conclusive answer could be found only through the discovery *above* the Second Step of relics from Mallory and Irvine's final climb.

PUZZLE #7: How did Mallory and Irvine die? Before the discovery of Mallory's body in 1999, two basic scenarios were considered likely. Either Mallory and Irvine had fallen to their deaths from the point where Irvine's ice ax had been found in 1933, or they had frozen to death in an open bivouac after failing to return to their high camp before dark. Another theory had Mallory and Irvine separating above the Second Step, with Irvine dying in a fall from the ice-ax site and Mallory either falling or freezing to death high on the mountain on the descent from the summit.

THE PIECES: When Mallory's body was found, it showed unmistakable signs of a fall—a severe head injury over the left eye, a broken right leg, and several cuts and bruises along the body's right side. Mallory was tangled up in a length of broken climbing rope, indicating that he and Irvine had been together at the time of the accident.

Mallory's body lay below, but not necessarily in line with, the ice-ax location. A fall line from this point (as indicated on the diagrams from 1933), drawn perpendicular to the altitude contours on the aerial photos, runs 40–50 yards to the southwest (right) of Mallory's position, and the configuration of the terrain above makes a fall from the gullies leading through the Yellow Band more likely. Because Mallory's injuries were lesser than those of other victims who have fallen from the Northeast Ridge, many believed that his fall must have occurred from lower down, somewhere in or even below the Yellow Band.

Bloodstains on the left front of Mallory's jacket look blotted, and streaks on the left cuff appear as if he had wiped over a bleeding injury with the back of his hand. DNA sequencing of samples from the stains confirmed that the blood is Mallory's. This has led to speculation about whether he might have suffered another accident before the fatal one, or if this is an actual indication that he had briefly survived the fall.

Without finding Irvine's body and knowing its exact location, we cannot say whether he was killed in the fall with Mallory or if he survived the accident only to die later of cold, exhaustion, or injury.

PUZZLE #8: Could Mallory and Irvine have reached the summit? Most experts simply believe that their route was too long and too difficult for them to have succeeded—but a true estimation of Mallory and Irvine's chances depends largely on where they were last seen by Odell.

THE PIECES: Had Mallory and Irvine been climbing the First Step when last seen, at 12:50 P.M., it would have been too late to reach the summit and return to the site of the fatal accident during the remainder of the day, even if they had found a way around the Second Step.

If Mallory and Irvine were instead seen surmounting the Second Step at 12:50 P.M., they would have done so at a crucial time. Based on the experience of later expeditions, they should have taken about four hours to reach the upper part of the Second Step from below the First Step, where they had discarded their first oxygen bottle. By the time they climbed the Second Step, Mallory and Irvine would thus have been about to finish their second and perhaps last cylinder of oxygen. Without oxygen, it is unlikely they could have covered the remaining distance to the summit *and* back to the accident site before dark, and it seems impossible that they could have survived a night out in the open with only their clothing as protection.

However, if Mallory and Irvine had switched to a third cylinder near the Second Step or been at the Third Step when last seen (which would have been possible only with a third cylinder anyway), they *could have* reached the top—which is still a far cry from saying that they did.

The possibility that Mallory and Irvine reached the summit of Mount Everest before they died remains rooted in both factual basis and idealistic wish. No matter how inconceivable one thinks it might be, the incomplete and conflicting evidence has to allow for the chance that they made it. But the idea is also carried on by the captivating image it holds—two men standing on top of the world, the perfect culmination of a climb that embodied the essence of human endeavor and spirit. Sir Edmund Hillary, who, with Tenzing Norgay, will always remain the first to successfully climb Mount Everest and return, recognized the power and significance of that image. In an interview for the film *The Mystery of Mallory and Irvine* (Arcturus Motion Picture Company/BBC, 1987), Hillary said:

> *Mallory was the one who not only stimulated his companions, but he stimulated the whole world into an interest in the ascent of Mount Everest. . . . It would have been a very fitting reward for all his efforts if on that final day he had set foot on the summit of the mountain.*

Perhaps one day the mountain will reveal additional pieces of the puzzles to complete the picture of Mallory and Irvine's final day. Until then, nobody will know for certain what happened on June 8, 1924.

CHAPTER 8

A SINGLE TRACE

The ice ax looks surprisingly new. Its long wooden shaft is light and smooth except for a distinctive triple-nick mark. Sandy Irvine had marked his properties that way. On the polished steel head of the ax is a stamp of its maker, "Willisch," of Täsch, Switzerland. It is a trusted tool, used for cutting steps into the ice in the classic mountain-guide fashion, long before the advent of curved picks and twelve-point crampons.

Since 1933 the ice ax has been housed in the rooms of the British Alpine Club in London, occasionally put on display for a curious public. For nine years before that, it lay on a slab amid the broken waste of Everest's Northeast Ridge. Then a climber named Percy Wyn-Harris came across it and took it down—a single trace from Mallory and Irvine's final day. But the ax turned out to raise more questions than it answered.

Jake Norton still remembers vividly how he first found the 1933 British expedition's high camp in 1999. He wrote afterward, "A bit of a pack frame seemingly jumped out of the snow beneath my feet and nearly threw me on my face. I pulled it out, strapped it to my rucksack, and carried it down to Camp VI. Later the same day Tap [Richards] and I were in the Yellow Band again to lend a hand to a tired Conrad Anker and Dave Hahn as they returned from their summit day. Now, in darkness broken by my headlamp beam, I could make out the tatters of a couple brown down sleeping bags and bits of paper and tin. But it was not the time for excavation, and I forced myself to put it off till another time."[1]

On April 29, 2001, this time had come as he and Brent Okita woke up at our Camp VI to their second day of searching. Their goal for the day was twofold: to prepare the route to the crest of the Northeast Ridge for upcoming summit bids as well as looking for more artifacts along the way.

Norton and Okita had set themselves on the trail of the 1933 British expedition. They wanted to closely examine the expedition's high camp, Camp VI at 27,495 feet (8,380 m), to gain further insights into the equipment and circumstances of the 1933 summit attempts. Most important, they hoped to relocate the spot where Percy Wyn-Harris had found Irvine's ice ax. Ever since the day it was found, a debate had raged among researchers whether the ax had marked Irvine and Mallory's fatal fall. Would a visit to the location yield a conclusive answer?

Above our Camp VI towers the Yellow Band, a steep staircase of alternating rock walls and ledges rising 1,000 feet (300 m) to the skyline of the Northeast Ridge. It is the first serious hurdle climbers face on the way to the summit, when they have to find a way through the broken cliffs in the early morning darkness. It is also the last obstacle they have to overcome on the way down, when limbs are weak from a long day and concentration lapses. Okita and Norton's task was to equip the route with fixed ropes to protect the ascent and descent over the steep rocks.

The early British and Chinese expeditions hardly used any fixed ropes, apart from a few stretches on the North Col. By contrast, it is now usual to "fix" the whole mountain from the base of the col to the summit—an Ariadne's Thread almost 3 miles (4.8 km) long. Although some purists condemn fixed ropes for downgrading a mountain's true challenge, most expeditions see them as paramount to safety, because they offer a quick way of descent as well as orientation, in bad weather, for example.

To string a line of fixed ropes, Norton, who was leading, would run out a coil of rope and tie it to an anchor, in most cases a metal spike (piton) driven into a crack in the rock. Okita would then follow, climbing along the fixed line with a mechanical ascender—a metal clamp that can be pushed up the rope but locks when pulled down. Connected with the climber's harness, the ascender (often called a jumar after the name of a popular brand) thus acts as a "movable handhold," while at the same

The relics of the 1933 Camp VI
(Photo © Jake Norton)

128

time attaching the climber securely to the fixed line. While climbing, Okita would tie the rope at intervals to additional anchors, so it would keep to the route as it wound its way up the cliffs.

After two hours, Norton and Okita reached the exit from the gully cutting through the lower part of the Yellow Band where it gave way to a wide, sloping ledge, dividing the cliff at half-height. This was the spot where the 1933 British expedition had placed their Camp VI. At first Norton was confused. He had been in this place before in a snow squall. Now there was no fresh snow covering the ledges, and the surroundings looked very different. He noticed some tent fabric protruding from the gravel. In some places the cloth was faded, in others it had retained its original green color, looking comparatively new. Moreover, there was an oxygen bottle on top of the pile with Russian writing on it. Norton called Base Camp.

Down in the mess tent, his mentioning of "an old camp, possibly Russian" had us jumping from our seats and made us instantly think of the rumored Soviet expedition of 1952. There were reports in certain European climbing journals and in *The Times* of London that the Soviets had launched an attempt to climb Everest from the north in late autumn that year. Apparently they tried to snatch success at the last moment from the British expedition from the south the following spring, the one that was to put Hillary and Tenzing on the summit. Yet disaster struck the Soviets when the six-member summit team disappeared above their high camp at 26,970 feet (8,220 m)—or such was the story. Without any supporting clues, it was believed to be either a hoax or a massive cover-up.[2]

The first summit team in 1933: Lawrence Wager, left, and Percy Wyn-Harris, right. *(Photo © Royal Geographical Society, London)*

Had Norton found the first solid evidence of this attempt? If so, it would put the Soviets tantalizingly close to the summit. Fantasies were running wild. "It would be a hammer if we find evidence that the Soviets had indeed been high on Everest in 1952, perhaps even reached the summit!" ". . . and on the summit had found traces of Mallory and Irvine!!" "Yeah, that would make Hillary and Tenzing the . . . hang on; two, three, four . . . ninth and tenth persons to have reached the top!!!"

Later that day, however, as he and Okita were descending, Norton recognized the place again and realized he had merely rediscovered the old camp he had found in 1999. The Russian oxygen bottle had been a false lead; it was a rusted "Poisk" type used by many commercial expeditions. The tent was the 1933 Camp VI after all.

1933: THE BRITISH RETURN—AND FIND A TRACE OF THE PAST

Morning dawned bright and clear on May 30, 1933. In their tiny tent at Camp VI, two men readied themselves for the final stage of their climb to the summit of the world. Lawrence Wager, twenty-nine, was a geologist from Yorkshire and an experienced arctic traveler; and Percy Wyn-Harris, thirty, was a colonial administrator resident in Kenya, where four years earlier he had made the second ascent of difficult Mount Kenya, Africa's second-highest peak.

Northeast Ridge

FIRST STEP   SECOND STEP   THIRD STEP

Shipton's high point

Irvine's ice ax

Gray Band

Subsidiary Couloir

Yellow Band

1938 Camp VI
(27,250 feet/8,305 m)

1933 Camp VI
(27,495 feet/8,380 m)

1924 Camp VI
(26,700 feet/8,140 m)

Great (Norton) Couloir

North Ridge

(Photo © Jake Norton)

The 1930s

1933

——— Wager & Wyn-Harris

- - - - - Smythe & Shipton

·········· Smythe's descent route

— · — · Longland's descent route

× Highest point reached in 1933 by Wager & Wyn-Harris, and by Smythe, 28,125 feet/8,572 m

1938

——— Shipton & Smythe, Tilman & Lloyd

Although there was little wind and the cold was bearable, Wager was in a bad mood. He had slept badly, perhaps not surprising after the previous dinner's odd mix of Brand's essence of chicken, tinned loganberries, biscuits, and condensed milk. Moreover, the floor of their encampment tilted outward, making for an uncomfortable bed. After getting up at 4:30 A.M., he had also found his leather boots frozen solid. Now Wager was trying for what seemed ages to light one of their "Tommy Cookers" to thaw them. He struck match after match to no avail before finally throwing away the offending tin of solid fuel in disgust. He opened another and this time it worked. Soon a flickering blue flame rose, producing what little heat it could in the rarefied air of high altitude.

After a meager breakfast, the two were off at 5:40 A.M. The summit stood 0.75 mile (1.2 km) away and less than 1,600 feet (490 m) above. The day ahead looked hopeful.

1924 TO 1933—THE YEARS IN BETWEEN

Because there were three expeditions in rapid succession during the 1920s, why had there been a nine-year hiatus before the next attempt in 1933?

In the aftermath of 1924, the Tibetan authorities had complained about some of the post-expedition activities. One had been an unauthorized survey by John Hazard, during which he had exceeded the geographical bounds of the expedition's passport. Another was the promotion of John Noel's expedition film, for which he had a group of Tibetan monks brought to England to perform dances and religious ceremonies at various movie theaters. To "parade their religion for pecuniary gain" had apparently upset Tibetan authorities. As a consequence of these complaints, no further expeditions had been allowed to enter the country.

The deeper reasons, however, lay with the British Political Officer of Sikkim at the time, Major Frederick Bailey. He had been directly responsible for relations with Tibet, and more than once had put words in Lhasa's mouth to underscore his personal dislike of the Everest ventures. The reasons for Bailey's obstructive behavior remain unclear, but there are suggestions that it had to do with his own ambition of climbing Mount Everest, which was curtailed by his political career.

Only after Bailey had left his position in 1928 did relations between Tibet and Great Britain improve again, and four years later permission was finally granted to resume activities on the mountain.

It was a new generation of climbers who hoped to continue where the pioneers of the 1920s had left off. The leader was Hugh Ruttledge, a forty-eight-year-old ex-commissioner from the Indian Civil Service. Like General Bruce before him, he was chosen for his capacity in military organization rather than for his mountaineering experience. But his team's climbing expertise was considerably greater than that of their predecessors.

Besides Wager and Wyn-Harris, the expedition included the "Kamet Four": Frank Smythe, Eric Shipton, Bill Birnie, and Dr. Raymond Greene, who two years earlier had ascended Kamet in India's Garhwal Himalaya, the first peak over 25,000 feet (7,620 m) to be climbed. Among the other members were ace rock climber Jack Longland and two old hands from 1922 and 1924, Colin Crawford and Edward Shebbeare, the latter joining the team as transport officer.[3]

Following the traditional route of the 1920s, the expedition arrived at Rongbuk Base Camp in mid-April 1933. At first everything had gone according to plan, and Camp III was established at the head of the East Rongbuk Glacier on May 2. Then bad weather hit.

For two weeks, violent storms prevented progress to the North Col. The slopes of the col had changed considerably since 1924, now steeper and more broken. The crux was a large crevasse, overhung by a 40-foot (12-m) wall, which required some of the most difficult ice-climbing seen on Everest at the time.[4] On May 15, Camp IV was finally erected on a wide shelf below the actual col.

A disagreement over the severity of the weather and the porters' ability to continue stopped a first attempt to put up Camp V on the North Ridge on May 20.

"It may be that we lost not two days but twenty years," Greene wrote afterward—a remarkably prescient statement in the light of how Everest's history was to unfold.[5] When the camp was eventually established two days later, the climbers became trapped there in a blizzard. All were forced to retreat to the North Col.

The summit attempt began anew on May 28 with Wager, Wyn-Harris, Longland, and Birnie moving up to Camp V. Birnie was left in charge of the camp, while the others continued up with eight Sherpas. They managed to place Camp VI on the Yellow Band at 27,495 feet (8,380 m). This was 800 feet (240 m) higher and about 400 yards (360 m) closer to the summit than Camp VI was in 1924. After leaving Wager and Wyn-Harris at the new camp, Longland and the porters descended. As they fought their way down the North Ridge in a gale, they stumbled upon the remnants of the 1924 Camp VI—a poignant remainder of their predecessors.

The beginning of Wager and Wyn-Harris's ascent on May 30 was grueling. For the first hour they remained in the icy shadows of the North Face, following a system of ramps leading across the flank in a gently rising traverse. Neither climber was using supplementary oxygen, because the expedition had dispensed with it as a climbing aid and took only a few sets along for medical purposes. Every step required tremendous effort, and the men frequently stopped to lean on their ice axes and catch their breath. Wager especially was struggling; his frozen boots made him feel as if he had put his feet in an icebox. He feared the onset of frostbite. As soon as the pair climbed into the sunlight, he took off his footwear and tried to massage some warmth back into his clammy toes. His partner meanwhile continued.

Wyn-Harris was just a short way below the crest of the ridge when he caught a glimpse of something metallic among the ocher-brown boulders. Drawing nearer, he recognized it, to his surprise, as an ice ax, lying free on a smooth, easy-angled slab, supported by neither crack nor ledge. The ax looked remarkably shiny and undamaged, with no rust staining the steel. Realization came slowly. . . . This must have belonged to Mallory or Irvine! Was it not a curious quirk of fate that they, the first party to come this way in nine years, had found a trace of the missing pair in this maze of broken rocks?

But what had happened here? Had Mallory or Irvine, for whatever reason, left his ice ax behind? Or did the ax mark the spot where they had fallen to their deaths? There was little time to dwell on a possible answer. With a glance down the steepening slabs to where they broke off into the void of the North Face, Wyn-Harris and Wager left the ax where they found it and went on.

They were now some 250 yards (230 m) from the First Step, a massive two-tiered tower blocking the ridge. In fact, the First Step is formed where a band of harder dark-gray limestone intersects with the ridge crest. This Gray Band overlies the Yellow Band and girdles the summit pyramid of Mount Everest in an almost continuous line of steep crags. Farther along the ridge the same rock band forms an even more prominent cliff, the Second Step. It is a fearsome obstacle, jutting from the crest like "the sharp bow of a battle cruiser."

The 1924 expedition had demonstrated the basic problem of climbing the last 1,000 feet (330 m) of Mount Everest from the north. Was it possible to surmount the Second Step and follow the Northeast Ridge all the way to the summit, as Mallory had intended to do? Or were climbers inevitably forced on a traverse of the North Face below the steps and into the Great (Norton) Couloir? This was the route Edward Norton had followed, and from his highest point on the far side of the couloir, it seemed possible to break through the Gray Band and find a feasible way up the summit slopes.

It was 7:00 A.M. when Wager and Wyn-Harris arrived at the base of the First Step. Their initial idea was to circumvent the step and climb straight to the ridge beyond. They moved along a shelf running below the step's bulk. As they turned around the corner, they were greeted by a daunting sight. The ridge was a serrated blade of rock interrupted by narrow snow crests. Realizing that it would be too difficult and time-consuming to cross, the two climbers decided to continue their horizontal traverse in hope of finding a better way to the base of the Second Step farther on. Keeping a line directly underneath the steep crags of the Gray Band, Wager and Wyn-Harris frequently stopped to scan the cliffs overhead for a line of weakness. But there was none.[6]

When the team had watched the Second Step from afar, they had seen a wide crack splitting the northern face. Now, from their foreshortened perspective directly beneath, Wager and Wyn-Harris could no longer trace this. They could not even reach the base of the step, because the rocks below were equally devoid of any passage. Some distance to their right, however, appeared a gully of fair promise. It seemed to cut through the lower cliffs as well as the Second Step itself. Increasingly steep and treacherous ground brought the climbers to the entrance of the gully, which they reached around 10:00 A.M.

"The gully was a delusion, a mere shallow scoop in the smooth walls," wrote Ruttledge in the expedition account. "Moreover, it did not even continue to the ridge. The party roped up here. In general, the rock was of a uniform, treacherous smoothness; in detail, a few knobby excrescences could be found which, with less snow about, would afford a tolerably good foothold. For the hands there was nothing. Wyn-Harris made an attempt to lead up the shallow scoop, but was brought to a standstill almost at once."[7]

Percy Wyn-Harris pausing on a ledge at the base of the First Step, May 30, 1933
(Photo by Lawrence Wager
© Royal Geographical Society, London)

Looking down the North Face toward the
North Col from the top of the Yellow Band;
note ill-defined rib on the left.
(Photo © Brent Okita)

Wager and Wyn-Harris had spent three hours trying to find a feasible way around the Second Step. In their opinion, Mallory had been wrong. His ridge route was impracticable. Norton's couloir was the only option.

Yet the couloir itself and the far side were plastered with bottomless powder. Fifty feet (15 m) above the top of the Yellow Band, Wager and Wyn-Harris ended up in a snow-filled cleft, which they found too dangerous to cross. The word was given for retreat.

On the way back to Camp VI, Wager summoned his last strength and dragged himself up to a notch in the ridge below the First Step, from where he was able to peer down the stupendous East or Kangshung Face of Everest. As a last task, Wyn-Harris retrieved the ice ax from its slab and carried it down, leaving his own in its place.[8]

After the old ax was brought back to England, it soon became known as Mallory's. It was readily assumed that Irvine, the less-experienced climber, must have fallen and that Mallory had tried in vain to hold him by grabbing the rope with both hands, dropping his ax. However, in 1962 it was discovered that a triple-nick mark on the ice ax's shaft matched another on a military swagger stick belonging to Irvine. The ax was therefore very probably his—and the meaning of the find became more unclear than ever.

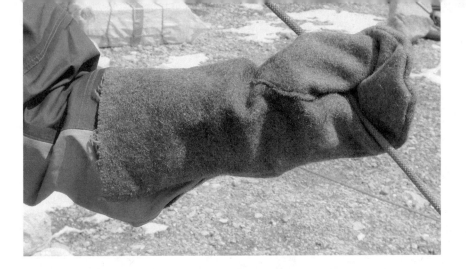

The mitten found by Jake Norton at the exit from the Yellow Band (Photo © Andy Politz)

In the early afternoon of April 29, 2001, Brent Okita and Jake Norton had almost completed the climb through the Yellow Band. They had chosen a steeper line than their predecessors from sixty-eight years earlier, and were now heading for the crest of the Northeast Ridge. Coming up the side of a cone-shaped rock tower, Norton was looking for where to go next when something caught his eye. Protruding from a hole between a rock and a patch of snow at his feet was a piece of brown cloth. Norton reached down and pulled out an old woolen mitten.

The mitten is crudely shaped, like the long asbestos oven gloves of steelworkers. It is made of thick woven wool with almost a feltlike texture. The palm and back of the cuff are slightly faded, and the cuff is torn along the seam.

There are a number of references in the old Everest literature to "Polar Mittens," or mittens of "Arctic pattern." Back in 1924, Edward Norton had written about his clothing for the summit attempt, "On my hands I wore a pair of long fingerless woollen mits inside a similar pair made of gabardine,"[9] a tightly woven, canvaslike wool fabric. The material of the mitten seems to predate the canvas and down used by the Chinese expeditions of the 1960s and 1970s. Could the mitten have stemmed from the early British attempts?

Only three parties, one in 1924 and two in 1933, were known to have reached the crest of the Northeast Ridge, and the latter two took a traverse below the point where the mitten was found. The mitten must have been Mallory's or Irvine's.

Why would they have left behind a mitten? Because it had not been particularly cold during the first part of their ascent? Because they wanted to mark this crucial spot, the point where they would have had to descend from the ridge? Edward Norton had also written, "When step-cutting necessitated a sensitive hold on the axe-haft, I sometimes substituted a pair of silk mits for the inner woolen pair." Had Mallory or Irvine shed his inner mittens to obtain greater dexterity for down-climbing the crags of the Yellow Band?

The least the mitten suggested was that Mallory and Irvine had taken basically the same route to the Northeast Ridge as today's expeditions. But if the mitten was

Brent Okita at the 1960 Camp VII site,
First Step and summit beyond
(Photo © Jake Norton)

left on the descent, it would disprove the theory that both men had fallen from the ice-ax site—because the mitten was found lower down the route, implying that one of the men must have made it past the spot alive.

Jake Norton recovered the artifact and resumed climbing. When Okita reached the site, Eric Simonson reminded him over the radio not to forget placing a marker. Okita replied with a very casual "Oh yeah," bringing a smile to the faces of the listeners at Base Camp—we all knew that Okita had spent a night out in the open in that area on his descent from the summit in 1991, precisely because he had not been able to find the then-unmarked turnoff in the dark.

Both Norton and Okita were now at 27,700 feet (8,440 m), poised on the very spine of the Northeast Ridge. In front of them, the undulating crest rose gradually to the dark towers of the First Step and on to a distant summit. To the right, the North Face dropped away steeply in a series of overlapping slabs. To the left, precarious snow cornices overhung the Kangshung Face, a cauldron of jumbled hanging glaciers, tottering rock buttresses, and billowing clouds. Soon they were on the trails of history again.

First they came across another Chinese camp, marked by an old tent and a stack of oxygen bottles. It was the lower site of the 1960 Camp VII. Nearby was the boulder from where in 1999 Norton and Tap Richards had recovered one of Mallory and Irvine's oxygen bottles. Now Norton and Okita searched the vicinity for more relics, possibly a second bottle, but without finding anything.

The First Step was now some 250 yards (230 m) away. Okita and Norton had thought of going as far as the step's base, perhaps even climbing the lower tier of the

Looking along the crest of the Northeast Ridge toward the Northeast Shoulder, 1960 Chinese Camp VII in the foreground *(Photo © Jake Norton)*

cliff, but now figured they did not have enough rope left to equip the route. There was a cave a little farther up the ridge, which they decided to investigate.

Norton reached the shoulder-high hollow first. He leant forward to peer inside—only to flinch back in horror. His voice burst out over the radio, "I've found a down suit . . . with a person in it!" The body was one of the three Indians who had died descending the ridge during the fatal storm of 1996, which killed another five climbers on the south side of the mountain in one of the worst and surely the most publicized tragedies in Everest history.

It took Norton a few minutes to regain his composure; then we told him to climb straight down from the cave onto the slabs of the North Face. Somewhere down there, among the mist-enshrouded cliffs, lay the goal of his and Okita's search and a major key to the mystery of Mallory and Irvine—the place where Irvine's ice ax had been found in 1933. Wyn-Harris, the finder of the ax, had left his own in place as a marker, which the searchers now hoped to rediscover. Their planned task at the site: to check out the likelihood of a fall as well as the exact direction of the fall line from there.

As he descended, Norton discovered below him a broad, sandy bench running along the mountainside. It provided a natural line of ascent and was in all probability the route that Wager and Wyn-Harris had followed in 1933. From indications on contemporary photographs, we knew the ice ax must be close, yet when Norton and Okita scoured the slabs above the bench, it was nowhere to be found. Perhaps a rockslide or avalanche had washed it away during the intervening sixty-eight years.

Nonetheless, their general observations in the area were revealing, "Gazing downward, I could see the basin in which we found Mallory," Norton recalls. "There is absolutely no way that the ice ax could mark the site of a fall that led eventually to Mallory's (and presumably Irvine's) death. . . . A fall to the basin would not only be unconditionally fatal, but would be completely body-shattering as well. Mallory's body position and condition clearly indicated that he had survived his accident—albeit for a short time.

"Regardless of this, there is another strong indication that the fall did not originate here: When I talk about 'limestone sidewalks' in the Yellow Band, I am not exaggerating. One would have to try quite hard to fall out of the Yellow Band at this point. A normal slip or fall would land one on his butt, and gravity and friction would do the rest of the stopping naturally. Climbers of Mallory and Irvine's caliber simply would not have fallen here, let alone have a fall that would get out of control. Clearly, the fall did not originate from the ice-ax site; there must be another explanation."[10]

After taking a few photographs of the surroundings, Norton and Okita needed to head down. It was already past 4:00 P.M., storm clouds were encroaching on the ridge, and a light snow had begun to fall. They walked down the bench until they found a way to cross over to their line of fixed ropes, and in the gathering mists started the series of rappels back down the gullies to the 1933 Camp VI.

1933: SMYTHE CHALLENGES MOUNT EVEREST SOLO

Wager and Wyn-Harris's attempt had not been the end to the story of the 1933 expedition. When the two men returned to Camp VI in the afternoon, utterly spent, they were already awaited by the second summit team of Eric Shipton and Frank Smythe.

The second summit team in 1933:
Frank Smythe (left) and Eric Shipton (right)
(Photo © Royal Geographical Society, London)

Shipton, twenty-five, was at the time working as a planter in Kenya. But his mountaineering exploits in Africa and the Everest expedition proved to be a launch pad for an outstanding life of travels all over the world, making him one of the most distinguished explorers of the last century. Smythe, thirty-two, was one of the best British mountaineers between the wars. Besides a number of difficult ascents in the European Alps to his credit, he also had considerable Himalayan experience, having joined an expedition to Kangchenjunga as well as having led the successful ascent of Kamet. Smythe was also close to a professional mountaineer, one of the earliest of its kind, living off his writings, photographs, and lectures. Together, Shipton and Smythe formed a highly skilled and experienced party, perhaps the strongest to attempt Everest before the Second World War.

After listening to Wager and Wyn-Harris's tale and seeing the two off on their descent, the new party tried their best to make themselves comfortable among the confined quarters before settling down for the night. Like their colleagues, both men suffered from the cramped and sloping tent. Smythe later commented wryly, "I spent the night rolling at frequent intervals on to Eric, whilst Eric spent the night being rolled on at frequent intervals by me."[11]

As the night went on, gusts of wind started to shake the tent, and by dawn a full gale was blowing. There was no way to attempt the summit, and the climbers spent the day lying side by side in their tenuous shelter, packed like sardines in a tin. Besides the discomfort, there was also fear that the increasingly heavy snowfall would cut off their retreat. Yet toward evening the sky cleared, and although the wind was still blowing hard, there was a spark of hope for the next day.

Smythe and Shipton had planned to leave at 5:00 A.M., but the wind in addition to the intense cold made this impossible. After they waited for another hour, the wind suddenly dropped. Both men had a rushed breakfast, then struggled out of their sleeping bags and into their protective wind suits.

For the ascent, under the canvas outer garment Smythe wore a Shetland wool vest, a thick flannel shirt, a heavy camel-hair sweater, six light Shetland wool pull-overs, two pairs of long Shetland pants, and a pair of flannel trousers. His head was protected by a Shetland balaclava and a canvas helmet, his hands by woolen mittens underneath an outer pair made of lambskin. His feet were encased in four pairs of woolen socks inside nailed leather boots insulated with felt and asbestos. Shipton was similarly dressed, and he wrote that they felt "as suitably equipped for delicate rock climbing as a fully rigged deep-sea diver for dancing a tango."[12]

They left camp at 7:00 A.M. Right from the start, however, it became obvious that Shipton was far from his usual form. He had eaten little and was complaining about stomach pains. They had climbed for two hours and were just below the First Step when Smythe suddenly heard a weak cry behind him. Turning around, he saw Shipton leaning heavily on his ice ax, then slumping down on a rock. His stomach disorder had finally proven too much for him.

Smythe asked his partner whether he felt fit enough to return to Camp VI safely. Shipton answered yes and added that he would slowly follow. In fact, he had no intention of doing so. He only wanted to encourage his partner and relieve him of additional worries. For Frank Smythe had now set himself against the biggest challenge of all—attempting the highest mountain in the world solo.

There was no question about the route he would take. If the descriptions by Wager and Wyn-Harris had not told him already, Smythe could now see it for himself. The Second Step looked impregnable, and he headed straight for Norton's traverse.

Before long, the deeply incised gorge of the Great (Norton) Couloir opened up before him. To enter it, he followed a narrowing ledge until he was forced to edge along it facing inward, spread-eagled "like some beast of ill repute nailed to the wall of a barn." Twice he tried to do the final move—twice he retreated for fear of toppling over backward into the void. Smythe felt foolish about failing at what was obviously a climbable passage. But being alone and at this altitude made all the dif- ference. He lowered himself to another ledge 20 feet (6 m) below, which brought him without difficulty to the bed of the couloir.

Norton's traverse and the Great Couloir, Subsidiary Couloir at far right; the highest point reached in 1933 is the head of the narrow snow gully near the center of the picture. *(Photo by Frank Smythe © Royal Geographical Society, London)*

Wager and Wyn-Harris had found the Great (Norton) Couloir full of loose powder. So had Norton in 1924. Where Smythe wanted to cross it, the snow was wind-packed and hard. He reached out with his ice ax to produce two steps for his feet. Then, carefully balancing and breathing hard from the strain, he held the shaft in both hands and swung out again, cutting another set. The angle of the slope was a full 50 degrees, and to Smythe's right the blank chute of the couloir dropped away in one giant sweep to the glacier, 8,000 feet (2,400 m) below. About a dozen steps, and he was across.

The rocks on the far side were even steeper, but Smythe could see a feasible ledge some 50 feet (15 m) higher, leading off to the right around a shallow buttress. Yet because this was facing away from the wind, snow had accumulated deeply on the shelving ledges. One probe with his ax told Smythe that he was leading a forlorn hope. So far the climbing had been more dangerous than difficult. Now it was both dangerous and difficult.

> *I was a prisoner, struggling vainly to escape from a vast hollow enclosed by dungeon-like walls. Wherever I looked, hostile rocks frowned down on my impotent strugglings, and the wall above seemed almost to overhang me with its dark strata set one upon the other, an embodiment of static, but pitiless, force.*[13]

With his arms at breast-level, he started shoveling away the snow, watching as it cascaded into the depths in billowing streaks of white. After several minutes, he had cleared a ledge wide enough to lift himself up on his knees. Kneeling, he paused "like a supplicant before a priest," lungs desperately heaving for air. Then, with another effort, he cautiously stood up. More sweeping and pushing gained him another couple of feet.

Next came a steep slab with a bank of deep snow, into which he sank to the knees before his right foot caught hold on a knob. Stretching out, Smythe wedged the pick of his ice ax in a thin fissure and pushed up. There was a sharp grinding sound and the knob broke away. His feet shot out from underneath him, and for a split second Smythe's whole weight rested on the ax alone. A short, frantic scramble and he regained control, finding purchase on another edge. It was a close call.

Smythe looked at his watch. It was 11:00 A.M. An hour had passed since he had crossed the couloir, and during this hour he had hardly gained 50 feet (15 m). Above him, a band of dark-gray overhanging rocks ran horizontally across the face, and he would have to traverse for at least another 300 feet (90 m) over snow-plastered, downsloping slabs before the breach of a subsidiary couloir would allow access to the easier ground of the final pyramid. Under the prevailing conditions, it was an impossibility.

From his precarious stance high on the walls of the couloir, Smythe gazed over the Rongbuk Glacier, a whitish-blue river of ice flowing miles below, and all the way to the brown hills of the Tibetan Plateau stretching endlessly to the horizon. Only three men—Norton, Wager, and Wyn-Harris—had reached this place before him. The summit was somewhere above, hidden from view by the towering buttresses of striated limestone. He sensed the almost superhuman strength it would require, both physically and mentally, to surmount this last stretch.

The last 1,000 feet of Everest are not for mere flesh and blood. Whoever reaches the summit, if he does it without artificial aid, will have to rise godlike above his own frailties and his tremendous environment. Only through a Power within him and without him will he overcome a deadly fatigue and win through to success. . . . In climbing at great altitudes, when mind and body are in the grip of an insidious lethargy, it is on the subconscious, rather than the conscious, that the climber must rely to push him forward. Therefore, it is essential that the will to reach the summit of Everest be strengthened by a prior determination to get there. Perhaps it is not too much to say that Everest will be climbed in England.[14]

View across Tibet from near the Great Couloir, June 1, 1933 *(Photo by Frank Smythe © Royal Geographical Society, London)*

Frank Smythe
(Photo © Royal Geographical Society, London)

141

Smythe turned to descend. He had equaled Norton's height record from 1924.

After recrossing the couloir, Smythe stopped for a short rest. Throughout the day, since he had left Shipton, he was possessed by the feeling of being accompanied by an invisible partner. This "presence," as Smythe called it, felt as if it was there to protect him during his solitary journey. Now he instinctively divided his mint cake and offered half to his "companion." It almost came as a shock when he realized he was alone.

A while later he witnessed another strange phenomenon, "I saw two curious-looking objects floating in the sky. They strongly resembled kite-balloons in shape, but one possessed what appeared to be squat, underdeveloped wings, and the other a protuberance suggestive of a beak. They hovered motionless but seemed slowly to pulsate, a pulsation incidentally much slower than my own heart-beats, which is of interest supposing that it was an optical illusion. The two objects were very dark in color and were silhouetted sharply against the sky, or possibly a background of clouds."[15]

Was he hallucinating? Smythe did not believe so and put himself through some mental tests. He had no trouble identifying the surrounding peaks and glaciers, and the objects did not follow his vision. His eyes and brain were OK. As Smythe rose to continue his descent, mist started to drift across the North Ridge and the objects gradually disappeared behind it. When the mist cleared a few minutes later, they were gone.

On the way back to Camp VI, Smythe found easier going near the bottom of the Yellow Band, where the angle decreased before the slabs broke off in a huge precipice. On this lower route, he passed beneath the ice-ax site. Noting a gently sloping expanse of snow, scree, and broken rocks at the foot of the Yellow Band, it occurred to him that if the ax had indeed marked the point of a fall, the bodies of Mallory and Irvine might have come to rest there. Sixty-six years later, Smythe's prediction about the search area was proven true.

Smythe was close to exhaustion when he arrived back at Camp VI, where Shipton had waited. After a rest, hot drinks, and sharing their stories, the latter opted to descend to Camp V. Smythe, on the other hand, was too tired and decided to stay for another night. Despite a raging storm during the afternoon[16] and a bitter cold evening, he slept soundly until 7:00 A.M. the next day. Here, at the highest place man had ever camped up to that time, Smythe had spent his best night on the expedition. He had not even noticed the spindrift leaking through a hole in the wall and covering the lower half of his body almost tent-high in powder.

So refreshed did he feel that he briefly fancied the idea of another reconnaissance of the Second Step. But the very first effort of brushing away the snow instantly bent him over double with heavy panting, showing the true extent of his exhaustion. With the weather looking more than ominous, he needed to get down immediately.

With the remaining fuel, Smythe prepared a last drink of café au lait and hot chocolate. After collecting his few possessions, he crawled out of the tent, closed the flaps of the canvas behind him, and started his descent. "One backward glance I took at the little tent—the sole evidence of man's handiwork on that most desolate and inhospitable mountain-side. It had served us well."[17]

Jake Norton's eyes twinkle when he talks about his personal "relationship" with the 1933 Camp VI, reminding us that research at high altitude also has a lighter side to it. Recalling how he almost stumbled over the relics in 1999, he said with mock seriousness, "This year the same was not going to happen to me. . . . I was determined to find the camp without it finding me first." Late in the afternoon of April 29, 2001, the moment had come to settle the score as Norton unclipped from his rappel rope and stood again in front of the heap of green tent fabric. Kneeling down, he carefully parted the sheets of canvas.

It was not exactly like opening Tutankamen's tomb, more like time-traveling back into a London grocery store of the 1930s. "The bits of paper I saw in 1999 turned out to be a virtual treasure trove of tinned goods. Carefully chipping away the ice and rock, I slowly gained access to the portion of the tent hiding the goods. One by one, the cans were extricated: Nestlé's Condensed Milk—'By appointment to H. M., The King George V'; Stelna Beef; Selected Ginger; Heinz Spaghetti; Heinz Baked Beans; Tabloid Tea, black tea extract pressed in pellets and saccharine pills, an early form of instant sweetened tea; Salmon and Shrimp Puree; Kendal Mint Cake with Ernest Shackleton's endorsement, and many other fascinating tidbits."

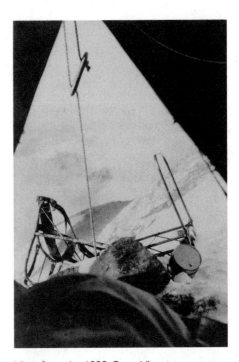

View from the 1933 Camp VI; note rope tighteners, top, and cooker, right.
(Photo by Frank Smythe © Royal Geographical Society, London)

Bar of Kendal Mint Cake, front and back views, recovered from the 1933 British Camp VI. Note endorsements on wrapper.
(Photos © Jochen Hemmleb, left, Jake Norton, right)

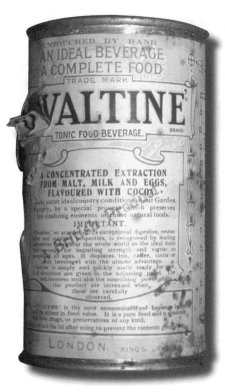

Above:
Ovaltine tin, recovered from the 1933
Camp VI (*Photo © Jochen Hemmleb*)

There was equipment as well: several "Tommy Cookers"; sachets of "Meta," a solid fuel; an aluminum pot and windscreen, misshapen by the weight of the snow and rocks burying the tent; a candle, still standing upright in its makeshift holder after sixty-eight years; a cup, a tin opener, and a tablespoon. Chunks of chocolate adhered to the spoon, still preserving the lip and teeth marks of the last person who had eaten there.

With his pack loaded with artifacts, the snow falling in sheets, and the exertions of the past hours making themselves notable, Norton was eager to leave. He decided to explore one last nook of the tent before calling it a day, and a bit of shining metal and greenish paper caught his eye. "Again, carefully chipping, I was able to remove an opened and partially eaten box of Huntley & Palmers Superior Reading Biscuits.

Right:
Still edible biscuits, found (and tasted) at
the 1933 Camp VI (*Photo © Jochen Hemmleb*)

The crackers had sat in the elements at 27,500 feet on Mount Everest for sixty-eight years, and looked no worse for wear. I was quite curious . . . and more than a bit hungry. I couldn't resist. Perhaps it was an archeological faux pas. Regardless, it was great. There I was, sitting in the Yellow Band in a snow squall, eating a biscuit from 1933! It made my head spin to think that the last person to eat out of this box may have been Wager, Wyn-Harris, Shipton, or Smythe."

Later, at Base Camp, Norton reflected with a chuckle, "I reckon the camp and I are now even. It may have tripped me in 1999, but I took a bite out of it in 2001."[18]

1933 climbers' food and drinks (clockwise from upper left):
Nestlé's Milk Coffee, crystalized ginger, condensed milk
(Photos © Jochen Hemmleb)

Provisions and equipment from the 1933 Camp VI (clockwise from upper left): instant sweetened tea, guy lines, corned beef, Heinz spaghetti, and baked beans *(Photos © Jake Norton)*

1933 climbers' utensils (clockwise from upper left): cup, tablespoon, can opener, matches, candle in makeshift holder, aluminum pot and windscreen, sachets of solid fuel, solid fuel cooker
(Photos © Jake Norton)

After the British expedition of 1933, twenty-seven years were to pass before climbers would tread again the uppermost reaches of Mount Everest's Northeast Ridge. Shipton's expedition of 1935 was a reconnaissance, and the next attempt at the summit, in 1936, was a complete failure due to the early onset of the monsoon. By contrast, Bill Tilman's lightweight expedition in 1938 managed to place Camp VI on top of the North Ridge at 27,250 feet (8,305 m), but above, bottomless snow on the Yellow Band stopped them after only one rope length.

After the Second World War, the north side of Everest was visited twice by soloists—Earl Denman in 1947 and Klavs Becker-Larsen in 1951—but they both retreated from the North Col slopes. At the time of the latter attempt, Tibet's borders were already closed, and Larsen had entered the country illegally from Nepal. Edmund Hillary and George Lowe did the same when they paid the north side a visit in 1952—one year before Hillary, with Tenzing, made the first confirmed ascent of Mount Everest, via the Nepalese south side. He and Lowe hiked partway up the East Rongbuk Glacier.

Then it was the turn of the Chinese.

MAY 29, 1953: THE HILLARY AND TENZING ASCENT

"I always thought that . . . Everest, only a little way outside [our territory], and the English being the first mountaineering race in the world, an Englishman ought to be the first on top . . . of Everest."

So had written Lord Curzon, then Viceroy of India, shortly after the turn of the twentieth century. Mount Everest was always regarded as a "British mountain," and neither the interruption of the British attempts by the Second World War nor the closure of the north side through Tibet would change this attitude. It was the great explorer-mountaineers Bill Tilman and Eric Shipton, veterans of the 1930s expeditions to Everest's north side, who reconnoitered a new way to the mountain via the south side through Nepal in 1950 and 1951.

The other of the world's leading mountaineering nations, however, would not accept the British claim to Everest. The Swiss had nearly succeeded in 1952, coming to within 800 feet (250 m) of the summit on the Nepalese Southeast Ridge, and the Nepalese government had given permission to the French for their own attempt in 1954. It was clear that the mountain would not hold out much longer—the British expedition to the south side in 1953 simply had to succeed.

The expedition needed to be organized like a large-scale military operation, with all efforts directed toward a single goal—the summit. And for this, it needed a leader suited for the job. Shipton, who otherwise would have been an obvious choice, was an explorer who believed in the freedom and agility of small expeditions. So, despite his Everest experience and to the consternation of many, the Himalayan Committee (which had superseded the Mount Everest Committee of pre–World War II days) sacked him. Instead, they chose a forty-three-year-old British Army officer, John Hunt.

The burden placed on Hunt was huge—but he managed the task superbly.

For his team, he selected an all-climbers group of ten, almost all of them with previous Himalayan experience. They were completed by a physiologist, a cameraman, and a reporter. For the equipment, Hunt requested the best—and got it. Clothing, tents, and oxygen apparatus were all newly designed and tested for the expedition. Once in Kathmandu, the team also hired twenty Sherpas with proven high-altitude capability. Their Sirdar (leader) was Tenzing Norgay, who had already been on two of the pre–World War II expeditions and nearly climbed Everest with the Swiss the year before.

The 1953 expedition established Base Camp at the edge of the Khumbu Glacier in the second week of April and began their ascent along what is now a familiar succession of Everest landmarks. They forced their way through the chaotic jumble of the Khumbu Icefall and sweated in the heat of the Western Cwm, the high glacial valley surrounded by the horseshoe of Everest, Lhotse, and Nuptse. Higher they went, over the steep and arduous Lhotse Face. Finally, after several determined attempts, they reached the windswept saddle of the South Col.

From there, Tom Bourdillon and Charles Evans set out on May 26 to make a first attempt at the summit. It was a grueling day. After a good start, the going along the Southeast Ridge became more and more difficult. Soft snow and unstable rock slowed their progress, and they were further hampered by malfunctioning oxygen sets. It was not until 1:00 P.M. that they arrived at the apex of the crest—the South Summit, 28,712 feet (8,751 m). They were now higher than man had ever been on Earth.

Bourdillon and Evans gazed along the ridge leading to the main summit. It was a fearsome knife-edge, narrow and exposed, with huge cornices overhanging the bottomless void of the East Face. Would they press on? Their oxygen reserves would probably get them to the top—but not back again. Forced to decide between success or survival, they chose the latter and retreated.

Now all hopes rested on the second summit team, thirty-three-year-old New Zealander Edmund Hillary and Tenzing Norgay. The two had climbed together since the early stages of the expedition and had formed a forceful partnership.

The two left the South Col on May 28. They were supported by George Lowe, Alfred Gregory, and Sherpa Ang Nyima, who broke trail to the Southeast Ridge and established a last camp, Camp IX, on its crest.

After a reasonable night, Hillary and Tenzing were off at 6:30 A.M. Being a trained snow and ice climber, and perhaps for the sake of speed, Hillary avoided the rocks of the ridge and aimed for the snow slope to the right—which was dangerously avalanche-prone. But on this day, he thought it was worth the gamble.

In his book *High Adventure,* Hillary remembered saying to himself, "Ed, my boy, this is Everest—you've got to push it a bit harder."

Tenzing agreed, and the two moved on. They crossed the South Summit and embarked on the final ridge—the bridge to the top.

There, the mountain rose its last defenses; a 40-foot (12-m) rock step barred the crest. A gap between the steep rock and the cornice on the right seemed the only possibility. Hillary wedged his body into the slot and levered himself up, praying that the snow behind him would hold. It did, and he arrived at the top of the step, gasping for breath. Then he belayed Tenzing up.

Above, the knife-edge broadened to a humped crest, the true roof of the world. It seemed to go on forever. But then . . .

I realized this was the last bump, for ahead of me the ridge dropped steeply away in a great corniced curve, and out in the distance I could see the pastel shades and fleecy clouds of the highlands of Tibet. To my right a slender snow ridge climbed up to a snowy dome about forty feet above our heads . . . I waved Tenzing up to me. A few whacks of the ice ax, a few very weary steps, and we were on the summit.

It was 11:30 A.M., on May 29, 1953. The British finally had climbed "their" Everest. And with a good sense of drama and symbolism, the expedition timed the dispatching of the news so it would arrive in Great Britain on the coronation day of Queen Elizabeth II.

While on the summit, Hillary had in mind his bold predecessors from the early expeditions. He looked briefly around for signs of Mallory and Irvine, but saw nothing.

CHAPTER 9

THE INVISIBLE SUMMIT

The lone Chinese climber gazed across the frozen plateau. It had been a miserably cold night at 28,500 feet (8,690 m). Above him, the summit pyramid of Mount Everest was just touched by the first rays of the morning sun. He knew that somewhere up there his three partners from the 1960 Chinese expedition were wrestling with the final slopes to the top of the world.

He, Liu Lienman, had not been able to keep up with them, exhausted as he was after their grueling climb of the Second Step—the great barrier that had turned back so many of their British predecessors. Once the Chinese were above it, they had walked into territory no one had ever seen—with the possible exception of Mallory and Irvine, who had vanished nearby...

Suddenly Liu spotted three dark figures etched against the snow at the tip of the pyramid. They were descending, ever so slowly, toward him. Had they made it? Was Mount Everest finally climbed from the north?

Mountaineering as a sport was not established in China until 1955. Immediately, it became a governmentally organized affair, with military-style training camps and a strong ideological background. Much of the Chinese knowledge in mountaineering was gained from the Soviets, and by early 1958, plans were laid for a joint Sino-Soviet expedition to Mount Everest—or Qomolangma, as the Chinese call the mountain—the following year.

After training climbs in the Russian Pamir mountains, seven Chinese and three Soviets reconnoitered the approaches to Everest in the autumn of 1958, climbing as far as the heads of the Main and East Rongbuk Glaciers. Also, a 190-mile-long (300-km-long) road was built from Shigatse in Tibet to the Rongbuk Monastery for the sole purpose of ensuring the transport of supplies for the main expedition. In early 1959 the Chinese postponed the expedition by one year because of the uproar in Tibet against the Chinese occupation, but then the growing political tension between Beijing and Moscow brought any plans of a joint venture to a halt. The Chinese went ahead on their own.

"We wanted to climb Qomolangma for three reasons," explained Chinese climbing veteran Zeng Shusheng. "First, after the Soviets had abandoned us, we wanted to prove that we were able to climb the mountain by ourselves to retain our self-respect. Second, Qomolangma had been climbed from Nepal, but not from the Chinese side. At the time, Nepal had firm ties to India, while on the other hand China was in conflict with India over the border along the Himalayas. By climbing the mountain from the north, we hoped to strengthen the Chinese position in the border negotiations. And last, in the years around 1960, China had been plagued by a great famine and people were suffering. By climbing the world's highest peak, we wanted to inspire the whole Chinese nation."[1]

Outwardly, however, a climb of Mount Everest by the very side on which the British "capitalists" had failed was to demonstrate the superiority of communism under the leadership of Chairman Mao. Gone were the days when the highest mountain in the world was climbed just "because it's there."

1960: THE CHINESE GO FOR THE PRIZE

True to the socialist principle of working together unselfishly for common goals, the Chinese sent a virtual army to the mountain in 1960. The expedition consisted of 214 members, one-third of them Tibetans.

On the lower mountain, they followed the British route via the East Rongbuk Glacier to the North Col[2] and the North Ridge. Like their predecessors, they suffered hardships from the weather and altitude. Two members of the scientific staff died in the early stages, Wang Ji of pulmonary edema after climbing partway to the North Col, and Shao Ziqing of a stroke or heart attack at Camp IV. Later, storms hindered their progress to Camp V and beyond. Camp VI was finally established out onto the North Face at 26,640 feet (8,120 m), and on May 3 they began their push for the upper mountain.

They left at 8:00 A.M.[3] in two three-member groups. In the first were expedition leader Shi Zhanchun, Wang Fengtong, and Lhakpa Tsering, a Tibetan. Deputy leader Xu Jing was in the second party, together with Shi Ching and another Tibetan, Gonbu. Their aim was to reach the Northeast Ridge and place a last camp there, at about 28,000 feet (8,530 m). Time permitting, one group would reconnoiter the Second Step the same day. All were using oxygen, but decided to save their supplies by using it intermittently.

After four hours of laborious climbing, the six Chinese were up in the cliffs of the Yellow Band. Xu Jing was struggling hard, and a little while later collapsed on a

Members of the 1960 Chinese expedition ready to tackle Mount Everest (*From* Mountaineering in China, *Beijing: Foreign Languages Press, 1965/Jochen Hemmleb collection*)

ledge, exhausted. After some time he recovered and eventually felt fit enough to return to Camp VI on his own. The others continued upward.

Soon after, Shi Zhanchun's party came across the remnants of an ancient campsite. There was a torn tent with a messed-up brown sleeping bag inside, and a piece of hemp rope protruding from a nearby patch of snow. At the corner of the camp stood a small wooden pole. It was the 1933 Camp VI, the last and highest trace the Chinese said they found of any previous expedition.

Two hours later, Shi, Wang, and Lhakpa clambered onto the crest of the Northeast Ridge. It was already past 3:00 P.M. Lhakpa was very tired, and it was decided that he should wait for the other group to arrive and help them in establishing Camp VII. They eventually found a small platform on the ridge at around 27,750 feet (8,460 m), where they pitched tents. Meanwhile Shi Zhanchun and Wang Fengtong would attempt to reach the Second Step, look for a possible way to the summit, and try to return before dark.

But the pair did not make it back to Camp VII that night. They rounded the First Step on the right, as Wager and Wyn-Harris had done in 1933, but then climbed steep rocks to the crest above. A narrow snow ridge led on, from which the frontal face of the Second Step rose abruptly in a vertical cliff some 25 feet (7 to 8 m) high. Shi and Wang thought it too difficult and exposed to warrant an attempt. But upon further observation, they could see that the right side of the step, though three times as high as the prow, showed a line of weakness. They moved farther along the ridge, which was hardly 3 feet (1 m) wide, then traversed right to approach the base of the cliff.

Now Shi Zhanchun and Wang Fengtong faced the obstacle that had so dominated the minds of the British expeditions before them. Nobody had actually got to grips with it, with the possible exception of Mallory and Irvine on their last climb.

Chinese climbers in the Camp VI area; note oxygen gear. (*From* Mountaineering in China, *Beijing: Foreign Languages Press, 1965/Jochen Hemmleb collection*)

The lower part of the Second Step was cut by a slanting chimney filled with broken stones. Shi and Wang found the exit from the chimney awkward, because it was blocked by a high bench covered with snow. By 7:00 P.M. they arrived in a corner by a vertical slab. Because the cliff shielded the wind, snow had accumulated in the cleft. With their ice axes the two climbers scraped out a hollow and, huddling together, waited for the dawn. They managed to survive the intense cold, even though they had switched off their oxygen to save it for the way down. They descended safely to the high camp the next morning.

After recuperating at Base Camp and waiting for suitable weather, the Chinese headed up again toward the Second Step. On May 22, the summit team of Xu Jing, Wang Fuzhou, Liu Lienman, and Gonbu, together with a twenty-seven-member support group, carried 550 pounds (250 kg) of supplies to Camp VI. The four proceeded the next day and reached the high camp, Camp VII, at noon.

They were followed by a nine-member support group, led by Qu Yinhua. The latter's task was to remain at the high camp during the summit climb and shoot film. With ample time at hand, they shifted the camp some 100 yards (90 m) farther along the ridge to the base of the First Step at 28,000 feet (8,530 m).

Upon arrival, they learned to their dismay that of the ten oxygen bottles brought up, two were already empty, perhaps due to an accidentally triggered valve. During the night they breathed from bottles that had been partially used on the ascent.

The summit team was off shortly after 7:00 A.M. on May 24. They had not gone far when Xu Jing was displaying signs of altitude sickness. Immensely disappointed, he turned around. His place was taken by Qu Yinhua.

By noon they were back at the previous high point, Shi Zhanchun and Wang Fengtong's bivouac site at the Second Step. Up to this point, they had been breathing oxygen at 3 liters per minute, and their first bottles were three-quarters empty. To save a supply for the descent and shed some weight, they cached the partially used bottles at the spot. Above them now loomed the final 16-foot (5-m) vertical part of the Second Step.

Liu Lienman attempted the crux first. He drove a piton in a crack above his head and tried to climb up. Four times he fell back when his crampons skidded off the tiny edges of the friable rock. After each attempt, it took him ten to fifteen minutes to recover. Then Qu Yinhua placed another piton and tried also, as did Wang Fuzhou, but without success. Time was running out and they were getting desperate. As a last resort, Liu voiced the idea of a "human ladder." He crouched on a square-cut boulder and offered Qu a leg up.

To avoid hurting his partner, Qu took off his crampons and all of his footwear apart from one pair of socks, then clambered onto Liu's shoulders and stood up. He gained another couple of inches by stepping onto a piton with one foot and wedging the other into the wide corner crack on the left. With Wang and Gonbu paying out the rope, he stretched out until he could just get his hands into a horizontal slot at the top of the slab. He wanted to place another piton, but it took him almost an hour to get the metal spike in, because the only size he had were some foot-long French ice pitons. Finally, secured by the rope running through a carabiner clipped to the piton's eye, Qu stepped out to the right and pulled up to a shelf just wide enough to stand on. He stood on top of the cliff, the crux now below him.

A few feet away from the edge, Qu found a rock bollard and tied his rope around it. He pulled on his boots, then, with the aid of the fixed rope, the others followed him up to his stance. It was 3:00 P.M. The 15-foot crux of the Second Step had taken them three hours.

Above the step, the four Chinese entered a different world. Ahead of them stretched a gently rising plateau of scree and boulders. At the end of it rose the great snowfield of the final pyramid, suspended across the sky like a giant triangular wing. Beyond it, the summit. After they had slowly carried on for another 300 feet (100 m), it became painfully apparent that Liu Lienman was at the end of his tether. The Second Step episode had taken too much out of him, and now he was stumbling and falling every few steps. The others eventually helped him to a shelter beneath another cliff, where they all gathered together. The altitude was 28,500 feet (8,690 m).

The three knew they could go on and try to reach the summit; with the hopes of the expedition and the Communist Party resting on them, they almost had to. On the other hand, to leave Liu behind would put him in grave danger. He was not in a state to safely descend on his own, and to stay where he was meant the risk of freezing to death. In the end, it was Liu Lienman himself who said he would spend the night out in the open and that the other three should continue. For a while, Liu could watch them as they moved on into the twilight.

As darkness fell, the intense cold crept into Liu's body. He found himself drifting in and out of sleep, occasionally shaken wide awake by a gust of wind. He took some oxygen to restore circulation, but turned it off again, thinking of his partners somewhere above. At one point, when Liu felt he might not make it through the night, he jotted down some instructions for them to use the food and oxygen he had saved. Before long, however, the light of the stars above him gradually faded, and he knew he would live another day.

He sat up and looked again toward the summit—and soon enough he could see three figures slowly coming down the slope. One of the figures stopped and started gesticulating, pointing at Liu. Then they all quickened their pace, stumbling and rolling down the snow, shouting. They all embraced, and Liu could see the incredulity and joy in the others' faces at seeing him alive. When they read his message about the food and oxygen, it moved them to tears.

The summit? Had they been there? "Yes," they replied to Liu. They had made it.

Qu Yinhua

屈银华

Wang Fuzhou

王富洲

Qu Yinhua (top) and Wang Fuzhou (bottom) during the 1960 Chinese expedition (*From Mountaineering in China, Beijing: Foreign Languages Press, 1965 / Jochen Hemmleb collection*)

Here is the story as the three later put it on record:

Shortly after leaving Liu Lienman, they had embarked on "a slope, about 100 meters long, covered with a thick layer of snow," into which they sometimes sunk to their knees. Their pace was reduced to a crawl, and at one point they got down on all fours to overcome a short, steep ice pitch. It was 10:00 P.M. when they reached the top of the slope. Above "was a cliff, which was difficult of access with a huge cornice on the south side." They opted "to make a detour to the right and head for the summit by the north slope, brushed past the cliff, and began to tackle a rocky slope."

Only the faint starlight reflecting off the snow now helped them to see the route ahead. They carried no flashlights, probably because they had expected to arrive on the summit slopes earlier in the day. As they gained the final ridge, they were overcome by a feeling of suffocation. Their oxygen supplies, already low since leaving the Second Step, had basically run out. Gasping frantically for breath, they pressed on.

"In the dim light we saw a steep slope in front, covered with ice and snow. We took it for the main peak, only to find that the summit was farther away to the southwest."[4] They staggered toward it, a snowy dome almost invisible against the dark sky. The last stretch of the undulating crest, perhaps 300 feet (100 m) in distance, took another forty minutes. At 2:20 A.M., on May 25, 1960, Wang Fuzhou, Gonbu, and Qu Yinhua finally stood on the summit of Mount Everest.

The three remained on the highest point for about fifteen minutes. With fingers already frostbitten, Wang scribbled down their names and the date in a notebook, tore out the page, and placed it inside a spare glove. Together with a Chinese flag and a small plaster bust of Mao, they placed it on the summit. As they started the descent, however, Gonbu retrieved the items for fear of them getting blown away, and buried them among the first rocks below.

At 4:00 A.M., still before dawn, they were back at the top of the traverse along the topmost part of the North Face, below the final ridge. They had kept one bottle that had a little oxygen remaining, which they now used to regain some strength before down-climbing this tricky section. Once past it, they carefully edged their way down the steep snow slope in the gathering light. Suddenly they heard Gonbu shouting, "Look! Liu Lienman is still alive. He is waving at us!"

It was 7:30 A.M. when the three reunited with Liu. The sun was well above the horizon, and there was finally sufficient light to take some pictures. Qu Yinhua pulled out his movie camera. Because his hands were stiff from the cold, working the mechanism was difficult, but he managed to shoot a brief panorama of the range of peaks to the northeast. Then he turned around and took another shot of the final pyramid in the bright morning light.

THE 1960 CHINESE ASCENT—DID THEY REACH THE SUMMIT?

At the time the first accounts of the 1960 Chinese climb of the north side were published, many details bordered on the improbable. Climbing the Second Step in stockings, surviving a bivouac at 28,500 feet (8,690 m), or reaching the summit in the dark after their oxygen ran out—to western climbers, it all seemed a bit too much. To this day, Reinhold Messner doubts the Chinese account and claims to possess "documents" that show that the climbers never made it out of the high camp (for example, see *Der Spiegel,* May 10, 1999). He has yet to make these "documents" public or come forward with any sources.

On the other hand, when I saw a copy of the 1960 Chinese expedition film, I found that the highest images that were included—Qu Yinhua's footage from the morning after reaching the summit—were without doubt taken from above the Second Step. They showed part of the Third Step with the summit slopes beyond, and matched exactly photos taken by other expeditions from the plateau at the base of the final pyramid.

Of the terrain above this point at 28,500 feet (8,690 m), the Chinese could provide only verbal descriptions. But even the earliest of their accounts, published in 1961, already hinted at crucial topographical details of the last 500 feet (150 m), such as the summit snowfield or the traverse along the upper North Face to bypass the summit tower. This dispels any suspicion that the Chinese could have added these details after their ascent in 1975. The deviation around the summit tower was found by later expeditions to be the easiest way to gain the final ridge from the tip of the summit snowfield. And both Eric Simonson in 1991 and Matt Dickinson in 1996 reported how they had first mistaken the initial rise of the final ridge for the main summit—just as the Chinese had done.

Further corroboration came when Eric Simonson and I interviewed Qu Yinhua and Wang Fuzhou in Beijing in 2001. Without being asked specifically, the two described to us essential aspects of their route, such as Liu Lienman's bivouac spot at the Third Step or the exact way up the final pyramid, and pointed them out on a photograph. Nothing they said contradicted any of the previous accounts. Even more important, they confirmed what was known independently through photographic evidence. The detail and comprehensiveness of their account made it hard to doubt that the Chinese in 1960 had indeed done what they said they did—the probable first ascent of Mount Everest from the north.

Image from the 1960 Chinese expedition film, showing part of the Third Step and the summit pyramid
(China Newsreel & Documentary Film, Beijing)

Modern-day picture taken from the base of the Third Step; note that boxed section of photo is almost an exact match with the 1960 image. *(Jochen Hemmleb collection)*

Wang Fuzhou (left) and Qu Yinhua (right) in 2001 *(Photo © Jochen Hemmleb)*

After a rest, the four Chinese groped their way down to the top of the Second Step. By the time they got there, the sky had clouded over and it started to snow. They rappelled the crux, leaving behind their rope. At the bottom of the Second Step, conditions became truly atrocious. Visibility was low, and thick snow cloaked the downsloping slabs and ledges. Every handhold needed to be cleared; feet burrowed blindly through the powder for purchase. Often the climbers assisted each other on awkward moves. In their already exhausted state, they were agonizingly slow—it was not until seven o'clock in the evening that they were back at their high camp.

The next morning saw the upper mountain covered in white. After his retreat from the high camp two days earlier, Xu Jing had waited at Camp VI, together with Zhang Junyan and Liu Dayi. Now, with bad weather upon them and neither sufficient food nor oxygen for a longer stay, they had no option but to descend. When they were back at the North Col in the afternoon, they could make out two solitary figures coming down after them. They were Gonbu and Liu Lienman, who told them that, up on the mountain, Qu Yinhua and Wang Fuzhou were apparently in trouble. As indeed they were, and more than anybody could know.

Qu and Wang had been lagging behind the others, being in bad shape after the ordeal of the summit climb. Qu was leading as they were nearing Camp VI, wading through deep snow. Suddenly he lost his footing, and in a split second was cartwheeling down the slope. Wang had no strength left to check the fall and was dragged off his feet. They rapidly slid toward the edge of a cliff and certain oblivion—then came a brutal jerk and they stopped. The rope had snagged on a protruding rock, saving them both.

Wang had hurt his hip badly and lost his left boot, so for the rest of the descent he had to replace it with a spare pair of socks and a mitten. He and Qu spent a miserable night at the deserted camp. They were severely dehydrated and suffered terribly from parched throats, regularly swallowing lumps of snow to ease the pain.

Early on May 27, the rescue party of Bianba and Bian Amin headed back up the North Ridge. In the afternoon, they bumped into Qu and Wang a short distance above Camp V and escorted them down to the North Col the same evening. There, the climbers were treated to drinks and boiled noodles—their first real meal in four days.

Two days later, all members of the climbing team were back at Base Camp.

The Chinese ascent of Mount Everest in 1960 meant the culmination of the early mountaineering history of Mount Everest's north side, which had begun almost forty years earlier with the British reconnaissance of 1921.

It was also historically important for another reason. Above 28,000 feet (8,530 m), the Chinese were the first to have followed Mallory's intended route via the crest of the Northeast Ridge. Their high camp was only yards away from where the highest trace of Mallory and Irvine's attempt—an oygen bottle—was ever found. Therefore the Chinese decisions and the times they took above this point, such as on the way to the Second Step, merit particular interest. The 1960 party was to encounter the route under the same pristine conditions as those that existed in 1924; they had to face the same difficulties in finding the correct way—and thus came perhaps closer than anyone to experiencing the circumstances of Mallory and Irvine's final climb. The Chinese in 1960 had only limited experience but an almost fanatical determination. They were somewhat better equipped than the 1924 party, and the 1960 high camp was some four hours closer to the summit. How much could Mallory's greater experience and equal determination have compensated for these disadvantages?

All in all, the 1960 Chinese ascent was a remarkable feat—perhaps one of the most remarkable ascents in the history of Himalayan climbing. Some performances were particularly noteworthy. In the course of the Second Step reconnaissance and the summit climb, eighteen members reached altitudes of 27,800 feet (8,470 m) or higher. Three survived open bivouacs at or above 28,200 feet (8,595 m), the highest for the next twenty-three years.

The Chinese success had come at a cost; upon arrival at Base Camp, Qu Yinhua was discovered to have sustained severe frostbite while climbing the Second Step. He later lost all of his toes down to the front part of the soles and suffered damage to six fingers. Wang Fuzhou had five toes amputated, plus the tips of four fingers. In the course of the expedition, Qu and Wang each lost more than 50 pounds (23 kg) in body weight. No serious injuries were reported of the third summit climber, Gonbu, nor of the fourth member of the party, Liu Lienman.

None of these climbers seem to have been particularly experienced or skilled, although they were well-trained and adapted to altitude. They owed their success to an unusual drive and sheer boldness. And they were lucky.

When looking at the timing of the 1960 ascent and the chain of events, one realizes how narrow the margin between success and disaster had become in the final stages of the expedition. Already on the summit climb, several members had been showing signs of altitude sickness. The accounts speak of "utter exhaustion, excessive panting, troubled vision, and feebleness." It was a thirty-six-hour epic of endurance, and on the descent at least two of the Chinese were on their last legs. They came back alive—but only just.

After the 1960 Chinese ascent, Beijing did not seem to be bothered by the widespread disbelief with which the western mountaineering world greeted the news. Unknown to the West, however, plans were made for a second ascent in 1967 to underscore the earlier success.

Ambitions were high. A simultaneous ascent by the West and Northeast Ridges was planned—and the summit was to be reached in daylight to provide irrefutable proof. In the spring of 1965, a first reconnaissance of the West Ridge was mounted. It reached the Lho La saddle on the border to Nepal. In autumn the same year, the Chinese explored the complete Northeast Ridge starting from the Rapiu La, the pass opposite the East Rongbuk Advance Base Camp. Wang Hongbao and Wu Zongyue, who were both later to die on Everest, attained about 24,500 feet (7,470 m).

Another expedition in 1966 consisted of around 400 members, mostly from the army, and was led by Xu Jing. It was intended to select members for the summit attempt the following year. Thirty-two climbers reached 26,580 feet (8,100 m). Shugao Ma was killed in a fall from the North Ridge when descending from Camp V.

It was the military nature of the reconnaissance and the relative inexperience of the participants that nurtured rumors of a massive disaster during the 1966 expedition. The German climbing magazine *Alpinismus* claimed that of a twenty-six-member climbing team, only two had returned to Base Camp, frostbitten and exhausted. The others had blindly marched on, inadequately protected against the cold, but "warmed by the thoughts of Chairman Mao." Another rumor, this time spread by the New China News Agency, claimed three individual solo ascents of Everest by surveyors in 1969. Both stories, unsupported as they were, did nothing to enhance the credibility of the Chinese accounts in general.

FIRST STEP
SECOND STEP
THIRD STEP
Summit tower
1975 Camp VII Mushroom Rock
Liu Lienman's bivouac
Northeast Ridge
1960 Camp VII
Snow
Terrace
1975 Camp VI
Great (Norton) Couloir
1924 Camp VI
Mallory's body
North Ridge

(Photo © Jake Norton)

1960 & 1975
Chinese Expeditions

By this time, however, the mountaineering community also lacked support in China itself. The 1967 summit attempt was cancelled by the leaders of the Cultural Revolution, and two further expeditions in post-monsoon 1967 and pre-monsoon 1968 were mainly scientific missions, getting no higher than the North Col. In 1969, Lin Biao, then number-two man in China behind Mao, declared, "athletics are useless" and dissolved the mountaineering team, despite personal intervention by Premier Chou Enlai. Climbers such as Wang Fuzhou, once Master of Sports and a national hero, were sent to "Labor Schools" to become farmers or plain workmen.

It was not until five years later that the Chinese mountaineering team was reestablished with the support of Vice-Premier Deng Xiaoping, and plans were renewed for the second Chinese ascent of Mount Everest, to take place in 1975. In the course of the preparation, a training climb to the North Col was undertaken in 1974.

1975: THE CHINESE CLIMB EVEREST AGAIN

The 1975 Chinese expedition was the largest team ever to attempt Mount Everest. It comprised 434 members, 179 of whom were climbers, including 36 women.

After the disappearance of Wu Zongyue on May 4 (see Chapter 6, Short Walk into the Past),[5] the first summit team was confined to Camp VII by a sudden storm. After waiting for fifty hours without oxygen at 27,750 feet (8,460 m), they were

The 1975 Chinese summit team climbing the Second Step headwall *(From* Another Ascent of the World's Highest Peak, *Beijing: Foreign Languages Press, 1975/Jochen Hemmleb collection)*

forced to retreat to Camp VI. One member, Xia Boyu, suffered severe frostbite, which later resulted in the amputation of both his legs below the knees. Another summit attempt four days later by Cheng Tianliang, Sodnam Norbu, Wang Hongbao, and Samdrup failed when the party lost their way near the First Step and ended up in the Great (Norton) Couloir.

Finally, on May 25, after moving the high camp to 28,120 feet (8,570 m), Sodnam Norbu and Kunga Pasang reached the Second Step, where they found the pitons and rope left behind in 1960. The next day, with the help of Lotse and Tsering Tobgyal, they rigged up a 15-foot (4.8-m) aluminum ladder on the step's headwall. Meanwhile, another five climbers—Hou Shengfu, Samdrup, Darphuntso, Ngapo Khyen, and a Tibetan woman, Phanthog—arrived at the high camp from Camp VI.

At 6:00 A.M. on the morning of May 27, all nine climbers set out for the summit together. Ninety minutes later, they were on top of the Second Step. Using oxygen only during rest breaks, they slowly made their way up the final pyramid. Near the tip of the triangular snowfield, where the angle steepened considerably, Kunga Pasang fainted from exhaustion. He recovered, and the climbers took a detour to the right to bypass the obstacle. Like the 1960 party, they traversed beneath the summit tower and regained the final ridge beyond.

At 12:30 P.M., everybody stood on the summit. They spent seventy minutes on top, taking film and still photographs as well as carrying out numerous scientific

Chinese climbers on the summit of Mount Everest, May 27, 1975; note survey target. *(From* Another Ascent of the World's Highest Peak, *Beijing: Foreign Languages Press, 1975/ Jochen Hemmleb collection)*

tasks. Phanthog even underwent an electrocardiograph test, which was transmitted by radio to Base Camp. The Chinese left behind a survey tripod, which remained on the summit for the next decade as irrefutable proof of their ascent.

Three years later, in 1978, the Chinese invited a group of Iranian climbers on a joint reconnaissance. The Iranians thus became the first foreigners to legally visit the north side of Everest after the Second World War. Plans of a Chinese-Iranian expedition in 1979 came to nothing. Instead the Japanese became the next foreign visitors when they explored the East and Main Rongbuk Glaciers in the autumn that year.

In November 1979, the Chinese Mountaineering Association officially permitted foreign expeditions to Mount Everest and other mountains in Tibet—the historic north side was open again.

CHAPTER 10

OUT OF THE DARKNESS

The night had swallowed the mountain. There was no moon, only the scattered pinpricks of light from the stars. The black silhouette of the Northeast Ridge was barely visible against the sky, with the snowfields above the Second Step faintly glowing like the sails of a ghost ship. We were staring at a deadly desert of cold and blackness. This was no place for life—but there were people up there.

This night of May 23, 2001, marked the beginning of some of the most frustrating, nerve-wracking, and inspirational thirty hours anyone on our team had ever been through; thirty hours that, in the words of Eric Simonson, "epitomized everything that is best and worst about mountaineering."

The month of May had so far been a difficult one for the 2001 Mallory & Irvine Research Expedition. More searches as well as summit bids had been planned for the first half of the month, but the first foray was cut short by our team's rescue of two Chinese glaciologists struck with cerebral and pulmonary edema below Advance Base

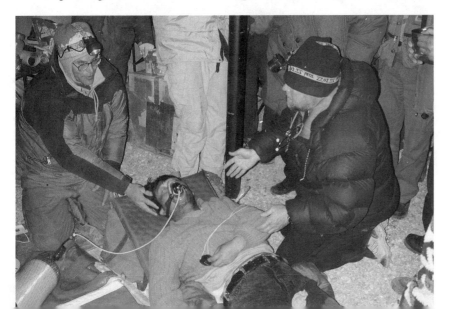

Eric Simonson (left) and expedition doctor Lee Meyers (right) at Base Camp, attending one of the ill Chinese glaciologists
(Photo © Andy Politz)

Mike Otis (left) and Terry LaFrance (right), our successful summit climbers
(Photo © Andy Politz)

Camp. During the rescue, Jake Norton badly injured his knee and had to withdraw from further climbing on the expedition. Two subsequent attempts at the summit were halted by deep snow above Camp VI and by marginal weather at Camp V, but clients Terry LaFrance and Mike Otis eventually made a flawless ascent on May 19, together with Sherpas Mingma Ongel, Ang Chhiring "Kami," Danuru, and Lhakpa Nuru.

With Norton out and John Race and Brent Okita leaving due to other commitments, it came down to our "Final Four"—Dave Hahn, Tap Richards, Jason Tanguay, and Andy Politz—to give it one last shot. The plan was for the first three to try for the summit and look for traces of Mallory and Irvine above the Second Step, while Politz was to conduct a final search for Irvine and the camera from Camp VI.

On May 23, the four moved up to Camp VI in preparation for the summit attempt the next day. For all except Tanguay, who had joined the team later as guide for the climbing and trekking program affiliated with the expedition, it was their third trip to 26,900 feet (8,200 m) over the course of the expedition—the equivalent of having climbed the world's sixth-highest peak, Cho Oyu, three times in five weeks!

Politz and Richards again followed the complete North Ridge to further investigate and film the site of the 1924 high camp. Hahn later joined them from Camp VI, which he had reached in a single push from the North Col the previous day. All were at the peak of their fitness and acclimatization.

Our "Final Four" (left to right): Tap Richards, Jason Tanguay, Andy Politz, and Dave Hahn
(Photo © Jochen Hemmleb)

Among the many expeditions on both sides of the mountain, the perfect weather caused a mass exodus upward, and we could see people reaching the summit by the dozen. On this day alone, there were a total of eighty-nine ascents from both sides—as many as in the first twenty-six years after Hillary and Tenzing's ascent. True to the words of British pioneer Alfred F. Mummery, the highest mountain had apparently regressed from "an inaccessible peak" to "an easy day for a lady." There were also the "Guinness Book" records: Frenchmen Marco Siffredi surfed down the Great (Norton) Couloir on his snowboard, and the day before a couple, Bertrand and Clair Roche, had flown from the summit with a tandem parapente.

But there was also a sense of foreboding. With everybody climbing to high altitude at the same time, it was almost inevitable that sooner or later something would go badly wrong.

May 23, 4:00 p.m., Base Camp: We were just settling down for a leisurely teatime when a startled cry came from behind the telescope. "There are still people up there!" We could see them clearly. One figure stood forlornly beside the Mushroom Rock, a curiously shaped limestone bollard halfway between the First and Second Step. Two other climbers, clad in yellow down suits, were still on the traverse from the base of the Second Step. One had slipped and was hanging from the fixed ropes some 15 feet (5 m) below the tracks. The other kept moving back and forth in an effort to help the fallen climber.

But their predicament was still not as bad as what was yet to come that evening.

Just before dinner our doctor, Lee Meyers, came over to the mess tent. "There are people below the Second Step, all right. But what about those on the Third Step?" With silent disbelief we turned again to the telescope—and indeed, there were two yellow dots, slowly groping their way down the prow of the cliff. At the base of the step, they finally stopped. Another yellow dot was seen moving up to join them in what was obviously an emergency bivouac. They were at 28,500 feet (8,690 m).

6:00 p.m., Camp VI, 26,900 feet (8,200 m): Just before sunset, Tap Richards got out of the tent one more time. Looking up to the summit pyramid, glowing golden in the last rays, he spotted two figures at the base of the Third Step, etched against the dark-blue evening sky. He was disturbed. Whoever that was, they were too high, too late.

8:30 p.m., Camp VI: Dave Hahn and Andy Politz were resting in their tent. Suddenly they heard rustling outside, a muffled voice, the sound of boots grating over frozen gravel. Their tent door was zipped open and a face poked inside. It was Chris Warner, one of the guides working for Himalayan Experience, a company run by highly experienced New Zealander Russell Brice.

"We had to abandon a client up there today," Warner uttered between gasps of breath. Hahn and Politz went quiet. They had just been discussing the empty tents they had seen around camp, tents they had expected to be occupied by then.

View of the Northeast Ridge from Camp VI; the Third Step is the dark knoll at the base of the summit pyramid, where the crest starts to rise steeply. *(Photo © Mike Otis)*

"Say that again," replied Hahn. "What happened?"

"We had to abandon a client up at the Third Step," Warner answered. "I was wondering if you could take up a foam pad and a thermos of tea for him when you get up there in the morning. We'll have two Sherpas on their way up to help him down."

The client—a Guatemalan named Jaime Vinals—and his two guides, Andy Lapkass and Asmus Norreslet, had been the last in a group of fifteen climbers from Himalayan Experience to summit Everest that day. On his descent from the summit, Warner had met them on the summit snowfield at 11:30 A.M., going up. Although Brice had warned them repeatedly over the radio of the potentially late hour, they were confident of reaching the summit and achieving a safe descent. For Vinals, climbing the world's highest mountain would make him the first Guatemalan to do so. Also, Everest was the last in his quest for the "Seven Summits," the highest points on each continent.

The trio reached the top at 2:30 P.M., but must have run out of oxygen shortly afterward. On the way down, Vinals developed vision problems that made walking increasingly difficult. By the time they were back at the Third Step, the group had almost ground to a halt. In a supreme effort, Norreslet forged ahead to the top of the Second Step, where their team had cached additional oxygen. He fetched some bottles and dragged himself back up to his partners. But as darkness fell, it seemed as if the guides had made the agonizing decision to leave their client behind.

At the latter notion, Politz shook his head in disbelief. "I had been with Andy Lapkass on Everest before and found him a highly ethical guy. It just didn't seem right that he should do such a thing." Hahn, on the other hand, wondered about the client. "If they had to abandon him, I reasoned he couldn't be coherent, that he hadn't responded to any drugs or oxygen. I told Warner that we would do what we could—but inwardly I thought we would find a dead body."

Meanwhile up on the dark ridge, Norreslet tried to find a way down the interminable ledges and crags by the beam of his headlamp. The young Dane, who worked and lived in Chamonix, France, started to hallucinate. For hours he thought he was on Mont Blanc. Only the steep descent through the Yellow Band made him realize where he truly was.

About midnight, Base Camp: I had decided to spend the night in our expedition's communications tent to monitor any radio calls coming in. Now I was abruptly awakened as the base station crackled to life once again. Norreslet was back at Camp VI, talking on Brice's frequency. My sleepy brain took a moment to register—but the content of the message shook me awake immediately; Norreslet was alone. Lapkass had *not* abandoned his client. He was still up there with Vinals at the Third Step and was also exhausted and affected by altitude.

There was no mention of other climbers on the ridge.

May 24, 1:00 a.m., Camp VI: Hahn, Richards, Tanguay, Phu Nuru, and Fu Dorji left their tents and headed up into the dark. They were going for the summit as planned, but at the same time prepared for a rescue if there was one.

It was a calm night, only moderately cold and with little wind. Conditions on the route were ideal. The many ascents over the previous days had left a trail of firm steps in the snow-filled gullies, and secure fixed ropes were in place.

After only two hours the men crested the Northeast Ridge. It was still dark when they climbed the First Step. As they turned the corner, a headlamp suddenly flashed at them. In the purple light of dawn they could see a lone figure next to the Mushroom Rock. The client must have made it down to this point during the night, they thought. But when Hahn came up the side of the tower, there was not just a single figure. There were three.

4:45 a.m., Mushroom Rock, 28,120 feet (8,570 m): Hahn contacted Base Camp: "Eric, this is Dave. We are at the Mushroom Rock, and we've just found three Russians who spent the night here."

They were members of a Siberian expedition. Two of them, Aman Eleushev and Stanislav Krylov, had reached the summit the previous day. On the way down, at 2:45 P.M., they were shocked to encounter the third, Alexei Nikiforov, above the Second Step, still struggling weakly upward. They talked him into turning back and descended together. Nikiforov could move only slowly and with difficulty, despite using oxygen. One by one their bottles ran out. Eleushev went ahead in search of

Climbing the First Step
(Photo © Mike Otis)

partially used bottles left behind for the descent, found some, and, with Krylov's help, ferried them back to Nikiforov.

It was Nikiforov whom we had seen in trouble on the fixed ropes the previous afternoon; at one point during the night, he must have made it across the rest of the traverse to his partners. Eventually all three sought shelter in a wind-carved hollow behind the Mushroom Rock. No one knew about their fate because they did not have any radios. A woman from their team had also summited that day and descended ahead of her partners, but nobody had talked to her that night.

Although the three Siberians had been breathing oxygen from discarded bottles left at the site, they had spent a tough night. Eleushev had lived through the ordeal least affected; occasionally he stood up and talked. The other two just lay in the snow, feebly kicking their feet and barely conscious. Richards described the scene:

"It was scary to see how out of it they were. They wouldn't realize that you were there until you stood right in front of their faces. I screamed and shouted at them. Although their eyes were open, it was like trying to wake someone from a deep slumber. They were like an engine that sat in the cold and needed to be jump-started."

Most bizarre, all of them had their down clothing zipped open and wore only thin woolen gloves. Their thick expedition mittens lay scattered around. This is a phenomenon often observed in victims of severe hypothermia, when at a certain core temperature the constricted blood vessels near the skin suddenly dilate, creating a sensation of warmth.

Hahn, Richards, Tanguay, and the two Sherpas did what they could to revive the Siberians. They gave dexamethasone pills to combat the effects of cerebral edema, fed them water and food, and put them on oxygen. Because the Russian regulators were not compatible with the American systems, they cobbled together a T-connection, so two could breathe from a spare bottle that Phu Nuru had been carrying. After nearly an hour, some vitality returned to the men. "One became quite coherent again," noted Hahn. "The other two were worse off, but eventually we figured if they worked together, they could make it down on their own."

At that point the team also could not expect much help from anybody below. Already two Colombians had been moving up the ridge and passed them, summit-bound. Lapkass and Vinal's colleagues were not able to support them either. If Brice's team had made any mistake, it was that everybody—guides, clients, and Sherpas—had gone for the summit at the same time, taking opportunity of the good weather. Most of them had descended to lower camps, and those remaining at Camp VI felt too exhausted to go back up and help. Even more critical, there was little oxygen left at the high camp.

Simonson at Base Camp and Brice at the North Col now arranged for Sherpas to carry up oxygen bottles from the lower camps. Simonson also called Politz at Camp VI to climb up to the Northeast Ridge and assist the team.

Through their conversations with Base Camp, Hahn and the others at the Mushroom Rock learned for the first time about Lapkass. Faced with a second person in emergency up high, they asked Phu Nuru for his oxygen set and sent the Sherpa down, thereby giving up his chance to summit Everest for the first time. He returned safely to the North Col on his own.

6:00 a.m.: While Hahn stayed until the Siberians were on their way, Tanguay and Fu Dorji continued toward the Second Step, as did Richards shortly after.

Tanguay, the youngest team member, was going exceptionally strong. "He had no qualms whatsoever," Richards said. "I remember how intimidated I had been by the traverse to the Second Step in 1999, when I turned around at this point. But Jason . . . He was just strolling along the brittle ledges, absolutely unconcerned. I could almost hear him whistle!"

Next, Tanguay virtually raced up the Second Step, followed closely by Fu Dorji. The two just hopped on the ropes and Chinese ladder, and all in all dispatched with the whole step in little more than ten minutes.

The Second Step *(Photo © Mike Otis)*

6:30 a.m., Second Step, 28,250 feet (8,610 m): Tanguay and Fu Dorji reached the top of the step, followed ten minutes later by Richards. "By then the ridge was basking in the sun, and we could see the rest of the route clearly," Richards recalled later. "Jason and I kept high-fiving. We were both climbing so well and it was a perfect day. We were so sure that we would be on the summit in no time."

But looking across the scree plateau ahead of them, they could see the red and yellow figures lying motionless at the base of the Third Step.

6:50 a.m., base of Third Step, 28,500 feet (8,690 m): Tanguay, Fu Dorji, and Richards arrived at the bivouac site of Andy Lapkass and Jaime Vinals. The guide and his client were huddled in an exposed spot near the ridge crest, unprotected from the wind, lower legs wrapped in the shredded pieces of a flimsy space blanket. Like the Siberians, they had their jackets unzipped. Lapkass had one hand tucked under an armpit, and one of the first things he asked was, "Where is my mitten?" They found it lying right beside him.

Lapkass's speech was slurred, and both he and Vinals complained about blurred vision, indicating cerebral edema. Tanguay and Richards rigged them up to one of their oxygen bottles, then tried to inject dexamethasone. But the ampoules were frozen and they had to feed them several rounds of pills instead.

After giving them some water and food, they tried to raise the men—with deeply discouraging results. Their balance was gone. Richards said, "It would take them a few minutes to get to their feet—and then their legs would just buckle underneath them. They'd fall back to the ground, limp.

"It was like dealing with someone with a broken back."

They could not walk—but they needed to if they wanted to survive . . .

As they stood there trying to help the men, other climbers showed up. First the two Colombians reappeared, whom the team had passed again above the Second Step. This time they stopped and shed some drinks and food, but did not lend manpower or oxygen. Several minutes later, two Spaniards and their Sherpa walked by. Richards asked them for oxygen, but they just shook their heads and continued toward the top.

In the meantime, Hahn had reached the top of the Second Step. He had worked for ninety minutes on the Siberians with his oxygen switched off. Moreover, he now continued his climb at a reduced flow rate to save the depleted oxygen reserves. We could see the effort it must have taken as he walked on, frequently stopping for brief rests.

8:05 a.m., base of Third Step: Hahn arrived at the Third Step and joined the others in their efforts to save Lapkass and Vinals. His heart sank when he first saw them.

"It was horrifying to watch Andy and Jaime trying to stand and walk, only to collapse back on the rock. . . . To make matters worse, the two were far from dead at the moment. In fact they were very much alive. Jaime was so alive, it was scary."

At one point he told Hahn about trouble with his contact lenses—and the latter realized that Vinals's vision problems might not have been signs of cerebral edema at all. Vinals was just downright exhausted. He and Lapkass had the will to live—but their bodies were not allowing it to happen.

Hahn, Richards, and Tanguay stared at the men as they lay at their feet, the sight bringing tears to their eyes.

Fu Dorji, in another great sacrifice, also gave up his summit chance and handed over his oxygen. Like Phu Nuru earlier, he descended without. "Bad luck," he murmured and pointed back at the summit, "bad luck. . . ." Then he disappeared down the slope.

At Base Camp we could only guess at the full scale of the drama—and, for a while, had still hoped our team would be able to continue to the top. They deserved it so much after all their hard work to make this expedition a success, after almost single-handedly putting in the route by which others were now making it. Simonson raised the idea, "What if you just run up, ring the bell, and take further care of Jaime and Andy on the way down?"

But in the meantime they might die.

Hahn looked at his partners. "You guys realize that there is absolutely no way we can do what Eric is suggesting, don't you?" For them there was only one answer . . .

8:30 a.m., base of Third Step: Hahn's voice came over the radio: "We are *not* going to the summit!" Sensing the questions and traces of disappointment in our voices, he added, "In such a moment, you don't even *think* about the summit . . ."

Looking back along the Northeast Ridge from the Third Step *(Photo © Mike Otis)*

It was a decision that, at this point, probably took more courage than to carry on over the remaining 500 feet (150 m) of elevation gain to the top of the world. The summit was so close, just an hour away. Everybody felt strong, they had most of the day still ahead, the weather was perfect. They all wanted to get there—it would never have been easier, and would never be more of a sure thing. Yet for the team it was never an option.

Richards said, "We had delved in to help, so we made the decision to essentially stay with these guys until their last moments—if that was what it meant. Just to give them that comfort."

And in this commitment there was hope. Richards continued, "I realized if there *was* any way they were going to get up and walk, it would be by staying with them and keep telling them to do so. And so I said to them repeatedly, 'You are not going to die, we are going to get off this thing—but you've got to do it by yourself! We can't carry you.'

"And they would look back at you with wide eyes, saying, 'I don't want to die. I don't want to die up here!'"

Although the rescuers saw the possible futility of their efforts, they continued to do what they could, giving more medicine, water, food, and oxygen. And slowly, almost indiscernibly at first, things started to change.

Lapkass's eyesight had improved. The main problem, he said, were his feet; he could not feel them. Richards checked for frostbite and saw that Lapkass could still move his ankles. So he should be able to walk. They got him to stand up. This left only his pack and oxygen bottle to take care of, which Lapkass found too heavy to carry by himself.

9:00 a.m., base of Third Step: Richards put the oxygen bottle in his own pack, from where the rubber hose led to Lapkass's face mask. Lapkass leaned against

Richards's back and shoulders while Tanguay held him from behind by the belt of his harness. And so, together, the three finally started walking. First three steps between each rest, then five steps, another rest, then more steps . . .

"Great," Richards thought, "we are finally getting somewhere—but there is *no way* we're going to be able to deal with the Second Step this way!"

10:00 a.m., Second Step: "At that altitude, it is really hard to rappel with someone attached to you," explained Tanguay. "We also didn't have any rope to lower Andy with. It was very plain that if he could do the rappel by himself, we'd keep going—if he couldn't, then it was over."

Richards rappelled down the headwall first, ready to receive Lapkass on the snow patch below. Tanguay made a final check of the anchors—and noticed that Lapkass had not doubled back his harness. "Had he leaned back on it . . . well, it could have been the end right there and then." He quickly grabbed Lapkass, fixed the problem, and sent him off the ledge.

At first it went well. But 5 feet (1.5 m) were enough to take everything out of the exhausted guide. He slowly pitched forward into the rock, losing his balance . . . then let go with his hands. But Richards was prepared for a "fireman's rappel," yanking hard on the rope, so Lapkass's rappeling device would grip and brake the slide.

"C'mon, Andy, you've got to do this!" Richards hollered from below.

Bringing himself together, Lapkass descended the remaining feet and crumpled on the ledge, gasping for breath. Richards climbed up to him.

"Way to go! We just have to do this one more time. You can do it!"

"Where are you, Tap?" Lapkass asked.

His vision had gone bad again.

After a rest, waiting for Tanguay to lower Lapkass's pack and come down himself, the three forced their way to the bottom of the step.

Meanwhile, above the Second Step, Hahn and Vinals had been entangled in their own personal drama. Half an hour had passed since the others had left, and since then the two had managed to walk down only a few yards over a patch of scree to some boulders, where they stopped again. And yet through all of this, Vinals had been lucid and attentive, painfully alive.

Hahn then tried everything to rekindle a spark of energy in Vinals. He started talking to him. "Jaime, do you have a family?" "Oh yes, my wife is pregnant." "You want to see them again, don't you?" "Oh yes!" "Then you better start walking!"

Slowly they moved from one boulder to the next, inch by inch, before Hahn would feel Vinals tapping his back to stop and sit down again. To relieve him of the weight, Hahn put Vinals's oxygen in his own pack—and together, connected by 2 feet (0.6 m) of rubber tubing, they could at last walk a few wobbly steps.

"The terrain between the Third and Second Steps is by far the easiest ground on the climb," said Hahn. "Even so, when we got walking along, I half expected to just hear a little 'pop' of that hose separating as Jaime tumbled off the Kangshung Face a few feet to our right. In fact, at one point I considered momentarily that Jaime might step over the cornice on purpose to save me from an unworkable future—for I had absolutely no clue how this day would end . . .

"I kept fogging up my sunglasses with tears, because I figured he would die. I didn't know how or when that would take place, but I thought I was going to have to witness it."

They still did not manage to make more than 20 feet (6 m) of progress between protracted sit-down rests, and their time was running out. The decision whether Hahn would soon have to abandon Vinals to save his own life hung in the air.

11:15 a.m., top of Second Step: Over the radio, Hahn heard Simonson winding up for a direct order. In despair, Hahn pulled the radio out of his down suit and held it out a few inches from Vinals's face. Simonson did not mince his words: "Dave, if Jaime can't do any better than he is doing now, you'll have to leave him up there!"

The reaction was profound. "I watched Jaime's eyes get wide as emotion flooded back into him," remembered Hahn. "He dug deep and found some as yet untapped source of strength and resolve.

"And then it was all Jaime. He clipped in the rope with his figure eight and rappelled the Second Step on his own—without oxygen, because I still had his bottle. 'Not bad for a dead man!' I thought as I accompanied him."

Just as the two were on the steepest part of the step, one of the Spaniards who had passed them on the way up was now returning from the summit and tried to overtake them. This earned him a verbal stop sign from Hahn, "Fuck off! Wait till we're down, all right?"

12:00 p.m., traverse from base of Second Step to Mushroom Rock: On the lower part of the Second Step, Vinals got tangled up in the rappel rope. Hahn, who had gone ahead, tried to climb back up the 6 or 8 feet (2 m or so) that separated them—but now the strain of the past few hours started taking its toll.

"I realized that not only was I not helping Jaime that much in this crucial place, but that I'd better keep track of myself or I was going to have an accident."

Luckily for both of them, it was right at this moment that Phurba, one of Brice's Sherpas, caught up with the rescue team. Phurba had summited the day before, but nonetheless had headed back up to help. He quickly climbed past Hahn, placed his goggles and oxygen mask on Vinals, and disentangled him from the ropes in about two minutes flat. "He made all the difference," Hahn acknowledged thankfully.

By the time Hahn, Phurba, and Vinals started climbing back toward the Mushroom Rock, the others had reached the end of the traverse. "The fixed lines were crap," said Richards, their pitons barely holding in the shattered rock. "If one of us had tripped, he would have pulled everybody off." With Tanguay and Richards at either end of a stretch, they pulled the rope tight between them, so Lapkass would

Tap Richards rappelling the First Step.
Note dead climber below.
(Photo © Andy Politz)

fall no distance at all in case of a slip. It was a scary tightrope act all the same, poised over the 8,000-foot (2,400-m) drop of the North Face to their left.

At the Mushroom Rock, Andy Politz was already waiting. "Hi!" he greeted them with a smile and gave his friend Andy Lapkass a long hug. "Now we have a problem—there are too many Andys here!"

And for the first time that day, they felt they all might make it . . .

2:00 p.m., base of First Step, 28,000 feet (8,535 m): The most difficult section of the route was behind them. After they left the Mushroom Rock, another of Brice's Sherpas, Lobsang, arrived. With so many helping hands, rappelling the slabs and cliff bands of the last rock bastion went like clockwork.

At the bottom of the First Step, the two Sherpas took care of Vinals and headed down the ridge. Tanguay followed with Lapkass in tow and the others brought up the rear. Securely clipped to the fixed ropes, with the terrain easing off and the sun still high in the sky, they started slowly to unwind. Soon they were at the entrance of the descent into the Yellow Band.

On the Northeast Ridge between the
First Step and the exit from the Yellow Band
(Photo © Andy Politz)

As they looked down the gully, they could see two figures in yellow down suits crouched on a ledge.

3:05 p.m., Yellow Band, 27,630 feet (8,420 m): Politz was the first to reach them. They were Krylov and Nikiforov, two of the Siberians they had helped to descend from the Mushroom Rock in the morning.

Politz had met all three of them four hours earlier on his way up, near the First Step. By then, Nikiforov had managed to walk only a couple of steps and repeatedly lay down to rest. Yet they had sufficient oxygen and would have been able to make it back to their camp, even at their slow pace.

But now Nikiforov had collapsed, and Krylov kept holding an oxygen mask to his partner's face. Politz quickly checked the pressure gauge of the bottle and noticed that it was already empty. He got doctor Lee Meyers on the radio, who advised them to inject dexamethasone. But even when they rammed the inch-long needle in Nikiforov's shoulder, the Siberian did not flinch. They feared the worst.

For fifteen minutes Politz, Tanguay, and Richards tried to resuscitate the man—to no avail. He showed no response to the dexamethasone injections, had no detectable pulse or breathing, his pupils were dilated and showed no reflexes to light. Based on this information, Meyers confirmed the inevitable—Alexei Nikiforov was dead.

Just as everything seemed nearly over, the mountain had claimed its price.

Krylov broke down in tears, grieving for his partner. After a silent prayer, the team gently pulled him away and accompanied him the last 650 feet (200 m) to the tents.

4:00 p.m., Camp VI: Rescuers as well as rescued were back at the camp. Minutes later, they watched in horror as a yellow-clad body and a backpack bounced down the crags and ledges of the Yellow Band. Nikiforov had somehow become detached from the ropes and slipped into the void.

He found his final resting place among the eternal snows of the North Face.

The First Step and summit pyramid *(Photo © Andy Politz)*

MATTERS OF LIFE AND DEATH

"Above 8,000 meters is not a place where people can afford morality . . ."—those were the infamous words of a Japanese climber who had walked past three ailing Indians on the Northeast Ridge after the deadly storm of 1996. Without help, none of the Indians survived. Despite the outrage these actions and words created, it subsequently became an accepted doctrine that no one could be rescued from such altitudes if they were not able to walk by themselves.

Yet the rescues of May 24, 2001, showed that with sufficient manpower, oxygen, and medicine it *is* possible to rescue climbers from near the summit of Mount Everest, even if at first they had not appeared able to walk and were stranded on a route of considerable difficulty. In this new light, some of the previous tragedies on 8,000-meter peaks under similar circumstances may need to be viewed differently—and future climbers who walk past victims without offering help may find it harder to justify their decision.

The success of the rescue was not rooted in technical aspects. The rescuers' gear, medical supplies, and oxygen had not been beyond what should be standard for a summit day on Everest. Luck with the weather and the victim's own ability to help also played a role. But it was the rescuers' attitude that became the decisive factor; a collective willingness of the five to put their personal ambitions aside and instead use all means at their disposal to help, and a refusal to give up anybody for dead before they actually were.

While still at Base Camp after the rescues, we began to discuss the events and their possible implications. Surely the rescue and the circumstances leading to it were to bring up again the debate over commercial expeditions, their guides, and their clients. There was no point in denying the mixed feelings the issue created within our team. Jason Tanguay spoke for many when he expressed his conflicting emotions after our return from the mountain:

"On one hand, I'm a little frustrated. We worked hard to make our own attempt as safe as possible—the preparation of the route, high camps stocked with adequate oxygen and supplies, the acclimatization, our trained ability to move fast and secure on summit day. All of this we had to sacrifice for

people who had made a bad decision. It wasn't a stroke of bad luck or rapid change in weather, not faulty equipment or an accident—just a plain error in judgment.

"On the other hand, they were people who needed help. In my mind, someone in need of help at 28,500 feet on Mount Everest is no different from someone in need of help at sea level in a city. And going on to the summit would never have been worth a lifetime of wondering if we could have changed the outcome."

Our team's decision to rescue was made from a pretty simple and familiar ethical base—Do unto others as you would have them do unto you. Being ready to lend a hand to an injured or sick climber seemed to us to have a legitimacy in itself. It seemed clean and unambiguous as a "right path" (in the Buddhist sense of finding the compassionate way). And despite the mixed feelings about the lost summit, we never doubted that our team had made the right decision.

As straightforward as this reasoning sounds, in reality it is not. In commercial expeditions, climbers pay up to $65,000 (U.S.) for their own participation. Whether the money comes out of their own pockets or from sponsors, the pressures on the individual to succeed are intense. This does not justify a climber's decision to walk past a victim or leave the rescue work to others, but it does show that the issue needs to be seen from different angles. The men on our team decided to help, while some others decided differently, for their own reasons.

As the highest mountain in the world, Mount Everest will continue to be seen by many as the epitome of human challenge, a prestigious goal independent of whether this is reflected in its actual mountaineering challenge. And in this role, Everest will always attract climbers and will always hold the potential to arouse the best and worst in human nature.

There is a tendency these days to measure success solely in absolutes, such as reaching the highest summit. More than 200,000 people greeted Everest summitteer Jaime Vinals upon his return to Guatemala. He came back a national hero—and the Guatemalan press took a long time to acknowledge that he had made it back down only thanks to the help of others.

There were few, if any, members of the press present when his rescuers returned to the United States.

Obviously, getting to the top is one kind of success—but should it be the only kind that is featured in the valuation and coverage of an expedition?

Dave Hahn, Tap Richards, Jason Tanguay, Fu Dorji, and Phu Nuru will not appear in the Everest summit statistics of 2001. Nor will Phurba, Andy Politz, and Lobsang. Their success on Everest was of a different kind, and in the team's eyes it was not even heroic. In our minds, they had just kept priorities right—what they did on May 24, 2001, was a plain act of humanity. Nothing more, nothing less.

There was no talking about it—the events of the day marked the end of our expedition. Nobody felt any need or wish to remain on the mountain any longer, and one by one the team bailed out of Camp VI in the evening.

Tanguay spent the night at Camp V, while Richards and Politz descended all the way to Advance Base Camp, arriving there at 10:00 P.M. Richards later told how he had fallen asleep in his tracks on the flat part of the glacier below the North Col. . . . Hahn, who had left after the others, was still at the top of the snow on the North Ridge when it got dark. But he had a working headlamp and figured he would be all right. He made it down to Advance Base Camp half an hour before midnight— more than twenty-four hours after he woke up at Camp VI.

Hahn's day ended with another search and bivouac: Already half asleep, Hahn had not found his sleeping bag in the storage tent—so he simply arranged some duffel bags and lay down, kept warm by his down suit.

Sleep came in seconds.

As for the original objectives of our 2001 Mallory & Irvine Research Expedition, the rescue had really put them in perspective. The detective work, the search—after all, they were just one of those self-imposed goals on which we sometimes tend to place a little too much importance. In the light of the events of May 24, 2001, they suddenly seemed pretty insignificant. . . . And in this insignificance, there was a healthy recognition and renewed respect for the mountain and its history. Despite all the changes over the years since Mallory and Irvine, Mount Everest had reminded us that the air around its summit was still thin, the cold freezing, and the winds ferocious.

And it could still kill people.

In the end, the rescue brought an unexpected twist to the expedition's conclusion. We had come to search for traces of two of the first climbers to fall victim to Mount Everest. Instead, we managed to help others avoid the same fate. Four lives had been kept from the grip of the mountain.

What the mountain had kept from us, though, was the secret of Sandy Irvine and his camera, perhaps containing the answer to the question we had set out to solve. Were George Mallory and Sandy Irvine the first to reach the top of Mount Everest?

THE 1999 AND 2001 MALLORY & IRVINE RESEARCH EXPEDITION—
A SUMMARY OF THE FINDINGS

1922 BRITISH EVEREST EXPEDITION

▶ Remnants of the **1922 Camp III** were discovered in 2001 at about 21,000 feet (6,400 m) on the right lateral moraine of the East Rongbuk Glacier below Advance Base Camp; recovered artifacts included three oxygen cylinders, food tins, stoves, and batteries.

▶ One **oxygen bottle from 1922 summit attempt by Finch, Bruce, and Tejbir** was recovered in 2001 from the North Ridge at about 24,850 feet (7,570 m).

1924 BRITISH EVEREST EXPEDITION

▶ The **body of George Mallory,** missing on Mount Everest since June 8, 1924, was discovered in 1999 at 26,760 feet (8,155 m) on the North Face; the body was photographed and conclusively identified from name tags in his clothing; recovered artifacts included samples of each clothing layer, altimeter, wristwatch, goggles, miscellaneous smaller items (matchbox, scissors, penknife, et cetera), personal letters, and notes. No camera or other clue was found as to whether Mallory had reached the summit before he perished.

▶ A discarded **oxygen bottle from Mallory and Irvine's summit attempt** was recovered in 1999 from 27,800 feet (8,475 m) on the Northeast Ridge.

▶ The **1924 Camp VI** was found in 2001 at 26,700 feet (8,140 m) on the North Ridge; recovered artifacts included tent poles, tent fabric, and miscellaneous smaller items (sock, mitten, food tins, spoon, et cetera).

▶ A **woollen mitten** of unknown provenance, but **very probably from Mallory and Irvine,** was recovered in 2001 from 27,700 feet (8,440 m) on the Northeast Ridge.

1933 BRITISH EVEREST EXPEDITION

▶ The **1933 Camp VI** was found in 1999 and rediscovered in 2001 at 27,495 feet (8,380 m) on the Yellow Band below the Northeast Ridge; a pack frame was recovered in 1999; artifacts in 2001 included several intact food tins and other provisions, stoves, solid fuel, cooking utensils, and tent fabric.

1934 MAURICE WILSON SOLO ATTEMPT

▶ Various **human bones, very probably belonging to Maurice Wilson,** who died during a solo attempt on Everest in 1934, were found in 1999 scattered along the right lateral moraine of the East Rongbuk Glacier below Advance Base Camp.

1960 CHINESE EVEREST EXPEDITION

▶ The **1960 Chinese "temporary camp"** below the North Col was found in 1999 and rediscovered in 2001 at about 21,750 feet (6,630 m) on the upper East Rongbuk Glacier; recovered artifacts included tent pegs, fabric, and poles; a piton hammer; ice and rock pitons; and food tins.

▶ The **1960 Camp V** was seen in 2001 at about 25,800 feet (7,860 m) on the North Ridge; the camp was identified from oxygen bottles found at the site; one bottle was recovered on a separate occasion.

▶ The **1960 Camp VI** was discovered in 2001 at about 26,640 feet (8,120 m) on the North Face; no artifacts were recovered. The camp's location was confirmed in a post-expedition interview with members from the 1960 Chinese expedition.

▶ The **1960 Camp VII,** was discovered in 2001 at about 27,750 feet (8,460 m) on the Northeast Ridge; recovered artifacts included three bamboo marker wands and an oxygen mask with regulator.

1975 CHINESE EVEREST EXPEDITION

▶ The **1975 Camp V** was seen in 1999 and 2001 at about 25,800 feet (7,860 m) on the North Ridge; the camp was identified from oxygen bottles found at the site. No artifacts were recovered.

▶ The **1975 Camp VI** was found in 2001 at 26,800 feet (8,170 m) on the North Face; recovered artifacts included parts of a survey tripod. At the same site, older equipment was found, possibly belonging to the 1960 expedition. This included a complete oxygen set (bottle, regulators, and valves) and an ice ax.

▶ The **1975 Camp VII** was found in 1999 at the Mushroom Rock, 28,120 feet (8,570 m), on the North Ridge; a piton hammer was recovered from the site but later left behind at Camp VI, from where it was eventually taken down in 2001.

REVELATION

I n 2001, Xu Jing was a handsome man with neatly combed silvery hair, a slender frame, and a liveliness that belied his seventy-five years. His was an aura of calm serenity. That is why I will never forget that moment when his whole expression changed. He went rigid in his chair, arms tight against his sides, his fingers curled, teeth clenched, and eyes wide open. It was when he described the body he had seen high on Mount Everest in 1960.

The 2001 Mallory & Irvine Research Expedition was over. We had not made a big discovery comparable to our finding of George Mallory in 1999. We had not found Sandy Irvine and the camera that could hold the answer to whether they were indeed the first to stand atop Mount Everest. But there was quiet satisfaction about the things we had found, the insights we had gained into the early British and Chinese expeditions. Our rescue of four climbers from above 28,120 feet (8,570 m) had of course made some headlines, especially in the climbing press.

While still on the expedition, I had discussed the possibility of joining Eric Simonson on one of his business trips to Beijing later that year to interview some of the Chinese climbers who had been on Mount Everest in the 1960s and 1970s. It would be an appropriate roundup to the detective work the team had done on the mountain and a splendid opportunity to fill in some of the gaps in the story of the Chinese expeditions. When Simonson sent his request to the Chinese Mountaineering Association (CMA), he was met with full support. A schedule of meetings was arranged, and on August 21, 2001, the two of us flew from Seattle via Tokyo to Beijing.

At Beijing Capital International Airport, we were greeted by the secretary of the CMA's exchange department, Li Guowei, and the head of the department, Wang

Yongfeng, who had summited Mount Everest himself from the north in 1993. As we drove through the night to our hotel, the illuminated streets of the capital revealed multistoried socialist architecture overlooking timeless Chinese pagodas, with the inevitable signs of westernization tucked in between: bright neon signs advertising McDonald's and Kentucky Fried Chicken—in Chinese script, of course.

The next morning we went to the CMA's headquarters, a plain brick building with a low annex that served as a conference room, surrounding a yard off Tiyuguan Road. The first persons we were to meet were members of the 1960 expedition. Among them were Wang Fuzhou and Qu Yinhua, two of the party who had become the first to climb Mount Everest from the north and return alive, and deputy leader Xu Jing.[1]

Before recounting the story of their expedition, they talked about how the Chinese activity on Everest had started with the Sino-Soviet reconnaissance in 1958. Of a rumored Soviet attempt in 1952, neither of the Chinese had any knowledge.

Most of the men's comments were delivered in matter-of-fact voices. But when Wang Fuzhou and Qu Yinhua spoke of how they had overcome the Second Step or of their near-demise during the descent, both men were visibly shaken. They gesticulated and shouted, vibrant with emotion. It was clear that they had been through a life-changing experience. Listening to their story made it difficult to imagine that we in the West had questioned the 1960 Chinese ascent of Everest for so long.

The authors with members of the 1960 Chinese Everest expedition, Beijing, summer 2001 (left to right): Wang Fuzhou, Xu Jing, Jochen Hemmleb, Eric Simonson, Qu Yinhua (Photo © Jochen Hemmleb)

Xu Jing then started to talk about the preparations and logistics of the 1960 expedition. After discussing routes and camp locations on the upper mountain, Simonson turned the subject to possible traces the Chinese had found of earlier attempts, especially of the 1924 Mallory and Irvine climb.

"Did they find anything from the British above the high camp?"

Wang Yongfeng translated. "At about 8,100 meters . . . to the left . . . he found this yellow tent, fixed by rope, from England. This was far away from our route, so others didn't go there to see this tent." From its altitude and position, this could have been the 1924 Camp VI, Mallory and Irvine's last camp, which our 2001 expedition thought to have revisited for the first time since the Second World War. Such a visit could also account for an enigmatic pair of old canvas-nylon mittens, which Jake Norton found in 2001 cached under a rock on the traverse between the Chinese Camp VI and the 1924 Camp VI, well to the left of today's route.

Then followed a long conversation in Chinese. Suddenly Xu rose in his chair, pressed his outstretched arms against his sides, and his eyes widened to a fearsome stare. It was an expression of such intensity and had come so unexpectedly, it made me shudder. But still neither Simonson nor I were prepared for the translation of Xu's words.

"At that time, he looked . . . there is a body, 8,200 meters high, one body . . . in a sleeping bag. That person is frozen there."

Simonson looked at me in disbelief. "Did he say he found a body?"

Only two climbers had been missing around this altitude on Everest before 1960—Mallory and Irvine . . .

Simonson turned to the Chinese. "At 8,200 meters?"

"He thinks, maybe it is at 8,200 meters or 8,300 meters, between that area"— which would have been 26,900 to 27,230 feet.

To make sure we had not misunderstood, I asked again. "A body?"

"Yes."

"You saw him?"

"Yes."

"In 1960?"

"Yes, in 1960."

As an afterthought, I remembered Xu's gesture again and wanted to confirm the impression it had made on me. "And he is lying on his back?"

"Yes."

Later Xu demonstrated the location by opening a book and pointing to the top of the pages. Then he ran his finger down the gutter, saying that the body was lying in a concave hollow or gully running down from the ridge crest. Again, he mentioned that the body was in a sleeping bag, but most of the bag was rotted away. The altitude, he now said, was 8,300 meters (27,230 feet).

Xu Jing admitted that his recollection was not all that clear after forty-one years, and he had trouble indicating the correct position of the 1960 Chinese assault camp, Camp VII, on a picture. But he estimated that the body was some 330 yards (300 m) or two hours away from that camp, and somewhat below it.

In 1999 we had picked up the rumor of a "mystery tent" that Gonbu, the third member who reached the summit in 1960, had allegedly found high on the mountain.[2] But when we asked the Chinese about this, their reply was unequivocal. "No, they didn't find anything at that height—only this body."

Simonson then showed Xu and the others a picture of the location where Mallory had been found in 1999, down on the North Face and well below where Xu had seen this other body. Xu looked at us. "But where is Irvine?" In the same instant, everybody in the room seemed to know the answer . . .

When we returned to our hotel room that night, our heads were spinning with the possible implications of what Xu Jing had told us.

We needed to approach the matter with caution, not reading more into it than had actually been said. There were the inevitable slips in Xu's memory after four decades, and a sleeping bag wrapped around the body sounded unlikely. In all probability, Mallory and Irvine would not have carried anything like a sleeping bag on their summit day for weight reasons. On the other hand, it seemed possible that Xu had confused layers of disintegrated old clothing with remnants of a bag or blanket. And as we started piecing together the available information, a lot in Xu Jing's story made sense.

We knew from earlier Chinese accounts of the 1960 ascent that Xu had twice climbed above the Chinese Camp VI, which was at 26,640 feet (8,120 m). On the first occasion on May 3, he had reached an area near the site of the 1933 British Camp VI, where he collapsed from exhaustion and returned to his Camp VI. Three weeks later, Xu climbed to the high camp, Camp VII, near the First Step. Originally he was to take part in the summit attempt the next day, but he developed altitude sickness and again had to descend.

In other words, on two occasions, Xu Jing had passed through long parts of the area between the Chinese Camps VI and VII, each time apparently on his own. This could explain others not seeing the body. There had been no fixed ropes and consequently no defined route through the Yellow Band in 1960, so Xu could have taken different lines each time.

Could we determine the location of the body more specifically? In the Chinese account of their discovery of the 1933 Camp VI, I noticed that they gave its altitude erroneously as 27,230 feet (8,300 m)—the same altitude at which Xu said he made his find. But the British camp was actually higher, at 27,495 feet (8,380 m). Perhaps the location of the body was likewise higher than Xu reckoned it to be, and was

The authors with members of the 1975 Chinese Everest expedition, Beijing, summer 2001 (left to right): Wu Peilan (Wang Hongbao's widow), Jin Junxi, Zhang Junyan, Jochen Hemmleb, Xia Boyu, Eric Simonson *(Photo © Jochen Hemmleb)*

somewhere near the 1933 Camp VI. The Chinese account said it took them two hours to reach their high camp from the 1933 Camp VI site, which is some 390 yards (350 m) away laterally. This tallies roughly with Xu's estimation of the body's location, which he said was some 330 yards (300 m) or two hours away from the Chinese high camp.

The day after Xu Jing's startling revelation, we met with Jin Junxi and Xia Boyu, members of the 1975 Chinese expedition,[3] during which Wang Hongbao had found his "English dead" (see Chapter 6, Short Walk into the Past)—the body we had previously assumed was Irvine. Also present was a resolute little woman in her fifties named Wu Peilan—Wang Hongbao's widow.

Even before we asked Wu Peilan anything about a discovery her husband had made on the mountain, she started leafing through a copy of *Ghosts of Everest*, our 1999 expedition's story of the finding of Mallory. When she came upon the pictures of Mallory's body, she immediately looked up and said, "You know, my husband told me he had found the old body of a foreign mountaineer beside a stone back in 1975."

The only remaining person who had been close to the actual event, Wang Hongbao's tent partner, Zhang Junyan, had not been found to ask to attend our meeting. But once again Li Guowei, Wang Yongfeng, and the other CMA staff worked their magic. They phoned around Beijing and finally were able to locate Zhang. Lunch arrived, and in walked the man.

He was an impressive figure. Almost as tall as Simonson, who is 6 feet 4 inches, Zhang was big for a Chinese, broad-shouldered, with a thick-set face and a military crew cut. His voice was powerful, and he was always ready to break out into a loud laugh, slapping one's back—a rough yet friendly giant.

We asked him about Wang Hongbao's discovery of an "English dead" during the time the two had spent at Camp VI. Zhang replied frankly that his recollections had not become any crisper since 1986, when he had been interviewed by Tom Holzel.[4] No, he did not remember any particular details from that day, such as the direction Wang had headed from their tent. But he did remember how Wang had told him of his find later at Base Camp.

Whom had Wang found, Mallory or Irvine? The question came up again, and the answer increasingly seemed to be George Mallory.

From the combined testimonies of Xu Jing and Wang Hongbao, we knew the Chinese had *twice* found a body high on Everest's North Face—one in 1960, and another in 1975. Wang said his "English dead" from 1975 was at 26,575 feet (8,100 m), while the corpse Xu found in 1960 was clearly higher—so the two bodies must have been different.

With rumors of a Soviet expedition and fatalities in 1952 now universally denied, Mallory and Irvine were the only climbers missing on the North Face before 1975—so the Chinese must have found both of them.

Our 2001 search team discovered the 1975 Chinese camp from which Wang had taken a walk and found a body. The searchers combed the surrounding area for any traces of Irvine but found none. However, this camp was in close proximity to where Mallory's body was found by our team in 1999.

Perhaps it is typical of a good mystery that there will be a lasting discrepancy between Wang's apparent description of the body he found and the actual appearance of Mallory's remains. But now, with Xu's report of in 1960 finding the only other missing body, considerably higher on the mountain, the conclusion seems obvious. Wang Hongbao had spotted Mallory's body, which we then rediscovered in 1999—and Xu Jing had found Irvine.

Somewhere in the lower reaches of the Yellow Band beneath Mount Everest's Northeast Ridge, probably near the 1933 Camp VI, lies the final resting place of Sandy Irvine—and with him perhaps the solution to mountaineering's greatest mystery.

As Eric Simonson and I walked the streets of Beijing for the last time, we felt an immense gratitude and respect toward the old Chinese climbers. These were pioneers of Everest in their own right, who, in another place and time, might have acquired the status of a Tom Hornbein or Willi Unsoeld. Those two Americans' ascent of the West Ridge in 1963, only three years after the Chinese success on the North Ridge, had turned them into international mountaineering legends. The

(Photo © Jake Norton)

Mallory & Irvine — The Chinese Revelation, 2001

——— 1960 Chinese Expedition

.... General area where Irvine's body may be located, estimated from Xu Jing's testimony in 2001

Chinese had remained unsung heroes outside their own country—and one of them, Xu Jing, had for more than forty years been the holder of a possible key to the mystery of Mallory and Irvine.

With fond memories we remembered the old man and his remarkable tale, which for the first time he had told to someone outside China. And we started wondering, would we go back to Mount Everest to finally solve the mystery?

Although a solution now seemed nearer than ever, there was no easy answer. First and foremost, the terrain where Irvine supposedly lies is higher and more difficult and dangerous to search than the ground around Mallory's location. On the two expeditions, in 1999 and 2001, our team had spent a total of eleven days searching in the "Death Zone"—and we knew that with every additional day at these altitudes, the risk of an accident would increase.

We also had to weigh the costs of such a venture, both financial and personal. An expedition swallows a whole lot of money, time, and energy. It puts one out of touch with home, family, and friends for three months, and its aftermath can keep one fully occupied for a year or more.

And still, the fascination remains. For years now we have been on the trails of Mallory and Irvine, and it would somehow seem appropriate if it was our team who became the ones to finally solve the mystery. We do not own it, though, and we know of other parties who share a similarly strong interest. We wish them luck in their efforts.

Perhaps we will never know what happened to George Mallory and Sandy Irvine, and whether they were the first to reach the summit of Mount Everest. But searching for an answer has sent us on an enthralling journey through history. The traces we found and the people we met along the way told tales of hardship and courage, of triumph and tragedy—from the days of the British pioneers to the Chinese who later followed them on to the summit. We were humbled by their achievements. Our admiration has grown deeper than ever, as has our respect for the mountain.

More than eighty years have passed since the very first expedition to Mount Everest, the British reconnaissance of 1921. The mountain and its mountaineers have changed since then, but its history endures. Mallory and Irvine, Smythe, Qu Yinhua, and all the others continue to inspire us—and in another eighty years, there will still be people who read of their adventures or walk in their footsteps, marveling.

CHRONOLOGY OF MAJOR ASCENTS AND EVENTS ON THE NORTH SIDE OF MOUNT EVEREST, 1921–2001

Two faces of Mount Everest are located in the northern or Tibetan aspect of the massif: the North Face, by which the mountain was first attempted in the 1920s, and the East Face. The following list covers the mountaineering history of the Tibetan aspect. Major events and ascents by the most-used summit approach, from the south or Nepal, are omitted from this overview.

1921

First British reconnaissance expedition. Exploration and survey of the northern and eastern approaches to Everest as well as the western areas toward Cho Oyu and Shisha Pangma. The North Col, 23,180 feet (7,066 m), was reached from the Kharta Valley via the Lhakpa La, and the North Ridge was recognized as a possible way to the summit.

1922

Second British expedition; first attempt to climb Mount Everest. The now common approach to the North Col via the East Rongbuk Valley was used for the first time. George Mallory, Edward Norton, and Howard Somervell reached around 26,640 feet (8,120 m) on the North Ridge on May 21 without using oxygen; on May 27, George Ingle Finch and Geoffrey Bruce climbed with bottled oxygen to almost 27,500 feet (8,380 m) on the North Face. A third summit attempt fell short when seven porters were killed in an avalanche below the North Col.

1924

Third British expedition—the mystery of Mallory and Irvine. On June 4, Norton and Somervell climbed to 28,000 feet (8,530 m) on a traverse below the Northeast Ridge. Norton continued alone to 28,125 feet (8,572 m). Neither climber used supplementary oxygen. On June 8, George Mallory and Andrew Irvine made another attempt with oxygen. At 12:50 P.M. they were last seen above 28,000 feet (8,530 m) on the crest of the Northeast Ridge, leaving open the question of whether they reached the summit before they died. Two native helpers died in mid-May after a blizzard.

1933

Fourth British expedition. Lawrence Wager and Percy Wyn-Harris reached 28,125 feet (8,572 m) on May 30, traversing into the Great (Norton) Couloir after a failed attempt on the Northeast Ridge (Mallory's route). Frank Smythe attained the same high point on June 1 in a solo attempt after Eric Shipton turned back from below the First Step. Wyn-Harris found Irvine's ice ax at 27,720 feet (8,450 m), just below the crest of the ridge, some 250 yards (230 m) before the First Step.

1934

Illicit solo attempt. Briton Maurice Wilson died of exhaustion below the North Col.

1935

New British reconnaissance. Detailed exploration was made of the glaciers and peaks surrounding Mount Everest, as well as study of snow and weather conditions during the monsoon. Twenty-six peaks over 20,000 feet (6,100 m) were climbed.

1936

Fifth British expedition. Failed to progress above the North Col due to the early onset of the monsoon.

1938

Sixth British expedition; first lightweight expedition to Everest. Bill Tilman's seven-member team approached the North Col from the west (Main Rongbuk Glacier) and reached about 27,360 feet (8,340 m) on the North Ridge before being turned back by deep snow.

1947

Illicit attempt. Canadian Earl Denman, accompanied by Sherpas Tenzing Norgay and Ang Dawa, made it partway up the North Col.

1950

North Side of Everest sealed off to foreign expeditions, after Chinese occupation of Tibet.

1951

Illicit attempt. Dane Klavs Becker-Larsen entered Tibet illegally by the old trade route over the Nangpa La. He and two Sherpas turned back from below the North Col.

1958

Chinese-Russian reconnaissance. The East and Main Rongbuk Glaciers were explored.

1960

First Chinese ascent; first recorded ascent of Mount Everest from the north. Wang Fuzhou and Qu Yinhua (Chinese) and Gonbu (Tibetan) reached the summit by the North and Northeast Ridges at 2:20 A.M. on May 25. They took nineteen hours for the final 1,000 feet (300 m) of the Northeast Ridge above their high camp, of which five hours alone were spent on the Second Step. A body was discovered at about 27,400 feet (8,350 m), possibly Irvine's.

1963

First American ascent; first traverse of Mount Everest. On May 1, Jim Whittaker became the first American to climb Everest when he reached the summit together with Sherpa Nawang Gombu via the South Col route. Three weeks later, on May 22, Tom Hornbein and Willi Unsoeld climbed a new route via the middle part of the West Ridge (which they accessed from the Western Cwm) and the upper North Face. They descended the Southeast Ridge, thus making the first traverse of the mountain.

1965

Chinese reconnaissances. The West Ridge (spring) and the complete Northeast Ridge (autumn) were explored.

1966

Chinese training expedition. Thirty-two climbers reached 26,575 feet (8,100 m) on the North Ridge; one member was killed on the descent.

1967–68

Two Chinese scientific expeditions. The North Col was reached.

1974

Chinese training expedition. The North Col was reached.

1975

Second Chinese ascent; first female ascent from the north.
Summit reached by nine members, including the Tibetan woman Phanthog, on May 27. Wu Zongyue died in a fall from 27,600 feet (8,410 m). An "English dead" was discovered at about 26,575 feet (8,100 m), probably Mallory.

1978

Chinese-Iranian reconnaissance. Nine Chinese and two Iranians reached 24,600 feet (7,500 m) on the North Ridge; one member (Shi Mingji) died of heart failure at Camp II.

1979

Chinese-Japanese reconnaissance. East and Main Rongbuk Glaciers were explored; exploratory attempt was made on the North Face (Hornbein Couloir direct). Three Chinese were killed in an avalanche below the North Col.

Everest reopened to foreign expeditions. In November the Chinese Mountaineering Association officially announced the opening to foreigners of twelve peaks in China and Tibet, including Qomolangma (Mount Everest).

1980

First solo ascent of Mount Everest without supplementary oxygen (South Tyrol). Reinhold Messner reached the summit on August 20. Snow on the North Ridge forced him to traverse into the Great (Norton) Couloir, which he climbed to the summit pyramid, finishing by the West Ridge. First ascent during the monsoon.

First ascent of North Face, Hornbein Couloir direct (Japan). Tsuneo Shigehiro and Takashi Ozaki reached the summit on May 10; on May 3 the classic North/Northeast Ridge was repeated with a new variation above Camp VI by Yasuo Kato (solo from the Third Step).

Expedition to East or Kangshung Face (United States). In October, Andrew Harvard became the first foreigner since 1921 to visit the East or Kangshung Face.

1981

First attempt on the East Face (United States). The very difficult (5.10, A3/A4) lower part of the central buttress was climbed to about 22,500 feet (6,860 m). The highest point was reached by Lou Reichardt on October 5.

1982

British attempt on complete Northeast Ridge. From the Rapiu La, Peter Boardman and Joe Tasker disappeared at around 27,000 feet (8,230 m) while attempting to cross the Pinnacles.

American attempt on the North Face, Great (Norton) Couloir. The party made it to 27,500 feet (8,380 m); Marty Hoey fell to her death.

1983

First ascent of East or Kangshung Face, central buttress (United States). Carlos Buhler, Kim Momb, and Lou Reichardt reached the summit on October 8; Jay Cassell, George Lowe, and Daniel Reid followed on October 9.

1984

First ascent of North Face, Great (Norton) Couloir direct (Australia). Tim Macartney-Snape and Greg Mortimer reached the summit on October 3, without supplementary oxygen.

American expedition established new variation on North Face. Traverse into the Great (Norton) Couloir from the North Col. Summit by Phil Ershler on October 20.

1986

Speed ascent of North Face, Hornbein Couloir direct (Switzerland). Erhard Loretan and Jean Troillet reached the summit in forty hours from the Main Rongbuk Glacier on August 30, without supplementary oxygen. In just under four hours, they descended the 8,000-foot (2,400-m) face by glissading.

First ascent of West Ridge/Hornbein Couloir from Tibet (Canada). Sharon Wood and Dwayne Congdon reached the summit on May 20.

American-British expedition. First attempt to search for Mallory and Irvine.

MAIN ROUTES

1. Northeast Ridge (Japanese 1995)
2. North/Northeast Ridge
   (British pre-WWII attempts, Chinese 1960)
3. North Face Traverse (Messner 1980)
4. Great Couloir direct (Australian 1984)
5. Great Couloir left side (Italian/Czech 1991)
6. Hornbein Couloir direct (Japanese 1980)
7. Hornbein Couloir from West Ridge
   (American 1963)

VARIATIONS

2a. Upper North Face Traverse from North
    Ridge (American 1984) [not to summit]
2b. Lower North Face Traverse from North
    Col (American 1984)
5a. North Face to North Ridge
    (New Zealand 1985) [not to summit]
6a. Hornbein Couloir left side
    (French/Spanish 1987) [not to summit]

(Photo by Chris Curry © Hedgehog House, New Zealand)

North Face

1988

International expedition; first ascent of Kangshung Face, "Neverest Buttress" to South Col. Robert Anderson (United States), Paul Teare (Canada), Stephen Venables (Great Britain), and Ed Webster (United States), without supplementary oxygen. From the South Col, the route followed the classic Southeast Ridge. On May 12, Anderson and Webster reached the South Summit; Venables continued to the top.

Chinese-Japanese-Nepalese "Friendship Expedition"; first north-south traverse of Mount Everest. Ciren Duoji (China), Noboru Yamada (Japan), and Ang Lhakpa (Nepal) climbed from north to south; Da Ciren (China), Renquin Pingcuo (China), and Ang Phurba (Nepal) climbed from south to north, all on May 5.

International expedition; first successful crossing of the Pinnacles on complete Northeast Ridge. Russell Brice (New Zealand) and Harry Taylor (Great Britain) were prevented from continuing to the summit by bad weather and descended the North Ridge.

1990

USA-USSR-China "Peace Climb." Twenty climbers from the three nations (eight Soviets, seven Tibetans, and five Americans) reached the top by the classic North and Northeast Ridges; Russians Sergei Arsentiev, Grigori Lunyakov, Andrei Tselinschev, and Anatoli Moshnikov and American Ed Viesturs made the climb without supplementary oxygen.

1991

International expedition; first ascent of North Face, Great (Norton) Couloir left side. Battistino Bonali (Italy) and Leopold Sulovsky (Czechoslovakia) reached the summit on May 17, without supplementary oxygen.

Swedish expedition; third ascent of the North Face, Hornbein Couloir direct. Sherpas Mingma Norbu and Gyalbu reached the summit on May 15, and Lars Cronlund (Sweden) on May 20.

First attempt on "Fantasy Ridge," aka East Ridge (Japan). Climbers reached 21,000 feet (6,400 m).

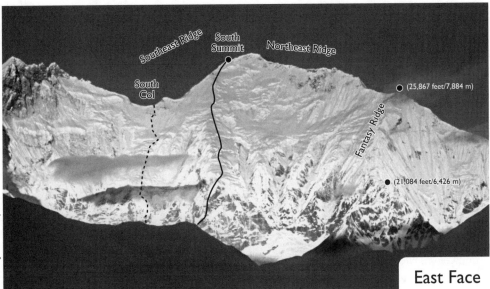

(Photo © Jake Norton)

East Face

—— 1983 American-Central Buttress
------ 1988 "Neverest Buttress" to South Col

1992

Second ascent of Kangshung Face, "Neverest Buttress" to South Col (Chile). Cristian Garcia-Huidobro, Juan-Sebastian Montes, and Rodrigo Jordan reached the summit on May 15.

Peter Boardman's body discovered. Members of a joint Japanese-Kazakhstani expedition found the remains on the Northeast Ridge's Second Pinnacle at 27,170 feet (8,280 m), ten years after Boardman's disappearance together with Joe Tasker.

1993

Lightweight Everest north-south traverse (Korea). Heo Young-Ho and Ngati Sherpa reached the summit by the North/Northeast Ridge on April 13; marginal weather and the difficulties of their route of ascent made them opt for descending by the easier Southeast Ridge. They bivouacked on the way down at 27,900 feet (8,500 m) and, because nobody had arrived on the South Col yet, had to continue all the way to the Western Cwm before finding other teams' assistance.

1995

First ascent of complete Northeast Ridge (Japan). Sherpas Dawa Tshering, Pasang Kami, Lhakpa Nuru, and Nima Dorje and Japanese Kiyoshi Furuno and Shiki Imoto reached the summit on May 11. The route was completely equipped with fixed ropes and oxygen was used—a stark contrast to the earlier attempts by Boardman and Tasker or Doug Scott.

Unsupported (solo) ascent of North/Northeast Ridge without oxygen (Great Britain). Alison Hargreaves made the ascent via the classic route.

Ascent via North/Northeast Ridge by Mallory's grandson (Australia). George Mallory II, descendant of the Everest pioneer, reached the summit by the route where his grandfather disappeared in 1924.

1996

First ascent of North Couloir (Russia). Peter Kuznetzov, Valeri Kohanov, and Grigori Semikolenkov climbed the face between the Northeast and North Ridges on May 20.

Speed ascent of North/Northeast Ridge (South Tyrol). Hans Kammerlander climbed from Advance Base Camp to the summit in seventeen hours, without supplementary oxygen. Most of the descent was done on skis.

Deadly storm of May 11. Three Indians on the North/Northeast Ridge were killed, as were five climbers on the Nepalese Southeast Ridge.

1999

Mallory & Irvine Research Expedition. George Mallory's body was discovered on May 1 at 26,760 feet (8,155 m) on the North Face, seventy-five years after his disappearance.

Third ascent of Kangshung Face "Neverest Buttress" (India). Amar Prakash and Sherpas Kusang Dorje and Sang Mudok reached the summit on May 28.

2001

Second Mallory & Irvine Research Expedition. Four stranded climbers were rescued from over 28,120 feet (8,570 m) on the Northeast Ridge. Expedition discovered further relics from the 1924 attempt as well as from the 1922, 1933, 1960, and 1975 British and Chinese expeditions.

First snowboard descent of Everest (France). Marco Siffredi surfed down the Great (Norton) Couloir of the North Face on May 23, taking 2.5 hours from the summit to the North Col.

Attempt on "Fantasy Ridge" (India). The highest point reached was about 22,000 feet (6,700 m).

2001 MALLORY & IRVINE RESEARCH EXPEDITION STATISTICS

EXPEDITION MEMBERS (AGE, AS OF JUNE 2001, IN PARENTHESES)

Search and Climbing Team

Eric Simonson (46)	expedition leader
Dave Hahn (39)	climber, videographer
Jochen Hemmleb (29)	researcher
Lee Meyers (54)	team physician
Riley Morton (25)	video and Internet technician
Jake Norton (27)	climber, photographer
Brent Okita (40)	climber
Andy Politz (41)	climber
John Race (32)	climber, videographer
Tap Richards (27)	climber
Jason Tanguay (26)	climber

Sherpas

Pa Nuru (33)	Sirdar
Lhakpa Nuru (28)	climber
Da Nuru (22)	climber
Da Chhiree (23)	climber
Phu Nuru (21)	climber
Nawang Jimba (37)	climber
Pemba Nuru (28)	climber
Pemba Geljen (29)	climber
Palden Namgye (28)	climber
Lakpa Nuru (39)	climber
Mingma Ongel (23)	climber
Fu Dorji (25)	climber
Ang Chhiring "Kami" (39)	climber
Man Bahadur Tamang (42)	climber
Pemba Gyalzen (26)	climber

Pema Tenzi (38)	climber
Dorjee (37)	climber
Kami Rita (31)	climber
Ang Gelzen (38)	climber
Pemba Tshiri (33)	chief cook
Mingma Chhiring (29)	ABC chief cook
Padam Bahadur Limbu (32)	kitchen staff
Kami (25)	kitchen staff
Tara Bir Yakha (35)	kitchen staff
Kelsong	Intermediate Camp maintainance

International Mountain Guides Climbing and Trekking Groups

Craig John	climbing guide
Heidi Eichner	trekking guide
Heather Macdonald	trekking guide
Karen Balaban	Advance Base Camp (ABC) trekker
Dick Dickerson	ABC trekker
Peter Gargiulo	ABC trekker
Thomas Gibbons	ABC trekker
Sally Gilpin	ABC trekker
Jonathan Gilstrom	ABC trekker
William Goss	ABC trekker
Maggie Gross	ABC trekker
John Hall	ABC trekker
Aaron Hamilton	ABC trekker
Laura Howat	ABC trekker
Larry Johnson	ABC trekker
Steven McClung	ABC trekker

Greg Milliken	ABC trekker
Robert Nordhaus	ABC trekker
Nancy Norris	ABC trekker
Ed Norton	ABC trekker
Carlos Porto	ABC trekker
John Proulx	ABC trekker
Rick Richards	ABC trekker
Edward Ryan	ABC trekker
Ken Sageser	ABC trekker
Peter Scoville	ABC trekker
Roger Scoville	ABC trekker
Lawrence Welk	ABC trekker
Nancy Houdeshell	North Col climber
Lanta Olito	North Col climber
David Smith	North Col climber
Jerry Gross	8,000-m climber
Timothy Lapham	8,000-m climber
Richard Martinez	8,000-m climber
Timothey Ramey	8,000-m climber
Chris Shiver	8,000-m climber
Jim Waldron	8,000-m climber
Ted Wheeler	8,000-m climber
Terry LaFrance	nonguided summit climber
Mike Otis	nonguided summit climber

Singaporean-Brazilian Everest Expedition

David Lim	leader
Tok Beng Cheong	climber
Wong Ting Sern	climber
Mohd Rozani bin Maarof	climber
Gil Piekarz	climber

SPONSORS
Companies

Abner Jones Signs	signs, stickers, banners
Adventure Medical Kits	first-aid kits
Aeroground Inc.	gear shipping
American Foundation for International Mountaineering, Exploration, and Research (AFFIMER)	contribution; handling of Mallory artifacts
Automated Media Systems	lithium video camera batteries
The Brunton Company	GPS receivers
Corbis Sygma	photo pool agent
Cord Camera Center	film
Craghoppers Ltd.	high-altitude down sleeping bags
Dermatone Labs	sunscreen and lip protection

Dupont Industrial Yarn Division	nylon fiber for fixed rope
Essex Industries	oxygen regulators
Eureka!	expedition tents
Honeywell Aviation Information Services	satellite phones
International Mountain Guides	trek organization
Kraft Foods	Balance bars
LeDuc Packaging Inc.	waxed boxes for shipping
Lowe Alpine Systems	packs, outerwear, fleece
Men's Journal	magazine reporting
Metrotech Corporation	metal detectors
Mountain Safety Research	fuel, stoves, cookware
Oberto Meats	beef jerky
Pigeon Mountain Industries Inc.	constructed fixed rope
Polo Ralph Lauren	leisurewear
Reisefieber (Bad Homburg, Germany)	down jacket and sleeping bag for Jochen Hemmleb
Rexall	vitamins, nutritional supplements
Seals Compressed Gases	oxygen cylinder filling
Seattle General Agency	insurance
Slumberjack	low-altitude sleeping bags, mattresses, camp furniture
Seattle Manufacturing Corp.	technical climbing gear
Structural Composites Industries	oxygen cylinders
Suunto USA	altimeter wristwatches
Swissphoto AG	maps, aerial photographs
Thai Airways Cargo	gear shipping
Thai Airways Sales	team airline tickets
Thorlo Socks	climbing and trekking socks
Travel Time	airline ticketing
Triple B Forwarders	oxygen cylinder shipping
U.S. Army Natick Labs Soldier Systems Center	U.S. Army Base Camp tents, MREs (Meals, Ready to Eat)
Vasque/Red Wing Shoe Company Inc.	approach boots
Washington State History Museum	Mallory collection storage and display
ZAAZ	website design

Individuals

Peter Bosland	financial contribution
Charles Corfield	digital air photos
Neal Dempsey	financial contribution
Paul G. Hoffman	financial contribution
Dee Molenaar	Mount Everest artwork
Bradford Washburn	air photos

NOTES AND REFERENCES[1]

Prologue

1. G. Winthrop Young, letter to D. W. Freshfield, in T. Holzel and A. Salkeld, *The Mystery of Mallory and Irvine* (London: Jonathan Cape, 1986; Seattle: The Mountaineers Books, 2000), 243.

2. F. S. Smythe, *Camp Six—An Account of the 1933 Mount Everest Expedition* (London: Hodder & Stoughton, 1937), 307.

3. R. Messner, *The Crystal Horizon, Everest—The First Solo Ascent* (Seattle: The Mountaineers Books, 1999), 236.

4. Film interview with T. Sors, in D. Breashears, *The Mystery of Mallory and Irvine* (Newton, Mass.: Arcturus Motion Picture Company/BBC, 1987).

5. E. Simonson, "Mallory's Body Found on Everest" (including dispatches by D. Hahn, C. Anker, T. Richards, A. Politz, and J. Norton), MountainZone, May 2, 1999 (*www.mountainzone.com*).

6. Quoted in footage from P. Firstbrook, *Lost on Everest—The Search for Mallory & Irvine* (Bristol, England: BBC, 1999), and L. Clark, *Lost on Everest* (Boston: WGBH/*NOVA*, 1999).

Chapter 1

1. Letter from John Mallory to Eric Simonson, August 17, 1999.

2. C. Anker and D. Roberts, *The Lost Explorer—Finding Mallory on Everest* (New York: Simon & Schuster, 1999), 63.

Chapter 2

1. In L. Clark, "Pieces of the Puzzle," *NOVA* online, May 6, 1999 (*www.pbs.org/wgbh/nova/everest.html*).

2. For another evaluation of Mallory's climbs, see M. Crook, "George Mallory—Just How Good a Rock-climber Was He?" *High Mountain Sports* 205 (December 1999).

3. In W. Unsworth, *Everest*, 3rd ed. (Seattle: The Mountaineers Books; Leicester: Bâton Wicks, 2000), 141.

4. T. H. Somervell, "In Memoriam. George Leigh Mallory," *Journal of the Fell & Rock Climbing Club* (1924), quoted in Holzel and Salkeld, *Mystery*, rev. ed. (London: Pimlico, 1999; Seattle: The Mountaineers Books, 2000), 316.

Chapter 4

1. Nongovernmental organizations representing every possible program and ideal are a common sight in modern Nepal, one of the largest per capita recipients of foreign assistance. Most of the NGOs perform vital and effective services for this poor nation; however, Jake Norton remembered the common thought circulating while he studied in Kathmandu in 1993–94: "Buy a pack of Trojans and a Land Cruiser and you've got yourself an NGO!"

2. C. K. Howard-Bury, *Mount Everest—The Reconnaissance, 1921* (London: Edward Arnold, 1922), 281f.

---

1. The symbols *f.* and *ff.* immediately following a page number indicate reference to the noted page number and the following page or pages.

Chapter 5

1 G. Mallory, "The Reconnaissance of the Mountain," in Howard-Bury, *Mount Everest,* 192.

2 G. H. Bullock, "The Everest Expedition, 1921; Diary of G. H. Bullock." *Alpine Journal* 67 (1961).

3 The remains of one of the porters were discovered in 1989 and buried above Advance Base Camp.

Chapter 6

1 The details of Wang's testimony are compiled from the following sources: Letter from Hiroyuki Suzuki, Foreign Secretary, Japanese Alpine Club, to Tom Holzel, February 7, 1980, in T. Holzel, "The Search for Mallory and Irvine," *Summit,* September-October 1981, and in Holzel and Salkeld, *Mystery,* rev. ed., 2f. D. D. Seiner, "Everest: A Few More Words," *Summit,* July-August 1982. Letter from R. Hasegawa, in A. Salkeld, *People in High Places* (London: Jonathan Cape, 1991), 129ff. These are the contemporary sources regarding Wang's testimony; any other circulating information, i.e., that Wang reported a body "sitting upright," is unsubstantiated by these sources.

Chapter 7

1 Smythe, *Camp Six,* 223ff.

2 Possibilities include the 1992 Kazakh-Japanese expedition, which descended the North Ridge after crossing the Pinnacles of the Northeast Ridge, or expeditions in the post-monsoon, if the North Face above Camp V had been avalanche-prone.

3 E. F. Norton, et al., *The Fight for Everest 1924* (London: Arnold, 1925), 108.

4 Although Peter and Leni Gillman's biography of Mallory, *The Wildest Dream—Mallory, His Life and Conflicting Passions* (London: Headline, 2000; Seattle: The Mountaineers Books, 2000), reveals that Mallory was bisexual, there is conclusive proof that Irvine was not.

5 Gillman, *Wildest Dream.*

6 Holzel and Salkeld, *Mystery,* 234f.

7 E. Norton, *Fight for Everest,* 109.

8 J. B. L. Noel, *The Story of Everest* (Boston: Little, Brown & Co., 1927), 213ff.

9 B. Okita, "Following 77-year-old Footsteps," 2001 Mallory & Irvine Research Expedition dispatches, May 4, 2001 (*www.mountainguides.com*).

10 E. Norton, *Fight for Everest,* 112.

11 Quoted in E. F. Norton, "The Mount Everest Dispatches," *Alpine Journal* 229 (1924), 215.

12 N. E. Odell, "The Last Climb," *Alpine Journal* 229 (1924), 266.

13 E. Norton, *Fight for Everest,* footnote to p. 116; see also J. Hemmleb, et al., *Ghosts of Everest* (Seattle: The Mountaineers Books, 1999), 163ff.

14 E. Norton, *Fight for Everest,* 125.

15 E. Norton, "Mount Everest Dispatches," 216.

16 Reproduced in E. F. Norton, "The Problem of Mount Everest," *Alpine Journal* 230 (1925), frontispiece.

17 Reproduced in Noel, *Story of Everest,* facing p. 214.

18 Quoted in E. Norton, "Mount Everest Dispatches," 223.

19 E. Norton, *Fight for Everest,* 138.

Chapter 8

1 J. Norton, "68-year-old Crackers," 2001 Mallory & Irvine Research Expedition dispatches, May 5, 2001 (*www.mountainguides.com*).

2 For details see Hemmleb, et al., *Ghosts,* Appendix 1.

3 E. F. Norton and Geoffrey Bruce had been considered as potential leaders, but were unavailable. Nor was Odell. Other members were H. Boustead, T. A. Brooklebank, W. McLean, G. Wood-Johnson, and wireless operators W. R. Smyth-Windham and E. C. Thompson.

4 The pitch was ably led by Frank Smythe. It was the first time ice pitons were used as climbing aid on Everest.

5 Quoted in Unsworth, *Everest,* 568.

6 Later expeditions have shown that it is possible to climb directly to the ridge from below. The first were the Chinese in 1960, followed by the Japanese in 1980, who all took a line up the Gray Band immediately beyond the First Step. Only Jon Tinker's Out There Trekking expedition in 1993 crossed the band farther to the west, halfway to the Second Step. The latter ascent in particular was helped by a solid snow cover on the slabs that had eluded Wager and Wyn-Harris.

7 H. Ruttledge, *Everest 1933* (London: Hodder & Stoughton, 1934), 139.

8 This is the official version, as given in Ruttledge, *Everest 1933,* 141, and other contemporary accounts. However, Wyn-Harris's grandson, Steve, told Hemmleb that his grandfather's unpublished memoirs state that he took both axes back to Camp VI (e-mail conversation, spring 1999).

9 E. Norton, *Fight for Everest,* 103.

10 J. Norton, "68-year-old Crackers."

11 Smythe, *Camp Six,* 235.

12 E. E. Shipton, *Upon that Mountain* (London: Hodder & Stoughton, 1943), 126.

13 Smythe, *Camp Six,* 256.

14 Ibid., 261.

15 Ruttledge, *Everest 1933,* 165.

16 Shipton almost lost his life in the storm, as did Smythe in similar conditions on his descent to Camp V the next day.

17 Ruttledge, *Everest 1933,* 167.

18 J. Norton, "68-year-old Crackers."

Chapter 9

1 Interview with J. Hemmleb and E. Simonson, August 23, 2001.

2 There is an anecdotal link here between the British and the Chinese Everest expeditions: In 1960 the Chinese encountered an ice chimney on the way to the North Col, similar to the obstacle present in 1924. They safeguarded this with a rope ladder they had bought from the Rongbuk Monastery—and which had been left over from one of the British prewar expeditions.

3 The timings given in the Chinese accounts are Beijing Time. To facilitate comparison with other expeditions' timings, these were converted for this chapter to local time on Everest, which is two hours behind Beijing Time.

4 All quotes are from Wang Fuzhou, "The Conquest of Mount Qomolangma from the North Side," in *High Mountain Peaks in China—Newly Opened to Foreigners* (Peking: CMA and The Peoples Sports Publishing House of China; Tokyo: Shimbun Publishing, 1981), 14.

5 A simultaneous search from Camps VI and VII found Wu's rucksack, ice ax, movie camera, and oxygen bottle at about 27,600 feet (8,410 m), near the exit from the Yellow Band. There were some tracks of a slide and bloodstains below. Wu's body was found three weeks later at 27,000 feet (8,230 m) by the successful summit team as they returned from the high camp.

Epilogue

1 The others were Zeng Shusheng and Wang Zhenhua, who later became the leaders of the Chinese team during the China-Japan-Nepal Everest traverse in 1988; and Liu Dayi, who had been on the first Chinese ascent of Minya Konka (Gongga) in China in 1957.

2 For details and discussion, see Hemmleb, et al., *Ghosts,* Appendix 1.

3 Jin Junxi reached Camp V and Xia Boyu got to Camp VII.

4 Holzel and Salkeld, *Mystery,* 327.

SELECTED BIBLIOGRAPHY

BOOKS
Everest, General Reference, and History

Gillman, P., ed. *Everest, Eighty Years of Triumph and Tragedy.* Seattle: The Mountaineers Books, 2000.

Kielkowski, J. *Mount Everest Massif, Monograph-Guide-Chronicle.* Gliwice, Poland: Explo, 1993.

Salkeld, A., and J. Boyle, comp. *Climbing Mount Everest—The Bibliography.* Clevedon, England: Sixways Publishing, 1993.

Unsworth, W. *Everest.* 3rd ed. Seattle: The Mountaineers Books; Leicester, England: Bâton Wicks, 2000.

1921 British Reconnaissance

Howard-Bury, Lieut.-Col. C. K., et al. *Mount Everest: The Reconnaissance 1921.* London: Edward Arnold, 1922.

Howard-Bury, C. K., and G. L. Mallory. *Everest Reconnaissance, The First Expedition of 1921.* Rev. ed., with new biographical material by Marian Keaney and extracts of Howard-Bury's 1921 diaries. London: Hodder & Stoughton, 1991.

1922 British Everest Expedition

Bruce, Brig. Gen. C. G., et al. *The Assault on Mount Everest 1922.* London: Edward Arnold, 1923.

Finch, G. I. *The Making of a Mountaineer.* 1924. Rev. ed., with a memoir "George Finch—The Mountaineer" by Scott Russell, London: Arrowsmith, 1988.

———. *Der Kampf um den Everest.* Leipzig: Brockhaus, 1925.

———. *Climbing Mount Everest.* London: G. Philip, 1930.

1924 British Everest Expedition/ The Mystery of Mallory & Irvine

Anker, C., and D. Roberts. *The Lost Explorer—Finding Mallory on Everest.* New York: Simon & Schuster, 1999.

Breashears, D., and A. Salkeld. *Last Climb—The Legendary Everest Expeditions of George Mallory.* Washington, D.C.: National Geographic Society, 1999.

Carr, H. R. C. *The Irvine Diaries: Andrew Irvine and the Enigma of Everest, 1924.* Reading, England: Gastons-West Col Publications, 1979.

Firstbrook, P. *Lost on Everest—The Search for Mallory & Irvine.* London: BBC Worldwide, 1999.

Gillman, P., and L. Gillman. *The Wildest Dream—Mallory, His Life and Conflicting Passions.* London: Headline, 2000; Seattle: The Mountaineers Books, 2000.

Hemmleb, J., L. Johnson, and E. Simonson, as told to W. Nothdurft. *Ghosts of Everest—The Search for Mallory & Irvine.* Seattle: The Mountaineers Books, 1999.

Holzel, T., and A. Salkeld. *The Mystery of Mallory and Irvine.* London: Jonathan Cape, 1986; rev. ed., London: Pimlico, 1999; Seattle: The Mountaineers Books, 2000.

Messner, R. *The Second Death of George Mallory.* New York: St. Martin's Press, 2000.

Noel, Capt. J. B. L. *Through Tibet to Everest.* London: Edward Arnold, 1927.

Norton, Lieut.-Col. E. F., et al. *The Fight for Everest 1924.* London: Edward Arnold, 1925.

Salkeld, A. *People in High Places*. London: Jonathan Cape, 1991.

———. *Mystery on Everest: A Photobiography of George Mallory*. Washington, D.C.: National Geographic Society, 2000.

Summers, J. *Fearless on Everest—The Quest for Sandy Irvine*. London: Weidenfeld & Nicolson, 2000; Seattle: The Mountaineers Books, 2001.

1933 British Everest Expedition

Ruttledge, H. *Everest 1933*. London: Hodder & Stoughton, 1934.

Smythe, F. S. *Camp Six: An Account of the 1933 Mount Everest Expedition*. London: Hodder & Stoughton, 1937.

Chinese Expeditions

People's Republic of China. *Mountaineering in China*. Beijing: Foreign Languages Press, 1965.

———. *A Photographic Record of the Mount Jolmo Lungma Scientific Expedition 1966–1968*. Beijing: Chinese Academy of Science/Science Press, 1974.

———. *Another Ascent of the World's Highest Peak— Qomolangma*. Beijing: Foreign Languages Press, 1975.

———. *High Mountain Peaks in China—Newly Opened to Foreigners*. Beijing: CMA and The Peoples Sports Publishing House of China; Tokyo: Shimbun Publishing, 1981.

Zhang, Caizhen, ed. *The History of Mountaineering in China*. Han Kou, China: Wuhan Publishing House, 1993.

Zhou, Zhen, and Liu Zhenkai. *Footprints on the Peaks: Mountaineering in China*. Seattle: Cloudcap, 1995.

PERIODICALS

Though a few citations may lack all the facts of publication, they include sufficient information to allow the interested reader to locate them.

A.J. is the abbreviation for Alpine Journal

Alpine Club. "Alpine Club Statement" (Irvine controversy). *High Mountain Sports* 220 (March 2001).

Anker, C. "Mystery on Everest." *National Geographic* 196, no. 4 (October 1999).

Bruce, Brig. Gen. C. G. "The Organisation and Start of the Expedition." *A.J.* 36, no. 229 (1924).

Bruce, Capt. J. G. "The Journey through Tibet and the Establishment of the High Camps." *A.J.* 36, no. 229 (1924).

Bueler, W. M. "New Information on Chinese Ascents of Everest." *Off Belay*, April 1980.

Burrough, B. "The Riddle of Everest." *Vanity Fair*, September 1999.

Crook, M. "George Mallory—Just How Good a Rock-climber Was He?" *High Mountain Sports* 205 (December 1999).

Finch, G. I. "The Second Attempt on Mount Everest." *A.J.* 34, no. 225 (1922).

———. "Equipment for High Altitude Mountaineering, with Special Reference to Climbing Mount Everest." *A.J.* 35, no. 226 (1923).

Gippenreiter, Y. B. "Mount Everest and the Russians 1952 and 1958." *A.J.*, n.d.

Goodfellow, B. R. "Chinese Everest Expedition, 1960—A Further Commentary." *A.J.* 66 (1961).

Hawley, E. "China and Everest." *Out There*, n.d.

Hemmleb, J. "Final Report: Mallory & Irvine Research Expedition Mount Everest 1999." Unpublished research paper. Schönau, Germany: author's collection, 2000.

———. "Research Outline: Mallory & Irvine Research Expedition Mount Everest 2001." Unpublished research paper. Schönau, Germany: author's collection, 2001.

———. "Neue Expedition—Alte Rätsel" (2001 expedition preview). *Alpin*, March 2001.

———. Response to "Alpine Club Statement." *High Mountain Sports* 222 (May 2001).

———. "Das höchste Fundbüro der Welt" (2001 research). *Alpin*, November 2001.

Hemmleb, J., and L. Johnson. "Discovery on Everest." *Climbing* 188 (September 1999).

Holzel, T. "The Mystery of Mallory and Irvine." *Mountain* 17 (1971).

———. Reply to "The Mystery of Mallory and Irvine." *Mountain* 26 (1972).

———. "The Search for Mallory & Irvine." *Summit*, September/October 1981.

———. "The Chinese 1960 Ascent of Mount Everest." *Mountain* 101 (January/February 1985).

———. "Mallory and Irvine: First to the Top of Everest?" *Summit*, September/October 1987.

———. "How Far Did Mallory and Irvine Get?" *High Mountain Sports* 223 (June 2001).

Howard-Bury, Lt. Col. C. K. "The 1921 Mount Everest Expedition." *A.J.* 34, no. 224 (1922).

Hoyland, G. "The Finding of Mallory." *High Mountain Sports* 201 (1999).

Kratzer, C., with J. Hemmleb and J. Norton. "Dem Tod von der Schippe geklaut" (2001 rescue). *Alpin*, August 2001.

Mallory, G. L. "Mount Everest: The Reconnaissance." *A.J.* 34, no. 224 (1922).

———. "The Second Mount Everest Expedition." *A.J.* 34, no. 225 (1922).

Merrick, H. "Everest: The Chinese Photograph." *A.J.* 67–68 (1961–62).

Norton, Col. E. F. "The Mount Everest Dispatches." *A.J.* 36, no. 229 (1924).

———. "The Personnel of the Expedition." *A.J.* 36, no. 229 (1924).

———. "The Climb with Mr. Somervell to 28,000 feet." *A.J.* 36, no. 229 (1924).

Odell, N. E. "The Last Climb." *A.J.* 36, no. 229 (1924).

———. "The Ice Axe Found on Everest." *A.J.* 46 (1934).

———. "The Ice-Axe Found on Everest in 1933." *A.J.*, 1963.

———. "Mallory and Irvine's Last Climb, 1924." *A.J.* 78 (1973).

Roberts, D. "Out of Thin Air—75 Years Later, Everest Finally Gives up Mallory's Ghost." *National Geographic Adventure*, fall 1999.

———. "Losing It on Everest" (2001 rescue). *National Geographic Adventure*, October 2001.

Ruttledge, H. "The Mount Everest Expedition, 1933." *A.J.* 45 (1934).

Shi Zhanchun (or Shih Chan-chun). "The Conquest of Mount Everest by the Chinese Mountaineering Team" (extensively annotated by T. S. Blakeney). *A.J.* 66 (1961).

Simonson, E., J. Hemmleb, and L. Johnson. "Ghosts of Everest." *Outside*, October 1999.

Simpson, J. "George Leigh Mallory—Of Mystery and Morality." *Rock & Ice* 94 (August 1999).

Unna, P. J. H. "The Oxygen Equipment of the 1922 Everest Expedition." *A.J.* 34, no. 224 (1922).

Venables, S. "Mallory's Body Found on Everest." *High Mountain Sports* 200 (July 1999).

Wager, L. R. "Mount Everest: The Chinese Photograph." *A.J.* 68 (1962).

Wang Fuzhou and Qu Yinhua (or Wang Fu-chou and Chu Yin-hua). "How We Climbed the World's Highest Peak." *Mountaincraft*, July-September 1961.

Wyn-Harris, Sir P., and J. Paine. "What Happened to Mallory & Irvine?" *Mountain* 21 (1972).

FILMS AND VIDEOS

Breashears, D. *The Mystery of Mallory and Irvine*. Newton, Mass.: Arcturus Motion Picture Company/BBC, 1987.

Clark, L. *Lost on Everest*. Boston: WGBH/*NOVA*, 1999.

Firstbrook, P., with G. Hoyland. *Lost on Everest—The Search for Mallory & Irvine*. Bristol, England: BBC, 1999.

Noel, Capt. J. B. L. *Climbing Mount Everest*. Privately produced expedition film, 1922. Copy available at British Film Institute, London.

———. *Epic of Everest*. London: Explorer Films, 1924. Expedition film.

People's Republic of China. *Conquering the World's Highest Peak*. Beijing: China Newsreel and Documentary Film Studio, 1960. Expedition film.

———. *Another Ascent of the World's Highest Peak*. Beijing: China Newsreel and Documentary Film Studio, 1975. Expedition film.

Wyn-Harris, P. *The Fourth Mount Everest Expedition*. Privately produced expedition film, 1933. Copy available at British Film Institute, London.

INDEX

ABOUT THE AUTHORS

Jochen Hemmleb (left) and Eric Simonson (right) in Beijing, summer 2001, holding an oxygen set from the 1938 British Everest expedition, which was recovered by the Chinese in 1960
(Photo © Jochen Hemmleb)

Jochen Hemmleb, born in 1971, was the researcher/historian on both the 1999 and 2001 Mallory & Irvine Research Expeditions. He currently works as a freelance writer and lecturer in the field of mountaineering history. A mountaineer for twenty years, he has climbed many of the classic peaks in the European Alps, and has also climbed and trekked in East Africa, New Zealand, South America, and the Himalaya. On the 1999 Mallory & Irvine Research Expedition, he reached Mount Everest's North Col, 23,230 feet (7,070 m). Hemmleb's archives on the mountaineering history of the Tibetan side of Mount Everest and the mystery of Mallory and Irvine is one of the most comprehensive private collections. He lives in southwest Germany.

Eric R. Simonson, 1999 and 2001 Mallory & Irvine Research Expedition leader, has been a professional mountain guide since 1973. He is a founding partner of International Mountain Guides and Mount Rainier Alpine Guides, based in Ashford, Washington. Since 1970, Simonson has summited Mount Rainier 265 times, summited Mount McKinley sixteen times and participated in more than eighty high-altitude expeditions on seven continents. He has conducted twelve expeditions to Mount Everest, summiting via the Northeast Ridge in 1991. Simonson is one of the most experienced and successful expedition leaders in the world. He lives in Tacoma, Washington.

THE MOUNTAINEERS, founded in 1906, is a nonprofit outdoor activity and conservation club with 15,000 members, whose mission is "to explore, study, preserve, and enjoy the natural beauty of the outdoors. . . ." The club sponsors many classes and year-round outdoor activities in the Pacific Northwest, and supports environmental causes through educational activities, sponsoring legislation and presenting educational programs. The Mountaineers Books supports the club's mission by publishing travel and natural history guides, instructional texts, and works on conservation and history.

Send or call for our catalog of more than 500 outdoor titles:

The Mountaineers Books
1001 SW Klickitat Way, Suite 201
Seattle, WA 98134
800-553-4453

mbooks@mountaineersbooks.org
www.mountaineersbooks.org

Other titles you might enjoy from The Mountaineers Books

Available at fine bookstores and outdoor stores, by phone at 800-553-4453,
or on the World Wide Web at *www.mountaineersbooks.org.*

Ghosts of Everest: The Search for Mallory and Irvine
Jochen Hemmleb, Larry A. Johnson, and Eric R. Simonson.
$24.95, paperbound. 0-89886-850-5.

Fearless on Everest: The Quest for Sandy Irvine
Julie Summers. $18.95, paperbound. 0-89886-796-7.

The Wildest Dream: The Biography of George Mallory
Peter and Leni Gillman. $18.95, paperbound. 0-89886-751-7.

The Mystery of Mallory and Irvine: Fully Revised Edition
Tom Hozel and Audrey Salkeld. $18.95, paperbound.
0-89886-726-6.

Everest: Eighty Years of Triumph and Tragedy, 2nd Edition
Peter and Leni Gillman. $35.00, hardbound. 0-89886-780-0.

Everest: The Mountaineering History, 3rd Edition
Walt Unsworth. $45.00, hardbound. 0-89886-670-7.

Everest: The History of the Himalayan Giant
Robert Mantovani. $35.00, hardbound. 0-89886-534-4.

Everest: The West Ridge
Tom Hornbein. $19.95, paperbound. 0-89886-616-2.

Everest: Expedition to the Ultimate
Reinhold Messner. $24.95, paperbound. 0-89886-648-0.

The Crystal Horizon: Everest—The First Solo Ascent
Reinhold Messner. $24.95, paperbound. 0-89886-574-3.

Chomolungma Sings the Blues: Travels Around Everest
Ed Douglas. $14.95, paperbound. 0-89886-843-2.

The Mountaineers Anthology Series: Glorious Failures, Vol. I
Edited by The Mountaineers Books Staff. $16.95, paperbound.
0-89886-825-4.

The Mountaineers Anthology Series: Courage and Misfortune, Vol. II
Edited by The Mountaineers Books Staff. $16.95, paperbound.
0-89886-826-2.

The High Himalaya
Photography by Art Wolfe, text by Peter Potterfield. $44.95,
hardbound. 0-89886-841-6.